DO THE POOR MATTER ENOUGH?

The Authors

Aidan Cox is Aid Coordination Adviser in the Bureau of Development Policy at UNDP (New York), concentrating on aid management and poverty reduction. Until recently he worked as a Research Fellow in the Poverty and Social Policy Unit at the Overseas Development Institute (ODI) in London. At ODI he focused on the effectiveness of donor poverty reduction approaches, looking at both headquarters and field levels. He was Team Leader and editor of the DAC Scoping Study of Donor Poverty Reduction Policies and Practice published in 1999. His most recent publication (with John Healey) examines the record of European development agencies: European Development Cooperation and the Poor (Macmillan: 2000). Aidan Cox studied at the Universities of Cambridge, Paris and Manchester.

Steen Folke is Senior Researcher at the Centre for Development Research, Copenhagen (Denmark). Previously Associate Professor at the University of Copenhagen since the 1960s. Member of the Danish parliament 1975-84. Has carried out development research in India, Bangladesh, China, Tanzania and Zimbabwe. Has studied agricultural development, conflicts over natural resources, South-South trade and evaluated development assistance. Studied in India 1959-60 (University of Mysore) and has all-together spent more than three years doing research in India, divided over 20 visits of shorter or longer duration. Has published more than 50 research publications and co-authored South-South Trade and Development. Manufactures in the New International Division of Labour (Macmillan, 1993) and Project Impact at the Local Level – A Study of LIFT-Patuakhali (Bangladesh) (Danida, 1999).

Lau Schulpen is lecturer at the Centre for International Development Issues Nijmegen (The Netherlands). After obtaining his master's degree in development studies in 1988, he worked as a volunteer for the Nijmegen based Centre for Development Cooperation and he conducted a study of consultants and development cooperation. In October 1989, he joined the co-financing organisation ICCO in Zeist at the India desk. In April 1991, he returned to the University of Nijmegen to undertake his Ph.D research on a comparative analysis of Dutch aid channels to India. Since 1994, he has also been affiliated with the Third World Centre as lecturer on such topics as development cooperation and NGOs. His Ph.D thesis under the title The same difference – a comparative analysis of Dutch aid channels to India (Breitenbach) was published in September 1997.

Neil Webster is Senior Researcher at the Centre for Development Research, Copenhagen (Denmark). He has worked on development issues in India for 20 years, publishing three books and more than 30 articles in books and international journals. Most recent works include (2000) 'Democracy, Development and the Institutionalised Participation of the Poor for Poverty Reduction', in Paul Collins (ed) Applying Public Administration in Development: Guideposts to the Future, John Wiley: London, and forthcoming this year with Zed Press In the Name of the Poor: Contesting Political Space for Poverty Reduction, co-edited with Lars Engberg-Pedersen.

DO THE POOR MATTER ENOUGH?

A COMPARATIVE STUDY OF EUROPEAN AID FOR POVERTY REDUCTION IN INDIA

AIDAN COX
STEEN FOLKE
LAU SCHULPEN
NEIL WEBSTER

CONCEPT PUBLISHING COMPANY, NEW DELHI - 110059

ISBN 81-7022-914-6

First Published 2002

Published and Printed by

Ashok Kumar Mittal
Concept Publishing Company
A/15-16, Commercial Block, Mohan Garden
NEW DELHI - 110059

Phones: 5648039, 5649024

Fax : 091-11-5648053

E-Mail: publishing@conceptpub.com

FOREWORD

Although India has been a recipient of foreign aid for over half a century and more, studies on aid have been few and far between. True, aid has not occupied a prominent place in the scheme of financing development in India. If we treat official development assistance as aid as it is generally done, aid has been only around 0.4 per cent of India's GNP during the last decade. The entire quantum of aid including non-official assistance has never been over 1 per cent of the GNP. Even so, aid does play an important role in India's development. It is not quantity but quality that matters. At any rate, it is difficult to subscribe to the view of economists like Deepak Lal who maintain that aid has been a historical anomaly whose time has gone (see Deepak Lal, 1999, *India in the World Economy*, Oxford University Press). On the contrary, I think that aid has a significant place in India's development however small it may be in relative terms.

The role of aid assumes special significance because of the renewed focus of several donor countries on poverty. Multi-lateral agencies like World Bank have declared poverty alleviation as their over-arching concern. In the 1990s, particularly after the Maastricht Treaty, European countries have developed, at least in theory, common objectives towards development programmes, viz., poverty reduction, promotion of democracy and human rights, gender equity and environment. India may do well to make special note of this. In the context of the unfolding paradigm of market-mediated growth which does not necessarily care for the poor, the renewed focus on poverty assumes greater significance. There is growing evidence in India that the economic reforms launched since July 1991 have not favourably impacted on the poor. The recent finding based on the 55th National Sample Survey Report (1999-2000) on household consumer expenditure, which shows a sharp decline in the population below the poverty line to 26 per cent at the all-India level, is widely contested. Even if it is accepted, the sad fact that remains is that the magnitude of poverty in the country is still of gargantuan proportion. In this context this volume entitled *Do the Poor Matter Enough?* With its subtitle *A Comparative Study of European Aid for Poverty Reduction in India,* is a timely and relevant publication. It should engage the attention of development theorists as well as policy planners in the country, particularly since it is the outcome of the work of a team of European scholars.

This publication is important for a variety of reasons. First, aid or no aid, the poor and poverty alleviation do matter. Second, poverty is approached in this study from a wider perspective embodying four dimensions—livelihoods, resources, knowledge and rights which indeed is in sharp contrast to the income poverty approach followed by Government of India. This wider conceptualisation is important because measurement, monitoring and policy initiatives are only as good as the conceptualisation followed. Third, the book forms part of a larger study which covers six other aid-receiving countries besides India and involves the European Union, Denmark, Germany, the Netherlands, Sweden and the United Kingdom as donors. Four, it contains several practical suggestions that should prove useful for both donors as well as for India, based on 33 aided projects spread over five Indian states and covering nine important sectors such as watershed management, forestry, drinking water, primary health and primary education. NGOs in India, many of whom have a clear focus on poverty reduction, can also benefit from this as the study devotes considerable space for NGO projects.

Whatever the voices of disapproval on aid, there is growing evidence to show that it should be strengthened not only qualitatively but quantitatively. Aid can definitely play an important role at state and sub-state levels. The Panchayati Raj institutions and urban local bodies can also be encouraged to play a critical role in the years to come in owning projects and evoking local participation given the autonomy they command under the new dispensation.

This book will be an excellent addition to the literature on aid and should be of great interest to all those interested in India's development and progress. As the authors of the work rightly observe: "Development aid can indeed be regarded as 'peanuts' at the all-India level. This picture changes dramatically when looking at individual states. Here development aid can contribute substantially to the development budget, even to such an extent that one can speak of increasing aid dependence. Still, at the end of the day, it is not so much the quantitative level of aid that counts but the extent to which this aid has managed to improve the lives of the poor in a sustainable manner."

Institute of Social Sciences, New Delhi
May 5, 2001

GEORGE MATHEW

PREFACE

There is a peculiar dearth of studies on the role of aid in India. To the extent this is at all taken up, the academic as well as the political debate focus primarily on the role of the international financial institutions, the World Bank and the IMF—and in particular such controversial issues as conditionalities and sanctions. In contrast neither the aid from UN agencies nor the aid from bilateral donors is hardly ever subjected to analysis or debate. One reason for this obviously is that aid only plays a marginal rôle in the Indian economy. But that is not the same as saying that aid is unimportant or irrelevant for India's development. Apart from its macroeconomic effect, aid often plays a vital role in certain sectors and localities, providing much needed resources for productive activities or basic social services. In spite of this there are few well-documented studies of the role of aid. Lipton & Toye's 'Does Aid Work in India?' from 1990 still stands out as the only authoritative book. Our study of six European donors' development cooperation with India aims at partly filling the void. While Lipton & Toye's study in particular focuses on the macroeconomic effects of aid, our study is more focused on donor strategies and, approaches as well as on analysis of a large number of European funded projects and programmes. The main question is: To which extent does the aid from European donors contribute to what is seen as India's overriding development concern, namely poverty reduction.

The study forms part of a larger "Study of European aid for poverty reduction", a collaborative European research project involving research institutions from a number of EU countries (Cox & Healey, 2000). Assistance from EU and EU-member states as bilateral donors to India, Nepal, Tanzania, Zambia, Zimbabwe, Burkina Faso and Bolivia has been studied as part of the project. The entire research project is largely financed by the involved European research institutes supported by their respective governments.

The India study has been carried out by Aidan Cox, Overseas Development Institute, London; Lau Schulpen, Third World Centre, Catholic University, Nijmegen; Steen Folke (study coordinator) and Neil Webster, both from Centre for Development Research, Copenhagen—in collaboration with eleven Indian researchers, namely: Dr. (Ms.) S. Banerjee, Consultant, Delhi; Dr. S. Benjamin, Consultant, Bangalore; Dr. (Ms.) Kripa A.P., Consultant, Mysore; Dr. D. Manti, Institute of Rural Studies and Administration, Guntur; Dr. K.N. Ninan, Institute for Social and Economic Change, Bangalore; Prof. M.A. Oommen, Institute of Social Sciences, Delhi; Ms. Rajamma G., Consultant, Secunderabad; Dr. D. Rajasekhar, Institute for Social and Economic Change, Bangalore; Dr. Somasekhara Reddy, Indian Institute of Management, Bangalore; Dr. R.S. Srivastava, Department of Economics, University of Allahabad; Dr. N.V. Varghese, National Institute of Educational Planning and Administration, Delhi.

The aim of the India study is to investigate the effectiveness of aid from the European Commission and selected EU-countries in contributing to poverty reduction. By poverty reduction we do not just mean improvement in income or consumption of the poor, but also amelioration of the conditions that are important for such improvement (e.g. health, education). We have conceptualised poverty reduction as a multi-dimensional phenomenon which involves changes in livelihoods, resources, knowledge and rights. We have selected six donors who have in common that they want to strengthen the poverty orientation of their development assistance, namely the European Commission, Denmark, Germany, The Netherlands, Sweden and United Kingdom. Among EU countries these donors, incidentally, are the most important in terms of the volume of aid they provide to India (among the remaining EU countries only France really matters). The study has assessed the donor strategies, the donor-recipient dialogue, the recipient's perception of aid as well as the effectiveness in terms of poverty reduction of the programmes as such and a number of selected interventions in nine different 'sectors': watershed, irrigation, forestry, drinking water, primary health, primary education, women's training, urban housing and self-help projects (NGO-supported). In each sector 3-5 projects supported by one or the other of the EU-donors have been selected and assessed from a poverty perspective. Most of the 33 projects under study are found in Uttar Pradesh, Orissa, Andhra Pradesh, Karnataka and Tamil Nadu, but one project is located in Madhya Pradesh, one in Rajasthan and one in Kerala.

The study was prepared in the autumn of 1996 and field work was carried out in the first half of 1997. In January the researchers involved held a planning-cum-methodology workshop in Delhi, and a second workshop, where preliminary results from field work were discussed, was held in Delhi in April. Most of the Indian researchers involved have spent 1½-2 months working on the project. Half of that time has generally been spent in the field, assessing the selected 3-4 projects in a particular sector, i.e. roughly one week per project (including travel time). This has resulted in nine 'sector reports', containing analysis and assessment of the projects as well as comments about the relevance of the aid to that particular sector.

These sector reports (listed in the references) are in themselves an important result of the research project and they form the basis for what we write in chapters 8-18 of this book. The authors have also paid brief visits to some of the projects studied and moreover build on previous knowledge about the various sectors, but it goes without saying that the reports written by our Indian colleagues form the backbone of this part of our study. Two special studies by our Indian colleagues have also been carried out as part of the overall study. R.S. Srivastava has written a report entitled 'Poverty in India: A review of Nature, Trends and Eradication Strategies'. M.N. Oommen has written a report entitled 'Foreign Aid and Poverty Reduction. Towards Understanding the Indian Perspective'. Both of these provide interesting perspectives on the topic. We want to take the opportunity to thank all our Indian colleagues and collaborators for their enthusiasm during the research project and their invaluable contributions to the results.

The four European researchers involved in the project have planned the research in December 1996-January 1997, carried out field work in March-May 1997 and prepared the consolidated report afterwards. Apart from visits to projects our main task during field work has been interviewing numerous persons engaged in the aid administration either on donor or recipient side. These include a number of staff members in the embassies and aid agencies in Delhi, officers both in the Ministry of Finance and in the line ministries and other government institutions in Delhi as well as a number of government officers in the five states where almost all the projects are located, i.e. Uttar Pradesh, Orissa, Andhra Pradesh, Karnataka and Tamil Nadu. We thank all those interviewed for their readiness to use their time and share their experiences and views with us.

An incomplete draft version of this book was prepared in 1997 and presented and discussed in three well-attended meetings in New Delhi in September 1997, one with Government officials, one with donor representatives and one with staff members of a range of multilateral donor agencies (organised by the UNDP). The many valuable comments we received during those meetings have informed the final version of our book. Since then several of the donors studied have imposed sanctions by freezing or cutting back their aid to India after the nuclear bomb tests in May 1998. Both Sweden, Denmark and Germany have imposed such sanctions whereas the UK, the Netherlands and the EU— although protesting verbally—have adopted a 'business as usual' attitude in terms of the aid. None of the donors, however, has opted out of India, so the projects and programmes studied here are still very much at the heart of the aid from EU donors for poverty reduction in India.

It is our sincere hope that this study will contribute to strengthening the poverty reduction objective in interventions in the various sectors dealt with—whether by Government of India, state governments or NGOs and whether or not these interventions are supported by foreign donors. Irrespective of funding mechanism and implementing agency the major development issues related to poverty reduction are the same.

A much abbreviated version of this book has previously been published as a Working Paper by Overseas Development Institute, London (Cox et al. 2000).

New York, Copenhagen and Nijmegen, December 2000

Aidan Cox
Steen Folke
Lau Schulpen
Neil Webster

CONTENTS

ABBREVIATIONS (AND DONOR COUNTRIES)

AAO-FW	Assistant Agricultural Officers—Farm Women
ADP	Area Development Project *(United Kingdom and Denmark)*
ADS	Aleppey Diocesan Society
AF	Agro Forestry
AP	Andhra Pradesh
APPEP	Andhra Pradesh Primary Education Project
ARWSP	Accelerated Rural Water Supply Programme
BAIF	Bharat Agro Industrial Foundation
BDCOD	British Development Cooperation Office Delhi
BMZ	Bundesministerium für Wirtschaftliche Zusammenarbeit und Entwicklung - Federal Ministry of Economic Cooperation *(Germany)*
BUPP	Bangalore Urban Poverty Programme *(The Netherlands)*
CAPART	Council for the Advancement of People's Action and Rural Technology
CIDA	Canadian International Development Agency
CSP	Country Strategy Paper
CSSS	Changanacharerry Social Service Society *(Germany)*
DAC	Development Assistance Committee
Danida	Danish International Development Assistance
DEA	Department of External Affairs
DFID	Department for International Development *(United Kingdom)*
DG	Directorate General *(European Union)*
DGIS	Directoraat-Generaal Internationale Samenwerking *(The Netherlands)*
DIETs	District Institutes of Education and Training
DKK	Danish Kroner
DoP	Department of Planning
DPAP	Drought Prone Areas Programme

DPEP	District Primary Education Programme *(European Union and United Kingdom)*
DRDA	District Rural Development Agency
DVP	Doon Valley Integrated Watershed Development Project *(European Union)*
DWCRA	Development of Women and Children in Rural Areas
EAP	Externally Aided Projects
EAS	Employment Assurance Scheme
EC	European Commission/Community
EGS	Employment Guarantee Scheme
EU	European Union
FA	Farmers Association
FD	Forest Department
FTC	Farmers Training Centre
GAD	Gender and Development
GoI/GOI	Government of India
GTZ	Deutsche Gesellschaft für Technische Zusammenarbeit — German Agency for Technical Cooperation
GTZ-SHF	GTZ Self Help Fund *(Germany)*
HADP	Hill Areas Development Programme
HDFC	Housing Development Finance Corporation
HUDCO	Housing and Urban Development Corporation
ICDS	Integrated Child Development Services Scheme *(Sweden)*
IDA	International Development Association
IEC	Information, Education and Communication
IJRY	Intensive Jawahar Rozgar Yojana
IOV	Inspectie Ontwikkelingssamenwerking te Velde *(The Netherlands)*
IRDP	Integrated Rural Development Programme
IRS&WSP	Integrated Rural Sanitation and Water Supply Project *(Denmark)*
IRWSS	Integrated Rural Water Supply & Sanitation Project *(The Netherlands)*
JFM	Joint Forestry Management
JFMP	Joint Forest Management and Planning *(United Kingdom)*
JRY	Jawahar Rozgar Yojana
KWAD	Karnataka Watershed Development Project *(United Kingdom)*
KfW	Kreditanstallt für Wiederaufbau *(Germany)*
KIWMP	Karnataka Integrated Watershed Management Project *(Germany)*

KWDP	Karnataka Watershed Development Project *(Denmark)*
LVAW	Lady Village Agricultural Worker
MNP	Minimum Needs Programme
NFTP	Non-Forest Timber Products
NGO	Non-Governmental Organisation
NGDO	Non-Governmental Development Organisation
NIPHAD	Naujil Integrated Project for Health and Development *(Denmark)*
NORAD	Norwegian Agency for Development Cooperation
NREP	National Rural Employment Programme
ODA	Official Development Assistance
ODA	Overseas Development Agency *(United Kingdom)*
OECD	Organisation for Economic Cooperation and Development
OLIP	Orissa Lift Irrigation Project *(Germany)*
O&M	Operation & Maintenance
OOF	Other Official Flows
OPEC	Oil Producing and Exporting Countries
PAG	Project Advisory Group
PAP	Poverty Alleviation Programme
PHCC	Palani Hills Conservation Council (Denmark)
PR	Poverty Reduction
PRA	Participatory Rural Appraisal
PRI	Panchayati Raj Institutions
PSC	Project Steering Committee
PSU	Programme Support Unit
RDO	Rural Development Organisation
RD&PR	Department of Rural Development and Panchayati Raj
RLEGP	Rural Landless Employment Guarantee Programme
RPDS	Revamped Public Distribution Scheme
Rs	Rupees
RWS/S	Rural Water Supply/Sanitation
SCs	Scheduled Castes
SDT	Slum Development Team
SHARE	Self Help Association for Rural Education and Employment *(Germany)*
SHF	Self Help Fund
SHG	Self Help Group
Sida	Swedish International Development Agency
SP	Special Project
STs	Scheduled Tribes

TEWA	Training and Extension for Women in Agriculture *(Denmark)*
TIPP-II	Tungabhadra Irrigation Pilot Project—second phase *(The Netherlands)*
TN	Tamil Nadu
TRP	Tank Rehabilitation Project *(European Union)*
TRYSEM	Training of Rural Youth for Self-Employment
UCD	Urban Community Development
UK	United Kingdom
UN	United Nations
UNDP	United Nations Development Programme
UP	Uttar Pradesh
UT	Union Territory
VISP	Visakhapatnam Slum Improvement Project *(United Kingdom)*
WID	Women In Development
WUAs	Water Users Associations
WYTEP	Women and Youth Training and Extension Project *(Denmark)*

1

POVERTY IN INDIA

The poverty situation

In the first three decades after independence the rate of growth of the Indian economy was fairly low, around 3.5% per year on average, mockingly referred to as the 'hindu rate of growth'. This rate was enough to be slightly ahead of population growth, but not enough to make a significant dent into the widespread poverty. In the 1980s, when liberalisation was initiated and combined with expansionary fiscal policies, the growth rate picked up and exceeded 5% for a number of years. The expansionary policies, however, resulted in growing fiscal deficits that became the main factor engendering the economic crisis of 1990-91 (Parikh, ed., 1997:3). After the introduction in 1991 of the New Economic Policy the growth rate has again exceeded 5% in most years, and now it is being debated whether this growth rate will be sustainable into the next century. In terms of growth per capita it helps that population growth has been decreasing—from 2.3% per year in the 1960s to 2.1% in the 1980s (Haq, 1997:150) and probably as low as 1.6% in the period 1994-2000 (UNDP, 1997a:195).

Economic growth in itself, however, though necessary, is not sufficient to ensure poverty reduction. The distribution of growth is decisive, and it is well known that in India the distribution has been highly unequal. In the rural parts, where the vast majority live and where the bulk of poverty is found, growth has been slow. In terms of growth rates agriculture has generally lagged behind manufacturing industry and services. The green revolution of the 1960s and 1970s did produce markedly higher yields and incomes in regions with access to irrigation. It also resulted in greater differences between rich and poor farmers and between regions with extensive irrigation (e.g. Punjab-Haryana) and regions dependent on rainfed agriculture. The high growth rates in the 1980s and 1990s have primarily been in the secondary and tertiary sectors and have first of all benefited people in the urban areas, not least the rapidly growing middle class. Again inequalities are on the increase.

There is a vast literature about poverty in India, but no agreement about the answer to even the simplest questions, such as: What is poverty? How many poor are there (now and before)? In this study we use a broad concept of poverty, embodying four dimensions, livelihoods, resources, knowledge and rights. In India, however, poverty is usually conceived in economic terms, i.e. focusing on income and consumption. The poverty line is defined as a minimum level of per capita household consumption expenditure (based on a calorie norm of 2400 cal per person in rural and 2100 cal per person in urban areas). The head count method simply identifies the number of people falling below this line. In principle this is very simple, but in practice there are a number of technical problems involved (e.g. adjustment for price variations) with the consequence that even overall figures of the number of poor may vary considerably. The technical problems were sorted out by an Expert Group, headed by professor D.T. Lakdawala, which in 1993 recommended new procedures in estimating the number of poor (cfr Srivastava, 1997:3-5, World Bank, 1997: 41-42).

Relatively speaking there has been a marked reduction in Indian poverty since the 1970s. A little over half (53%) of the population fell below the poverty line in the early 1950s (1950-55) as well as in the early 1970s (1970-74). But since then there has been a significant decline with the head count index falling to 37.8% in 1991-92 (Srivastava, 1997:5) and 36.3% in 1993-94 (World Bank, 1997:3). There is an ongoing debate over whether the New Economic Policy since 1991 has resulted in an increase in the aggregate poverty, but the figures are inconclusive. In 1992 a significant increase in poverty was measured, but the extent to which this can be ascribed to the macroeconomic stabilisation measures is uncertain (Datt & Ravallion, 1996a).

In terms of absolute figures the number of poor people has doubled since India's independence, from 164m in 1951 to 312m in 1993-94 (World Bank, 1997:xiii). It is often stated that there are more poor people in India than in the whole of Africa. Most of India's poor live in the rural parts, 241m (77%) out of 312 millions by 1993-94, and the poverty tends to be more severe in the rural areas (World Bank, 1997:3). There are also marked regional differences in the extent of poverty. A contiguous belt of northern states, namely Assam, West Bengal, Orissa, Bihar,

Madhya Pradesh, Uttar Pradesh and Rajasthan, have the highest poverty incidence, i.e. the highest proportion of the population living below the poverty line. At the other end of the scale are Haryana and Punjab, Gujarat, Andhra Pradesh, and Kerala (World Bank, 1997:8-9).

A broader concept of poverty includes other than purely economic factors. Being poor in this study means being denied or having only limited access to resources, knowledge and rights and being deprived on the whole of an adequate livelihood. Poverty is also about vulnerability and lack of the capabilities necessary to cope with crises, whether externally (e.g. drought) or internally (e.g. death of family member) induced (cfr Drèze & Sen, 1989, 1995). Hence poor health and lack of basic education are important dimensions in our concept of poverty. As a corollary poverty reduction encompasses not only improvements in income and consumption, but also improvements of the coping capabilities through human resource development.

UNDP (1997b:7) lists a number of examples of deprivation of basic human and social needs in India: More than half of all children under four years are undernourished, more than 2 million infants die every year from preventable causes, only 45% of the rural population is covered with sanitation facilities, 61% of the women were illiterate by 1991, 36% of the children drop-out before completing primary school etc. These depressing facts are important aspects of contemporary poverty in India. It goes without saying that human and social deprivation in the broader sense is closely linked to economic poverty in the narrow sense. But even so they are distinct aspects of our understanding of poverty.

Who are the poor then? The concentration of poor people in the rural parts of India and in particular in certain states of North India has already been described. Moreover, there is a concentration of poor among certain social categories. According to a human development profile from 1996 (here quoted from World Bank, 1997:10) the incidence of poverty was 52% for the landless on the whole, 68% for landless wage-earners, 50% for members of the scheduled castes, 51% for members of the scheduled tribes and 5% for households where all members were illiterate.

There is an important gender dimension in poverty and human deprivation. 47% of female-headed households in rural areas are poor (Srivastava, 1997:12). 66% of the women are illiterate compared to 38% of the men. In contrast to virtually all other countries of the World even the sex ratio in India is skewed in favour of men. The 1991 census revealed a sex ratio of 927 women per thousand men and the 'deficit' of women has been growing from decade to decade; it was 972 per thousand in 1901 (Srivastava, 1997:13). This tells perhaps more than any other figure about the plight of women in India. A gender-related development index (highlighting inequalities between men and women) for Indian states (1991-92) shows a great deal of regional variation. At the top is Kerala, followed by Maharashtra and Gujarat, at the bottom is Uttar Pradesh, followed by Bihar, Rajasthan, Madhya Pradesh and Orissa (here based on Srivastava, 1997:14). The pattern is clearly similar to the regional variation in poverty.

Thus class (e.g. landless labourers), caste (e.g. scheduled castes) and gender (women) are some of the main determinants of who the poor are in India. When it comes to the causes of poverty it is evident that these are often complex. People's actions and coping strategies are influenced both by structural factors, by their individual capabilities and by the (natural and other) resources they can access.

Since 65% of the total labour force—and almost 90% in the rural parts of India—is engaged in agriculture (1991 Census), it is clear that the conditions for and within agriculture play a decisive role for the livelihood of a majority. It is no surprise that poverty is more widespread in regions dominated by rainfed agriculture than those with extensive irrigation. Among the former the semi-arid regions that are drought-prone, make people's livelihoods particularly vulnerable. But everywhere the access to productive resources, notably land and water, is a key determinant of the distribution of wealth and poverty. It has already been noted that landless labourers are overrepresented among the poor. Among the agricultural labourers, it may be added, there is an overrepresentation of scheduled castes. Small and marginal farmers also constitute a fair share of the poor. Evidently medium and bigger farmers tend to be better off. Usually access to productive resources not only entails higher income, better housing and clothing etc., but also better access to credit, education and health services. There is a whole virtuous circle which contrasts with the vicious circle of low income, debt, inadequate diet, poor health, illiteracy etc., that the poor find themselves trapped in.

Apart from many agricultural labourers and small and marginal farmers there are many poor among artisans and craftsmen in the rural areas. In the urban areas poverty is widespread among people who are forced to gain their livelihood in the informal sector, as petty retail vendors, casual labourers etc. Many have migrated from the countryside in search of gainful employment, but end up being underemployed and underpaid in the informal part of the urban economy. Invariably the poor also end up in the extensive urban slums.

Thus the occupational status of the working members of a household is a main determinant of poverty. But the division between the have's and the have-not's is not just a matter of economic status. It is reinforced by social status which—at least in the rural parts—is largely determined by position in the caste hierarchy. And economic and social status in turn form the basis for political power of the well-to-do, that can be used to bolster vested interests and preserve the status quo. In the Indian villages generally there is a local power structure dominated by the bigger farmers, upper castes and men. The class, caste and gender dimensions of power must also be dealt with in any attempt to support the poor in their struggle for a better life.

Indian strategies and policies on poverty reduction

Poverty, and thus poverty reduction, eradication or alleviation, has been part of the development discussion since the very start of planning in India. An agreement on what constitutes poverty and what are the best means of reducing it has not been reached, however. Nevertheless, the discussions have shown that an assessment of the poverty situation requires a precise definition of poverty which can lead to effective monitoring of the changes in the living conditions of the poor (see, for example R. Srivastava, 1997). This section provides a review of the nature, trends and eradication strategies with regard to poverty in India.

The concern of the state with poverty reduction goes back to the beginning of the planned economic development (1951). In the beginning, the main thrust of the state was to accelerate growth and to give the (rural) poor a stake in the growth process through sufficiently radical redistributive measures aimed at abolishing landed intermediaries, providing land to landless through land ownership, redistribution and secure tenures. The patchy record of land reform in India is sufficiently well documented. At the same time, the literature on poverty in the early decades reflects the growing disappointment with the 'trickle down' effects of the growth process set into motion. With the adoption of the 'new agricultural strategy' in the 1960s, the inequalising and immiserising effects of agricultural growth raised new concerns about poverty, which were compounded by break-down of the political consensus around the Congress party and sweeping waves of disenchantment among the rural and urban poor and middle classes (1967-75). The containment of poverty and inequality acquired important political overtones for the government of the day.

The failures of the 'trickle down theory' with regard to poverty reduction led to the realisation that specific measures had to be taken to address the problems of poverty more directly. In 1962 the Planning

Commission issued a paper which 'drew attention for the first time to the problem of abject poverty and quantified its magnitude' (Gaika, 1991:129). A development plan was prepared aimed at meeting the basic needs of the total population. Important parts of this plan were land reforms, reservation and special schemes for scheduled castes and tribes, employment schemes, support schemes for small and marginal farmers, and a nationalisation of financial institutions to control investments and credits. Since the Fourth Plan (1969-74), the state put into effect a number of programmes attempting to bring petty cultivators in hitherto neglected regions into the ambit of the new agricultural strategy. Simultaneously also programmes to provide employment for the landless poor were started. The Fifth Plan (1974-78) continued these initiatives around the populist slogan of *'garibi hatao'* (eradicate poverty) and introduced the Minimum Needs Programme and the 'twenty-point programme' which contained an amalgam of measures aimed at redistributive (land reforms, debt relief and abolition of bonded labour) and growth-promoting measures for the poor.

Direct poverty alleviation strategies have been put on a new footing since 1978. The Integrated Rural Development Programme (IRDP) consisting of an integrated approach promoting asset creation and self-employment among the rural poor was launched in 1979. Two major programmes [the National Rural Employment Programme (NREP) and later the Rural Landless Employment Guarantee Programme (RLEGP)], representing a more coherent approach towards employment creation were merged in 1989 into the Jawahar Rozgar Yojana (JRY).

Since 1993-94, a number of new initiatives have been taken to provide a safety net for the poor through programmes specially targeted at backward blocks or districts with a high concentration of the rural poor. These include the new employment schemes, namely the Intensive Jawahar Rozgar Yojana (IJRY) and the Employment Assurance Scheme (EAS). A Revamped Public Distribution Scheme (RPDS) was earlier launched in 1758 backward blocks in 1992, and has been extended to the 2446 blocks in which the EAS is operational. The Scheme provides for an additional subsidy of Rs. 50 per quintal of food grain over the issue price (for a discussion on the Public Distribution System, see: World Bank, 1997: 26-29). A National Social Assistance Programme (NSAP) comprising a pension scheme for the old, a maternity benefit and a family benefit to cover the natural and accidental death of the bread-winner, was introduced in 1995-96. Further, the Central Government's budgetary support to the social sector has been stepped up. In the sphere of primary education, externally aided programmes to improve the educational infrastructure are being implemented in many of the educationally backward districts. At the same time, while pressures on the fiscal situation continue, an effort is being made to increase the level of investment in agriculture and rural infrastructure. Since 1996-97, new initiatives to alleviate poverty include (1) a concerted focus on provision of seven identified basic needs; (2) efforts to launch a Maharashtra-type Employment Guarantee Scheme at the national level; and (3) announcement of a scheme for provision of 10 kg of cereals per month at half the market price to all families below the poverty line.

Many of the PAPs are implemented by the Ministry of Rural Development but several other ministries, such as the Ministry of Social Welfare and the Human Resource Development Ministry, are also involved. Simultaneously, the 'normal' design and implementation structure for PAPs is characterised by a 'top-down' approach through hierarchically structured bureaucracies with a close nexus with powerful groups in society. The almost exclusive reliance on the bureaucracy to fight poverty was, however, already in the 1950s shown to go hand in hand with elite domination, politicisation, corruption, malpractices and favouritism (Khanna, 1994). This insight led to a call for what is known as democratic decentralisation, in which the role of participatory approaches and people's mobilisation in the elimination of poverty is emphasized. The main concern here is three-fold. First, 'top-down' and standardised approaches to poverty alleviation are often based on a flimsy and incorrect understanding of people's priorities and interlinkage between these. Second, such approaches ultimately rest on hierarchical delivery systems and power groups, and the poor remain literally at the receiving end. Third, inefficiencies and leakages are built into the system since the 'dispensers' of the programme are not its beneficiaries. On the other hand, the mobilisation of the poor around common concerns realigns power balances and this is important since poverty is also a 'relation', and their participation leads to better programme design and 'ownership' (which raises efficiency and reduces leakages).

Despite the wide range of programmes and the different spheres of poverty they touch there are certain general points of critique to raise with regard to the Indian PAPs. The critique on the poverty alleviation schemes of the Indian government can be divided in three types. The first type of criticism refers to the non-holistic approach, which briefly refers to the fact that 'the approach ... has been piecemeal and vertically compartmentalised, separately managed by different departments of the government' (Ghosh, 1992: 31). In the Seventh Plan it was mentioned that 'the total impact of the programme depends on the degree to which the different poverty alleviation programmes [...] are integrated with one another and with the overall development of the area'. The necessity of an integrated approach, in which there is a clear coordination between the different programmes set up to tackle poverty, is indeed one of the major hurdles encountered. As the Eighth Plan noted: 'there is a need for integrating the various anti-poverty programmes with the sectoral programmes in a specified area so as to ensure a sustainable increase in employment and income of the rural poor and the infrastructural and environmental development of the area' (Government of India, 1992: 37).

The second general criticism with regard to the Indian PAPs refers to the fact that the programmes have been expenditure-oriented: Funds available had to be disbursed without sufficient attention being paid to, among other things, coordination of activities, backward and forward linkages, follow-up and the needs of the target group. The latter issue leads us to the third point of critique: 'the people, the rural populace in particular, have also been excluded from participation in the planning or decision-making process, even in matters which concern them (and their habitat) directly' (Ghosh, 1992: 31). The consequence of this non-participation has been that the government has relied almost exclusively on the official machinery (i.e. the bureaucracy) to fight poverty.

As a consequence, among others, of the abovementioned weaknesses, many of the PAPs have at best had a limited success. With regard to the IRDP, Rath (1985) pointed out that leaving aside selection of beneficiaries who were above the poverty line in the first place, 18.7% beneficiary households or about 6.6% rural households crossed the poverty line during 1978-85. However, if loan repayments are also deducted as cost, the percentage of rural households crossing the poverty line comes down to three. The success of the Development of Women and Children in Rural Areas programme (DWCRA) rests critically on linkages, and facilitation which are not easily achieved in the governmental delivery system. The impact of the Jawahar Rozgar Yojana employment scheme has been shown to be modest. Micro studies revealed high leakage, much lower wage labour component than stipulated and negligible role of the village assembly and village councils in project planning and supervision (*also see:* Srivastava 1997: 23-38).

The World Bank (1997) has identified a number of causes for the sometimes low impact of the Indian anti-poverty programmes. A distinction is made between causes which are amendable to change and causes which are not. The latter type of causes include the fact that 'the problems that the programmes are designed to address [...] are too massive to be resolved through public resources allocated to these programs, however efficient the use of these resources is'. Also the fact that many anti-poverty programmes have become highly politicised should be mentioned here: 'India's complex socio-political environment makes it very difficult to change existing programmes'. The causes 'amendable to change' mentioned by the World Bank include (1) ill-definition of objectives and existence of multiple objectives; (2) little effort in direct targeting of beneficiaries and no consistent definition to identify intended beneficiaries; (3) lack of adequate resources (e.g. programmes are underfunded, workers underpaid, undertrained and poorly motivated); (4) highly centralised programme administration and inadequate coordination between agencies involved; (5) high administrative costs including high leakages and corruption; and (6) the impact of the programmes is judged too often solely on the basis of fulfilling predetermined physical targets.

In sum: An evaluation of existing direct anti-poverty programmes and social services confirms leakages and inefficiencies in the governmental delivery system. The performance of these programmes varies across regions and is the poorest in regions where poverty is concentrated. There are major questions with regard to channelising investment in these programmes towards investment in infrastructure and agriculture, and relative efficacy of some of the major programmes (asset creation *versus* employment creation, protective *versus* promotional social security), as well as questions relating to the design of each of these programmes. While employment generation programmes can (up to a point) be geared towards creation of productive infrastructure, this has not always happened. On the other hand, the absorption of IRDP loans is clearly the lowest in backward regions and among the poorest groups. On the whole, direct strategies for poverty alleviation have probably mitigated poverty and risk of vulnerability to some extent, but with low efficiency, variable across regions. According to UNDP (1997b: iii), 'India's anti-poverty strategy could have reduced income poverty even more with better management, accountability, transparency and community involvement at all levels' and it calls for a focus on five important issues relevant to human development: (1) imbalances in investment; (2) impact of social expenditure; (3) decentralisation of development responsibilities; (4) convergence in programmes and action; and (5) accountability for use of public resources. Within this development assistance has a facilitating role to play.

The role of donors in poverty reduction

After 50 years of independence there is no doubt that the pervasive poverty remains India's number one development problem. The sheer magnitude of the problem implies that effective poverty reduction, not to speak of poverty eradication, will require vast resources and take considerable time. Clearly this is first and foremost the responsibility of Indian government institutions, both at the centre and state level. The record so far is a mixed one; government policies on the whole have not been pro-poor and the numerous poverty alleviation programmes have not been sufficient just to keep pace with the growing numbers of poor.

The role of foreign aid in India's development in general and poverty reduction in particular is at best little more than marginal. The scarcity of financial resources relative to the magnitude of the problems in our view necessitates that the aid to the largest extent possible is prioritised to contribute to the solution of the biggest problem, i.e. poverty reduction. This is increasingly also the view adopted by a number of both multilateral and bilateral donors, including the World Bank (to some extent), the UNDP and most of the donors studied here.

There is no commonly agreed strategy for poverty reduction. The pursuit of economic growth in itself, though necessary, is inadequate. The last fifteen years of Indian development have witnessed a fair amount of economic growth, but it is clear that the middle and upper classes have captured a disproportionate share of the benefits of that growth. Although there has been some poverty reduction, it is evident that a better (re)distribution is needed.

The success stories among Indian states regarding poverty reduction are Punjab-Haryana and Kerala. Datt & Ravallion (1996b) on the basis of a quantitative analysis argue that there are two routes to rural poverty reduction in India. The first is through (farm and non-farm) economic growth, of which Punjab-Haryana is the prime example. The second is through human resource development, with Kerala as the prime example. Although there may be an element of truth in this interpretation, we prefer to view economic growth and human resource development as closely interlinked and both vital for poverty reduction. In order to reduce poverty economic growth must be pro-poor, and this entails both employment, asset creation and improving capabilities of poor people, i.e. human resource development.

The World Bank's poverty alleviation strategy for the 1990s comprises three main elements (World Bank, 1990): promoting economic opportunities for the poor (labour-intensive growth), delivering social services for the poor (health, education) and providing safety nets for the poor (e.g. food subsidies). Without necessarily agreeing in general with the World Bank's policies and approaches, it is clear that these elements could well be used as part of a framework by the donors that are serious about contributing to poverty reduction in India, including the donors studied here. Any concrete strategy based on the World Bank approach would, however, need to be informed by a gender strategy; gender relations are an integrated part of the poverty problem, and the (different) needs of men and women must be addressed as part of the solution.

What is lacking in the World Bank's strategy is measures that attack the structural causes of poverty. One obvious example of such measures is land reform. Although a number of minor land reforms have been carried out in India since Independence, land ownership is still extremely unequal, and this is one of the main reasons for rural poverty. However, it may be argued that there is little donors can do about that, and that anyway such a crucial policy issue is a government prerogative. But at the local level donor-supported interventions may assist landless people, marginal farmers or tenants in getting access to and defending claims on land. Such interventions exemplify a type of development assistance that has gained prominence in the 1990s, the main purpose of which is to establish conditions for the empowerment of groups of poor people. In terms of our conceptualisation of poverty, empowerment is related to resources and knowledge as well as rights. In practice development assistance aiming at empowering poor people puts emphasis on capacity building and institution building among groups of poor. This is likely to be contested by the rural power elites, but empowering the poor is at least as necessary for poverty reduction as employment or asset creation and service delivery.

Bearing in mind the distribution of poverty in India there is a special need for donors to focus on rural areas particularly those that are dominated by rainfed agriculture, and more generally those that are poorest, most backward and remote. Even within these areas special attention should be given to landless people, to scheduled castes and tribes and to women. In order to reach the poor it will often be necessary to target interventions carefully, particularly in projects in the productive sectors where benefits of non-targeted assistance will tend to be captured by those who are well-endowed with productive assets (notably land).

Apart from support to concrete interventions donors can contribute to poverty reduction through policy dialogue both at the centre and state level. This policy dialogue may directly address poverty policies, but also wider issues concerning a policy environment that is conducive to poverty reduction through concrete interventions, e.g. distribution of income-earning assets or access to education or health services.

2

AID TO INDIA

For some countries in what is still often called the Third World, development aid is an important source of financing. This particularly holds for many African countries where aid may finance up to 70-80% of national investments. In India, however, development aid plays— certainly in quantitative terms — only a marginal role. Although aid used to contribute substantially to the total Indian budget in the 1960s, it has been reduced to a very small percentage of the total budget in the 1980s and 1990s. All this does not mean that development aid is not important. It is important for India, although perhaps more as a political sign. It is important for some of the states in India where aid continues to pay a substantial part of their annual budget. It is important for the donor, either for political, economic, humanitarian or geo-strategic reasons. Whether it is also important for the poor in India will be dealt with in another part of this book. In this chapter we will look into the quantitative background of development aid to India.[1] The chapter starts by discussing external financial (aid) flows to India, while also looking at utilisation and the relative (un)importance of foreign aid at all India level. In the second part, this 'relative (un)importance' of foreign aid is further worked out at state level. Examples from Uttar Pradesh and Andhra Pradesh show that development aid can be substantially more important at this state level.

All India level

External financial flows

Figure 2.1 clearly shows that over the period 1969-1997, the larger part of total net Official Development Finance stemmed from Official Development Assistance (ODA) or aid. It is only from the mid 1980s onwards that private sector investments and the other official flows (OOF) gained any momentum, although not for a very long time. In the beginning of the 1990s, private sector investments dropped substantially (and increased even more in 1996 and 1997), a few years later followed by other official funds. Of the total net amount of US$ 34,649 million disbursed as non-aid funds (i.e., OOF plus private sector investments) over the years 1968-1997, a total of 55% was disbursed over the years 1985-1991 only and nearly 21% over the two year-period 1996-1997.

Official Development Assistance (ODA)

Over the period 1968-1997, India received in total US$ 96,852 million of net ODA. Of this sum, 0.9% came from OPEC countries, 40.7% from multilateral organisations and the remaining 58.4% from bilateral DAC donors. Figure 2.2 shows the net ODA disbursements per group of donors for the period 1968-1997. The table clearly shows that OPEC only provided aid at any substantial amount in the years following the oil price hike of the early 1970s. It is further clear that there has been a substantial change in the share of bilateral and multilateral aid to total aid. In 1969, more than 83% of all net ODA to India came from bilateral DAC donors, while the remaining nearly 17% came from multilateral sources. Slowly, the share of multilateral aid increased and in 1980, 71.5% of all net ODA to India came from these multilateral sources. From 1980 to 1987, multilateral aid remained larger than bilateral aid. With a few exceptions, bilateral aid again became larger after 1987. One other important conclusion to be drawn from Fig. 2.2 is that total aid to India has shown an almost constant decline; particularly from the late 1970s onwards. During the 1970s, the average annual net ODA disbursements from all sources to India were US$ 3,660 million. During the 1980s, the average ODA disbursements were US$ 3,442 million and over the period 1990-1997, the average ODA disbursements were down to US$ 2.120 million.

The major multilateral donor for India is the soft-loan window of the World Bank: IDA (International Development Association). Of the total multilateral net ODA over 1968-1997 of US$ 39,417 million, nearly 75% came from IDA. Over the years 1978-1986, also the International Bank for Reconstruction and Development (IBRD) provided funds to India (less than 1% of the total amount received over 1968-1997). Within the United Nations (UN) organisations, the UNDP is by far the major donor. The European Union (EU), finally, contributed US$ 3,259 million

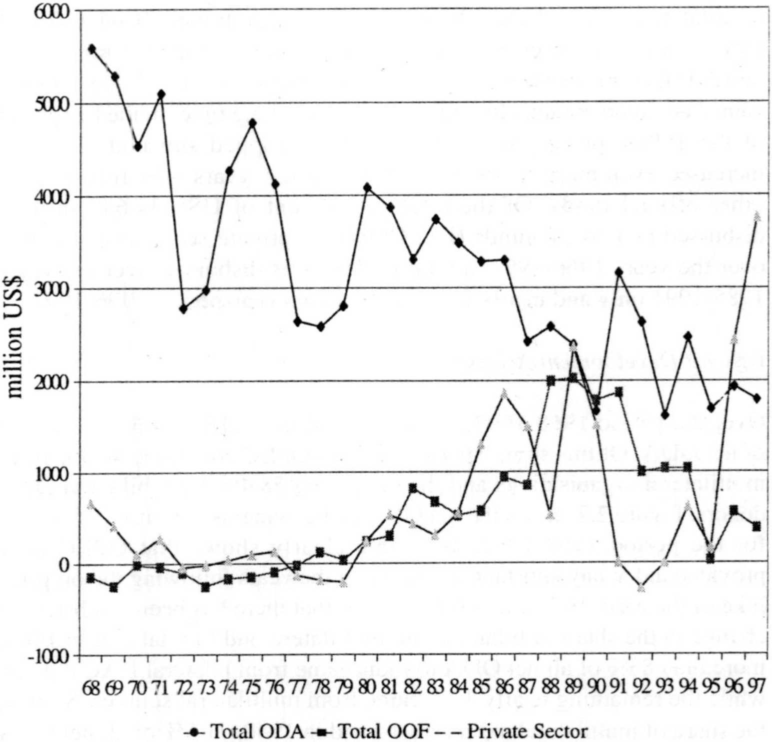

Figure 2.1: Official Development Finance (ODA + OOF + Private sector), 1968 – 1997

Source: Own calculations based on OECD

or 8.3% of all multilateral net ODA to India's development.

Aid from the European Union (multilateral aid) and the bilateral aid of individual European donor countries together form 30% of all net ODA to India over 1968-1997. Over the years the share of this European aid has fluctuated from 16% to slightly more than 48%. Within bilateral DAC aid, the EU donors form a major group. In 1969, bilateral EU donors contributed only 18.6% of all bilateral DAC aid. Three years later this had already increased to 52.6%. Up to 1990, the share of EU donors in total bilateral aid from DAC countries remained for most years well above the 50% mark, with a low of 49% and a high of 81%. The 1990s showed a decreasing share for EU donors. In 1994, only 29.3% of all bilateral ODA from DAC countries came from EU donors. This is mainly due to a substantial increase in the aid from Japan. Japan's net ODA to India totalled 23.7% of all bilateral DAC aid over the period 1968-1997.

Other non-European bilateral donors that have played an important role (quantitative-wise) in aid disbursements to India include the United States (14.5%) and Canada (5.9%)

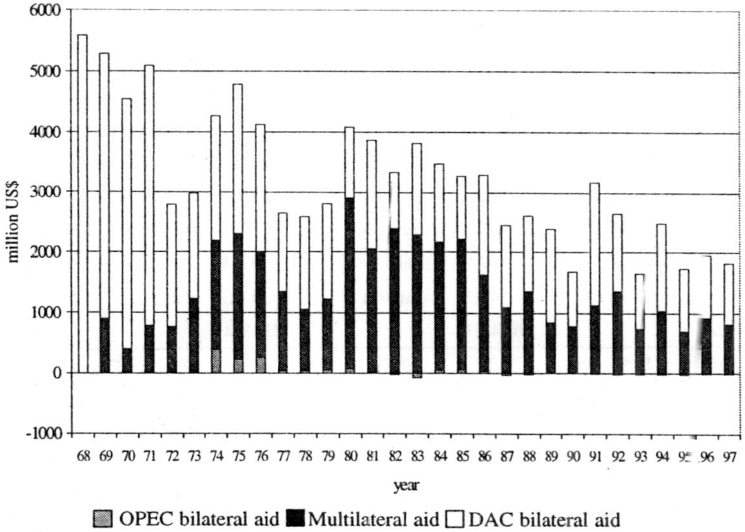

Figure 2.2: Net ODA to India from bilateral DAC donors, multilateral organisations and OPEC countries (1968-1997)

Source: Own Calculations based on OECD.

Among the European bilateral donors, there are six donors which together have provided the bulk of European aid to India: The United Kingdom (29.3% of all bilateral EU aid), Germany (22.0%), the Netherlands (12.9%), Sweden (10.0%), France (7.1%) and Denmark (3.9%). Except for France, these are the donors taken up in this study. Together these six donors provided 85.2% of all bilateral aid from EU countries over the period 1968-1997. Table 2.1 provides an overview of the major (bilateral) EU donors for India for selected years. The Table 2.1 clearly shows that the major change over the entire period refers to Germany taking over the position of major bilateral donor to India from the United Kingdom. For the rest there have been no major changes between the different periods distinguished.

Utilisation of ODA

One of the main issues that played an important role in development aid

Table 2.1: Net ODA from bilateral EU donors and the European Union (EU) to India (in million 1996 US$)

Years	1968-73		1974-79		1980-85	
1.	UK	2636.7	UK	2557.9	UK	1649.0
2	Germany	1854.0	Germany	1189.8	Germany	1184.2
3.	France	509.5	Sweden	1009.1	EU	1143.4
4.	Netherlands	394.2	Netherlands	1007.8	Netherlands	1079.9
5.	Sweden	251.3	EU	738.6	Sweden	620.4
6.	EU	217.7	France	441.2	France	418.2
7.	Belgium	136.0	Denmark	183.2	Denmark	324.6
8.	Denmark	102.6	Belgium	162.0	Belgium	59.7
9.	Italy	92.9	Italy	37.4	Austria	41.8
10.	Austria	40.5	Austria	34.6	Italy	29.1
Total		6240.1		7363.4		6554.4
Years	1986-1991		1992-1997		1968-1997	
1.	Germany	1337.3	Germany	874.1	UK	8578.2
2.	UK	921.0	UK	813.7	Germany	6439.4
3.	Netherlands	908.1	EU	448.8	Netherlands	3763.2
4.	EU	710.6	Netherlands	373.4	EU	3259.0
5.	Sweden	686.1	Sweden	368.1	Sweden	2935.0
6.	France	559.4	Denmark	200.3	France	2086.9
7.	Italy	337.9	France	158.8	Denmark	1132.6
8.	Denmark	322.2	Finland	14.4	Italy	480.2
9.	Spain	57.9	Spain	10.8	Belgium	334.0
10.	Austria	24.8	Luxembourg	9.2	Austria	127.7
Total		5868.6		3231.1		29255.7

Source: Own calculation based on OECD.

Note: Total refers to total net ODA from all bilateral EU donors (i.e., France, Germany, the Netherlands, the United Kingdom, Sweden, Austria, Belgium, Denmark, Finland, Ireland, Italy, Luxembourg, Portugal and Spain) plus the European Union.

to India is the utilisation figure (i.e., the percentage of aid utilised in relation to aid authorised). In 1993, for instance, the Indian government in the annual 'Economic Survey' (GoI 1993: 111) remarked that 'a worrying aspect of India's balance of payments in 1992-93 has been the low utilization of external assistance'. Over the entire period 1980-1992, India only managed to utilise 60.8% of all aid grants and loans committed by the international donor community.

Mishra (1995) identified several reasons for the under utilisation of Japanese development loans to India, which seem to be relevant for other cases as well (also see Oommen, 1997: 12-13): (1) sheer inefficiency of executing agencies; (2) difficulty in arranging local cost financing; (3) faulty project design, including choice of location requiring amendment of the agreement; and (4) time taken in arranging consultancy services, indenting bidding and procurement of materials against ODA loans after signing the contract. In the meantime, the Indian government has announced several measures to speed up disbursements. These measures include the agreement that all future borrowings from the multilateral/bilateral agencies by the Central and State Public Sector Undertakings will be undertaken without the Central Government's intermediation. More important perhaps is a change to the system under which aid allocations were forwarded to the states following the plan allocation formula (the so-called Gadgil formula) of 70 percent loans and 30 percent grants. By disbursing aid to the states on the same (concessional) terms on which the assistance has been received by the GoI is expected to enhance aid utilisation, as are the plans of a 25% advance and the setting up of a Project Management Unit within the Finance Ministry.

Utilisation figures are much higher for grants than they are for loans. Over 1990-91, for example, 81% of the aid loans committed in that year was indeed utilised, whereas this percentage was 102% in the case of grants. It should be mentioned in this regard that of the total net ODA to India over the entire period 1969-1995, a total of 42.5% was in the form of grants and the remaining 57.5% in the form of loans. Data on the grant-loan division of foreign aid to India show that from the mid-1970s onwards, between 40% and 60% of total net ODA annually was disbursed as a grant. At the same time, there are substantial differences between groups of donors. The grant part of multilateral aid, for instance, has exceeded the 40% mark only once and has for the larger part of the period 1969-1995 remained below 25% of total multilateral ODA. Bilateral aid from DAC countries showed a substantial increase in the grant part from 1975 onwards. During most of the 1980s, more than 75% of the annual net bilateral aid from DAC countries was disbursed as a grant. The EU members of the DAC even performed better: In 1994 and 1995 all net ODA from these bilateral donors was disbursed as a grant.

A comparison between individual EU donors, however, also shows that there are substantial differences when looking at the grant-loan division of net ODA to India. Over the last couple of years, four of the five bilateral EU donors central in this study have provided their entire

Table 2.2: Per capita ODA for selected countries in selected years (in 1994 US$)

	India	Israel	Indonesia	Tanzania
1969	9.35	108.21	15.91	17.08
1972	4.58	117.06	17.46	19.15
1975	7.95	379.40	14.93	57.06
1978	4.40	520.35	9.67	53.70
1981	5.06	353.55	11.94	67.32
1984	4.02	580.07	8.13	50.01
1987	3.06	378.09	9.67	50.06
1990	1.87	326.91	8.77	52.80
1993	1.72	258.19	11.43	38.06

Source: own calculations based on OECD.

net annual ODA as a grant: the United Kingdom since 1976 (with only a small loan attached in 1995), Sweden since 1978, Denmark in 1975 and 1976 and since 1990, and the Netherlands since 1992. Only Germany still provides a substantial amount of their annual net ODA as a loan to the Indian government. Over the larger part of the period 1969-1995, German net ODA to India was disbursed for less than 40% as a grant.

The relative (un)importance of aid

As already mentioned, aid to India used to finance a substantial part of the Indian budget for development in the 1960s. Nowadays, total aid inflows are relatively unimportant when looked at All India level. In 1969, total net aid per capita was US$ 9.35. In 1993 the per capita ODA for India was down to US$ 1.72. Table 2.2 shows that also for other countries per capita ODA decreased over the years, although the difference in absolute per capita aid is simply staggering between some of the countries.

Expressed as percentage of GNP, development aid to India is substantially less than, for instance, most of Sub Sahara African countries. In 1994, ODA constituted 100.1% of GNP in Mozambique, 30.3% in Tanzania and 22% in Mali. In India this was only 0.8% in the same year, down from 1.3% in the year 1980. Among the low-income countries, only Nigeria, China and Myanmar scored a lower percentage. In Sub Sahara Africa, ODA on average comprised 18% of all imports. In India, this was slightly more than 8.5%. Also with other comparisons (e.g., ODA as percentage of investments), India scores in general lower than many other countries, particularly Sub Sahara African countries. External assistance as support to import of goods is not substantial either. For India, domestic saving is the most important source of investment and external savings have only a marginal role. Even at its peak during the Reform period, the External Assistance/saving ratio is only 3.85%. Simultaneously, foreign aid formed only 4.5% of the aggregate public development expenditure of the country, a percentage which has been declining since then. All this shows that development aid is far less important for India than it is for those other countries.

Following this, the perceived lack of leverage in India felt by many donors becomes more clear. According to the Dutch embassy, for instance, their aid is so small that they can hardly pressurise the Indian government to follow their lead. Also Danida is convinced that its aid does not carry much leverage. The figures seem to support this. The bilateral aid from the Netherlands amounted to Dfl. 0.24 (at current prices some US$ 0.12) annually per head of the population over the period from 1971 to 1992. Nevertheless, the history of the aid programme of the EU donors proves them to be wrong. Also at central level, European donors, despite their aid being 'just a drop in the ocean', have managed to influence government policy and have their leverage (*see also* Chapters 4, 5 and 6). At state level, the possibilities for leverage seem to be more clear if only because foreign aid is substantially more important for individual states than for India as a whole.

State level

All foreign aid, except private aid to NGDOs, is routed through the Central Government in New Delhi (GoI). In effect, foreign aid is 'piled up' at the centre and then distributed to the states based on reimbursement requests from these states on expenditure already occurred. Furthermore, until recently the aid was provided from the centre to the state on a 70% loan (lately at 13% interest) and 30% grant basis no matter the conditions of the donor. This was because these funds were seen as part of the central assistance to the states (*also see,* Government of India 1994). Above we have seen that this so-called Gadgil formula has been changed in order to speed up utilisation figures. Simultaneously, foreign aided projects are part of the planning process in the respective states. As such, these externally funded projects are not additional but are already included in the budget. In general, disbursements from the centre to the states runs relatively smoothly. In many cases, such as in Andhra Pradesh, foreign aided projects have preference over other projects when it comes to releasing funds. In many states also, the government has set up specific

Table 2.3: Assistance to states for externally aided projects (1985-1990)

State	Allocated (in %)	Actuals (in %)	Actuals per Capita (in Rs.)	HDI rank	Population below poverty line*
Andhra Pradesh	4.96	3.57	16.60	9	27.20
Bihar	3.49	3.98	14.22	12	53.37
Gujarat	12.70	11.49	85.95	5	32.33
Haryana	2.48	3.04	56.97	4	16.63
Karnataka	4.88	5.94	40.76	7	38.14
Kerala	5.34	4.35	46.17	1	32.08
Madhya Pradesh	10.65	10.97	50.58	13	43.40
Maharashtra	14.06	14.91	58.42	3	40.10
Orissa	7.87	8.63	84.35	10	55.61
Punjab	0.85	1.09	16.62	2	12.70
Rajasthan	1.79	3.12	21.89	11	34.60
Tamil Nadu	7.33	8.67	48.03	8	45.13
Uttar Pradesh	19.34	15.93	35.38	14	41.99
West Bengal	4.26	4.33	19.63	6	43.99
All States	100.00	100.00	36.51		39.34

Source: Own calculations based on Government of Uttar Pradesh 1991: 180-181, R.S. Srivastava 1997: 5 and 9.

Notes: * = In % of total population (1987-88).

Per capita figures are worked out using 1991 census data.

units mostly within the Planning Department (e.g., Project Monitoring Unit in AP) to deal with the financial part of the foreign aided projects. These units do not deal with the construction part or the monitoring of the implementation, as that is the responsibility of the so-called Programme Implementing Agency (PIA) being either a state line department or an implementing body set up specifically for a project.

One of the reasons for the GoI to remain a kind of middleman between the foreign donor and the state government is that in this way it maximises its say in the foreign aid. Over the period 1990-1994, nearly two-thirds of foreign aid has been taken over by the centre, a large part of it being given as loans to Public Sector Undertakings. This means that only 28% of total foreign aid was available for allocation to states, which is not to say that these funds were allocated on an equitable basis. There are certain states in which hardly any of the donors works (and/or wants to work) and thus there is a large disparity between the states as far as their share in foreign aid is concerned. According to the Government of Uttar Pradesh (1991: 180-181), for instance, Maharashtra received 22% of all foreign aid released to the 14 major states. Uttar Pradesh itself received 7.7% in the same year despite it being the largest state. Although the share for UP picked up in later years, the GoUP is still convinced that they have been 'underpaid'. The above shows that the 'equity policy' said to be followed by the Central Government does not work out in practice. Some of the states clearly receive much more foreign aid than would have to be expected on the basis of their population, their HDI rank and/or the percentage of their population below the poverty line. Table 2.3 clearly shows the discrepancies between the states in this regard for the period 1985-1990.

Two examples: Uttar Pradesh and Andhra Pradesh

Whereas foreign aid for India as a total may be 'peanuts', this already becomes less the case when looked at state level. Uttar Pradesh has received an increasing amount in central assistance for externally aided projects over the period 1980-1991. In 1980, UP received nearly Rs. 9 crores while this was up to Rs. 292 ten years later (Government of Uttar Pradesh 1991: 170-173, 180-181). Over the Seventh Plan period (1985-1990), foreign aid made up 11.2% of total expenditure [while total outlay for the Seventh Plan was covered for 21% by Externally Aided Project (EAP) funds]. At the time of drafting the Eighth Plan there were in total 30 projects in the externally aided portfolio of which 19 were continuing and the remaining 11 new projects. Total outlay for these projects was Rs. 4,225.83 crores (or 15.1% of total outlay) up to 1997. If looked at specific 'heads of development', external aid is much more than the average percentage of 15% for total outlay. Activities in the field of tourism, for instance, are financed for more than 75% by foreign aid, while nearly 25% from the funds for power projects are envisaged to come from foreign donors. Also within agriculture and allied activities, some of the sub-sectors (e.g., forestry, soil conservation and fisheries) are to be covered for around 25% or more by foreign funds. Finally, also irrigation funds come for a major part from abroad (*also see* Table 2.4).

The GoUP has managed to cover an increasing part of its total annual outlay by foreign aid in the 1900s. Over the period 1985-90, a total of 21% of the total outlay was covered by EAPs. The first four years of the 1990s, this increased to over 30%. From 1994-95, this percentage declined and the GoUP noted that 'therefore it is required to formulate many more projects in different development sectors for posing to

Table 2.4: Uttar Pradesh: Externally aided projects as part of Plan outlay (1985-1995)

Year(s)	Total Outlay for The Plan lakhs	Externally Aided Projects Outlays lakhs	As % of total Plan Outlay	Expenditure lakhs
1985-90	11000	2306.28	20.9	1340.18
1990-91	3383	1049.68	31.0	731.53
1991-92	3892	1217.03	31.2	1310.21
1992-93	4040	1413.16	35.0	1407.83
1993-94	4250	1346.52	31.7	764.45
1994-95	4762	1344.24	28.2	824.48
1995-96	5702	1227.59	21.5	n.a.

Source: Own calculations based on GoUP 1995.

external agencies' (GoUP 1995). As with plan outlays, the outlays for EAPs do not say much about the actual expenditures. Of against an outlay for EAPs over 1993-94, for instance, of Rs. 1346.52 lakhs, total expenditures were only Rs. 764.45 lakhs or 57%. Table 2.4 provides an overview of the outlay and expenditure for EAPs in relation to total plan outlays for the years 1985 to 1994-95.

The discrepancy between outlays and expenditures mentioned above is quite common in Uttar Pradesh and is certainly not restricted to EAPs only. According to the Planning Department, the outlays expressed in the Five Year and annual plans should not be taken as rigid. These outlays are always put on a high side as this looks better politically. The possibilities for the GoUP to really spent all these funds is quite insufficient. This accounts also for EAPs. For 1997-98, there is a proposed outlay in the budget of Rs 1,500 crores for EAPs. However, this amount will not be reached mainly because this outlay is the outcome of political struggle and does not reflect any real possibility for implementation. Moreover: (1) it takes time to sanction new projects; (2) running projects can use less funds (like in power) or there are changes in the exchange rate; (3) procurement normally takes some time; (4) human resources and tenure uncertainty. The latter point refers not only to the quality of the staff implementing a specific project but also to the frequent shifts in personnel (interview, Planning Departments, Lucknow). Some of these points are confirmed in the Annual Plan 1995-96 (GoUP 1995) where it is stated that 'formulation, appraisal and processing for EAPs is relatively time consuming'. Consequently it takes lot of time before the assistance is actually received.

The same picture roughly emerges from Andhra Pradesh. Although

Table 2.5: Provisions in the Andhra Pradesh budget for major heads of development - 1996-97 and 1997-98 (in % of total budget provision per head)

	1996-97		1997-98	
	Normal Plan	EAP	Normal Plan	EAP
Economic Services	68.7%	31.3%	67.4%	32.6%
1. Agriculture	68.0%	32.0%	29.1%	70.9%
2. Rural development	100.0%	-	100.0%	-
3. Special area development	100.0%	-	100.0%	-
4. Irrigation & flood control	82.3%	16.7%	70.2%	29.8%
5. Energy	32.6%	67.4%	38.2%	61.8%
6. Industry & minerals	88.2%	11.8%	100.0%	-
7. Transport	74.4%	25.6%	100.0%	-
8. Communication	100.0%	-	100.0%	-
9. Science, technology & env.	84.6%	15.4%	96.0%	4.0%
10. General economic services	100.0%	-	100.0%	-
Social Services	90.6%	9.4%	75.1%	24.9%
1. Education	91.2%	8.8%	85.5%	14.5%
2. Health	77.4%	22.6%	45.0%	55.0%
3. Water supply & sanitation	82.4%	17.6%	32.0%	68.0%
4. Housing	100.0%	-	100.0%	-
5. Urban development	79.8%	20.2%	79.5%	20.5%
6. Information & publicity	100.0%	-	100.0%	-
7. Welfare SC, ST, BC & min.	90.8%	9.2%	78.9%	21.1%
8. Labour	100.0%	-	100.0%	-
General Services	100.0%	-	100.0%	-
Grand Total	75.1%	24.9%	69.6%	30.4%

Source: Government of Andhra Pradesh 1996.

aid (and particularly aid from European donors) may be relatively marginal when looked at the total budget (plan and non-plan) of the Andhra Pradesh government, it already becomes a different picture if looked at only the plan (or: development) budget and even more so if specific heads or budget posts are considered. Whereas of the total revised plan budget provision of Rs. 277,313.17 lakhs for the year 1996-97, nearly 25% came from external aided projects funds, it was substantially more for particular budget heads. Table 2.5 provides an overview of the total plan budget for the years 1996-97 and 1997-98 under specific heads dividing the budget in 'normal plan funds' and 'externally aided projects funds'. The Table 2.5 clearly shows that specific 'heads of development' can be financed for a substantial part by external or foreign donor funds.

It is also clear from the table that there is a growing dependency on foreign donors to provide the funds for developmental activities of the Andhra Pradesh government particularly in the field of social services. This highlights the budget constraints experienced by the state, exemplified by the relatively recent decision to come back on prohibition 'for development's sake'. Prohibition, which had been in effect since 1994, is said to have cost the State some Rs. 1,800 crores annually in income (Nagaraj, 1997: 11). It has led to 'restructuring' the finances and to a further exploration of 'the possibility of obtaining loans from international lending agencies such as the World Bank and the Asian Development Bank', both of which demand reforms for their assistance (Radhakrishna & Mainak, 1987: 26-28).

The importance of foreign aid for the development budget of specific states such as Andhra Pradesh, and particularly the importance for specific sectors in that budget, shows that the leverage of foreign donors is potentially bigger at state level as it is at central level in New Delhi. Of course, the bigger donors will potentially have a larger leverage than the smaller ones. For Andhra and Uttar Pradesh, the major donors are the multilateral donors (notably the World Bank and the Asian Development Bank) and Japan as bilateral donor. European donors only play a marginal role in the aid allocation to these two states. In financial sense, Uttar Pradesh' main donor is the World Bank (crop husbandry, soil conservation, fisheries, irrigation, roads and bridges, environment, education, water supply and sanitation). Of the 27 projects mentioned in the Eighth Five Year Plan, a total of 13 were from the World Bank. Simultaneously, of the total outlay mentioned in the Plan for these 27 projects, the World Bank covered the largest part. Also Japan (mainly active in power projects) takes, in financial terms, a large share in the EAPs. European donors are not a very common sight in UP, with the exception of the Netherlands (rural water supply and irrigation), Great Britain (power) and the European Union (soil conservation). The Project Monitoring Unit in the Government of Andhra Pradesh Planning Department regards the bilateral aid from European countries as 'small fish' and marginal not only when looked at the total budget but also in comparison with, for instance, the assistance from the World Bank or Japan (which is a large donor in power supply in the state). Also the Eighth Five Year Plan of the Government of Andhra Pradesh makes clear that power projects (e.g., co-financed by Japan and the UK) are in quantitative sense the most important, whereas the majority of funds come from the World Bank.

Concluding Remarks

For foreign donors, India remains an important country whether for political, humanitarian, economic or geo-strategic reasons. Data on (declining) ODA figures shows that bilateral DAC donors (and then particularly those that are central in this study) have provided an important part of total aid to the country. However, and despite the fact that India has been, and still is, a major aid receiving country, development aid is only of marginal importance to the country. Development aid can indeed be regarded as 'peanuts' at all India level. This picture changes dramatically when looked at individual states. Here development aid can contribute substantially to the development budget even to such an extent that one can speak of increasing aid dependence. Still, at the end of the day, it is not so much the quantitative level of aid that counts but the extent to which this aid has managed to improve the lives of the poor in a sustainable manner. Whether aid from the Netherlands, the United Kingdom, Denmark, Germany, Sweden and the European Union has contributed to this poverty reduction will be discussed in detail in following chapters.

REFERENCE

1. Unless otherwise stated, all figures are expressed in 1996 US$.

3

CRITERIA FOR ASSESSING AID FOR POVERTY REDUCTION

In order to assess the strategies and policies of the different EU donors covered by this study, it is important that we present the conceptual framework from which we approach poverty reduction and thereby the starting point for our assessment of the donors and their aid interventions. Moreover, we want to specify our views on the most important dimensions of development assistance and its operationalisation.

Hence in this chapter we start with a discussion of different concepts of poverty and presentation of the multidimensional concept that we use in this study. This is followed by a section on the need for targeting aid interventions on the poor in order to achieve poverty reduction. Next comes a section on the gender dimension of development and aid; gender sensitivity is necessary for successfully addressing the needs of the poor (men and women). A section on participation follows; it is evident that participatory approaches have a potential for increasing aid effectiveness and impact. Then comes a section dealing with various aspects of sustainability, economic, institutional, technological and environmental. Finally there are sections dealing with replicability of projects and programmes and monitoring & evaluation requirements.

This entire chapter in a sense can be seen as defining the 'yardstick' with which we have 'measured' or assessed the development interventions funded by the six European donors under study. In writing this we clearly present our views which in turn form the basis of our assessments. While we acknowledge that there is a certain subjective element in this, on the other hand we are reasonably sure that most of the views advocated here are in line with current donor thinking, notably that of the six EU donors.

Conceptualising poverty

Poverty reduction will only be as good as the conceptualisation of poverty which informs the way in which an aid intervention is identified, designed and implemented. Similarly, the assessment of the poverty reduction orientation in country strategies, programmes and projects; the evaluation of projects for poverty reduction; the assessment of their impact, are all heavily dependent upon the thinking on poverty, the definition of what constitutes poverty, the theoretical approaches that underwrite that definition, and the methodologies that they give rise to in investigating and monitoring the poverty condition (also see: Engberg-Pedersen, 1998).

The elevation of poverty reduction to an overarching objective for the majority of donor agencies in the 1990s has been parallelled by an increase in research on the meaning and measurement of poverty. The 'new poverty agenda' (Lipton & Maxwell, 1992) that these two trends reflect has, on the one hand, focused attention upon the continuing growth of the poverty problem in the world today, but on the other hand, has failed to reach any consensus as to how to define poverty, to target the poor better, to monitor and assess the impact of aid on poverty reduction better.

One can begin with a basic distinction between absolute and relative poverty. Absolute poverty is where basic necessities by any definition are lacking. Whether this is caused by natural, social or economic reasons is not of significance, what is important is that physical survival is in jeopardy. When absolute poverty approaches ultra-poverty, emergency relief is the response. Relative poverty, where there is a continual failure to meet the living conditions held to be minimal or acceptable within a locality, introduces dimensions of relation and perception and thereby turns attention more towards the processes giving rise to poverty and the different means by which to analyse and study poverty.

In current research on poverty, two analytical approaches predominate, namely the objective assessment approach and the people's perception of poverty approach. These utilise markedly different methodologies to research poverty, reflecting quite different epistemologies within the social sciences. At the same time, it can be argued that they both have a tendency to reflect poverty in terms of specific conditions for which the poverty reduction aim would be to treat these. While the former might emphasize assets, available resources, consumption, income, the latter would identify and prioritise the 'needs' of the poor quite differently, with the poor being active participants in the research. In both cases the tendency for the policy makers is to then design interventions according to the prioritised list of needs. What can be discussed is the extent to which this leads to the treatment of effects rather than causes. Throughout history, there has been a desire by the non-poor to see poverty as the poor's own problem and responsibility. To raise questions concerning the non-poor's responsibility for poverty that go beyond concerns with moral responsibility have been and remain contentious, not least because of the policy implications that can accompany such thinking.

Nevertheless, there is recognition today of the need to ensure that research and policy on poverty goes beyond the condition of poverty and stresses more the processes at work as reflected in such terms as 'ill-being', 'powerlessness', and 'vulnerability' (Baulch 1996). The problem of poverty is raised in relational terms, not least in terms of the production of wealth. Poverty reduction requires changes in relations secured through changes in ownership, rights, knowledge, capacities etc. Such an approach must lead to a more complex conceptualisation of poverty in terms of the characteristics or dimensions to be included in the poverty matrix. Common property resources are an example of a frequently neglected resource that has central importance to the poor in rural areas (Beck 1994), social capital is another (*see,* for instance, World Bank 1997, Putnam & Raffaella 1993, and Bourdieu 1991). But concepts of rights, dignity, autonomy take the relational discussion of poverty into the institutional arena and not least into a discussion of the nature and role of the state vis-à-vis poverty and the poor. They directly raise the issue of the political status of the poor and lines of demarcation that exist based upon gender, ethnicity, religion in addition to those based upon landownership, employment status, resource access, locality etc.

In identifying and designing a poverty reduction aid intervention, objective and perception-based assessments of poverty can be used to direct attention towards those with the problem of poverty; discussions of absolute and relative poverty should be the basis for deciding the desirable approach towards achieving poverty reduction; the more local analysis of vulnerabilities should enable a better needs analysis based upon an improved understanding as to the nature and dimensions of the problems that give rise to and reproduce poverty. In this way it should be possible to identify not only those who are poor today, but also those who could well be in poverty, possibly absolute poverty, tomorrow.

One further distinction can be usefully made when considering the different dimensions of poverty and the types of intervention for poverty reduction. This is between macro and micro forms of poverty. When a particular vulnerability or poverty condition is common to a large section of the population, for example illiteracy, landlessness, unemployment, poor health, or high infanct mortality, then one can speak of a form of macropoverty for which a sector-wide approach or programme is required. This could be a women and child literacy programme or the design and implementation of legislation to provide security of tenure to sharecroppers. Such interventions tend to be based upon one single dimension of poverty, taken up at a macro-cum-sector level and then implemented through a range of organisational instruments at meso and micro-levels. Micro- or local poverty can be used to describe more specific situations of poverty involving a number of overlapping vulnerabilities with consequences for a range of poverty characteristics. For example, women from landless or marginal landowning households in unirrigated forest areas, whose men migrate to find work and where the forest department denies access to its lands. A more integrated approach, not least bottom-up, that builds upon the localised patterns of poverty and seeks to reflect the complexity within the design and organisation of any aid intervention is required. Local decentralised government, if it is present, participatory and reflecting minority interests, might be the point for institutional intervention. Local NGOs might be another. In both instances, the participation and support of the beneficiaries in the identification, design and implementation of the PR intervention will play a far greater role.

In order to assess the strategies and policies of the different EU donors covered by the India study, a conceptual approach towards poverty and poverty reduction has been adopted that stresses the multidimensional nature of poverty and which seeks to capture characteristics of poverty that reflect not only the poverty condition, but the processes that lie behind. In other words, the dimensions selected are designed to reflect a way of thinking about poverty rather than a check list against which to set the strategies, programmes and projects. Undoubtedly, there are other dimensions that might have been taken into account, but those described below are believed to be sufficiently comprehensive to allow a balanced assessment of different donor approaches to and operationalisation of the poverty reduction objective (*also see* ODA, 1995).

Four main dimensions have been identified:

First, *livelihoods* covers the condition of a household and the means by which it reproduces itself. It covers factors such as employment and work conditions, income-generating activities, food security, state of health, literacy/illiteracy, asset ownership.

Secondly, *resources* refers to the resources to which the household has access including health care, education, credit, land, clean drinking water and sanitation, social support networks etc.

Thirdly, *knowledge* refers to the different types of knowledge possessed and the ability to utilise and expand it, for example, literacy, health knowledge, legal, technical and managerial knowledge etc.

Finally *rights* refers to the rights possessed, whether as individuals, women, minority groups, tenants, workers etc.; it covers formal legal rights as well as traditional and customary rights.

It is the view of the study that donor country strategy papers, sector strategy papers and project documents should reflect the complexity of poverty and in particular the need to handle the processes that give rise to poverty in developing a strategy for poverty reduction. In the case of projects, then from the identification through design, implementation and monitoring and assessment, poverty must be approached as multidimensional even when the project focuses on one specific condition in a particular sector.

Targeting the poor

The issue of whether or not and how to target the poor in development interventions (state-provided or donor-financed) is contested in India and more generally. In India targeted government programmes have a long history and many forms, e.g. the rural employment programmes, the rural integrated development programmes and a variety of basic needs programmes (housing, food provision, health etc.). In 1997 there has been a heated controversy around the United Front Government's plan to transform the Public Distribution System into a more narrowly Targeted Public Distribution System, aimed at providing subsidised food to those below the poverty line (cfr *Frontline,* Oct. 31, 1997). At stake in the debate are both fiscal concerns, vested middle class interests and the scope for leakage in this or that system. The controversy demonstrates that the issue of targeting is not merely a technocratic question dealing with effectiveness and efficiency, but a highly politicised issue.

At a more general level there are good arguments both for and against targeting the poor (Besley & Kanbur, 1993, Bamberger & Aziz, 1993). The main rationale for targeting the poor in development interventions is the desire to utilise scarce resources in a way that gives priority to those who need it most. In an open competition for access to resources the poor will generally lose out to economically and politically more powerful groups. The World Bank's poverty alleviation strategy has three main elements (World Bank, 1990, 1996): promoting economic opportunities for the poor (labour-intensive growth), delivering social services to the poor (health, education) and providing safety nets for the poor (food subsidies, employment schemes etc.). This can be viewed as a strong case for targeting.

There are, however, a number of arguments against targeting the poor. First, it is not easy to define who are the poor, whether by income or consumption criteria or according to a broader notion of poverty. Secondly, even if the group of poor is well defined it is administratively demanding and hence costly to identify the households or individuals that belong to the group and ensure that they receive the benefits. Thirdly, in spite of the best efforts to target the poor there will always be a certain amount of undercoverage, i.e. needy not being reached, as well as leakage, i.e. flow of resources to people who do not belong to the target group. Fourthly, the political economy of targeting often implies that powerful groups with vested interests will object to targeting the poor and try to undermine such efforts. All these arguments have been used in favour of more universalist schemes.

In order to overcome some of the practical difficulties involved in targeting the poor, several approaches have been devised that use proxies to identify poor groups and individuals. These can either take the form of geographic or social targeting.

In geographic targeting a given intervention is directed towards areas with a (more than average) concentration of poor people. This can be done at all geographic scales, e.g. by selecting poor states, districts, villages or hamlets. The problem in this approach of course is that although poverty in the geographic area targeted is above average, there is no guarantee that the better off people living in the area do not capture a disproportionate part of the benefits. At a macrolevel Datt & Ravaillon (1993) have argued that there is a potential for alleviating poverty through regional redistribution in India, but that the potential is quite modest. This result, however, is closely linked to the scale of their study which focuses on the states. In a different regional context Baker & Grosh (1994) have found that the outcome for the locality level targeting is distinctly better than that for the state level. It is evident that localised interventions can be more precise in geographic targeting of the poor, e.g. through selection of poor hamlets.

In social targeting the intervention is directed towards an easily identifiable social category with a (more than average) concentration of poor people. Targeting women is an important example, although the rationale for this entails other considerations than incidence of poverty. In an Indian context other social categories with a high concentration of poor people are landless agricultural labourers and scheduled castes *(dalits)* and scheduled tribes *(adivasis).*

A simple method to target the poor is by designing projects and programmes so that they become self-targeting. In India this has been done in employment programmes by setting the wage so low that only poor people would be interested in taking advantage of the programme (Besley & Kanbur, 1993). While this works well as a targeting mechanism it obviously has other drawbacks (foregone income and opportunity costs of time related to other work and household duties). In the health sector a good case can be made for viewing a sizable part of the public health system as self-targeting. Since the quality of health services is generally poor, and since there is a better alternative in the form of private doctors and hospitals, which the well-to-do can afford, it is largely poor people that are served by the public health system. Again, as a targeting mechanism this works well, but the drawbacks in terms of sub-standard services and continuous poor health are only too obvious.

In the context of the donor-supported interventions studied here there is scope for targeting the poor. A donor serious about addressing poverty would, logically, draw upon its understanding of the nature of poverty to identify who the poor are and design mechanisms for targeting as large a share of an intervention's benefits as possible towards them. This may necessitate the identification of the particular social, economic, and political dimensions that delineate the poor within a particular location, such as gender, minority status, occupation, landownership, religion etc. Even if poor groups are identified, project benefits are still likely to be captured by dominant groups unless special mechanisms are designed to target these groups, taking account of both supply- and demand-side aspects. The need and degree of targeting required, and the costs and benefits, vary from situation to situation. In terms of targeting policy, we would expect to find evidence of practices such as:

- account taken of existence/capability/willingness of institutions able to reach the poor;
- understanding of importance of targeting benefits to the poor and of designing mechanisms to facilitate this;
- using proxies to identify poor groups, e.g. geographical targeting of dry/backward/remote regions, poor states/districts/blocks/ villages, or hamlets rather than main villages, or social targeting of landless labourers, scheduled castes and tribes or women;
- recognition that quite precise targeting is especially important in productive sectors (as the poor are often assetless), whereas targeting in social sectors may be necessary, such as

expertise and simply required additional resources. Development assistance was a purely financial instrument, whereby the Community aid programme purchased a certain value of fertiliser and the Indian Government undertook to fund additional development projects to the same value. In the mid-1980s there was an attempt by some in the Commission to shift away from narrow provision of financial resources, to a more full-fledged development programme. This was resisted by the Government of India, which lobbied the Commission at a senior level and which, together with European industrial and fertiliser companies, succeeded in staving off significant change until 1990. The Community aid programme shifted away from its role as financial provider to being a catalyst for change which sought to enhance its impact by closer coordination with the member state programmes. This shift was reflected, belatedly, in a new Council Regulation in 1992 which included reference for the first time to human rights, democratisation and good governance. This was reinforced by the document *India and the European Community: cooperation strategy to the year 2000,* in 1994, which formally placed poverty reduction at the heart of its development strategy (as of course did the Treaty on European Union in 1992). A more recent document from the Commission, *EU-India Enhanced Partnership,* emphasizes the value of 'building a human dimension' as a parallel objective to economic development. Although it underlines the importance of improving basic social services, there is no detailed analysis of causes and potential solutions to poverty.

The positive nature of this groundswell in favour of a greater poverty orientation must, of course, be tempered by an acknowledgement that commercial interests continue to play a role. In all the donor programmes studied here, there are examples of business interests having distorted aid to India and made it less poverty-oriented. Despite clear evidence of a greater 'seriousness' in tackling poverty, ambiguity between developmental and business interest remains. To some extent this is inevitable; but the challenge is to ensure that hand directing each donor's approach is guided primarily by the desire to reach the poor.

Donor views of the Indian approach to poverty reduction

The donors considered here welcome the emphasis placed by the Government of India on tackling poverty through a raft of programmes. This commitment, many feel, contrasts sharply with the apathy towards poverty reduction characteristic of many Sub-Saharan African countries. However, donor impressions, shared by some within the GoI, are that most Central Government poverty reduction programmes have relatively little impact on their intended target group. The Danes, for example, expressed the view that by and large the policies are quite good, but implementation is a big problem. The dominant view among UK staff, shared by the Germans, was that often the policy environment itself was flawed, with distorted incentive structures causing massive 'leakage' of benefits to non-poor groups; most subsidies were felt to be misdirected.

The Dutch, the Danes, the European Commission, the UK, and no doubt others, felt that government programmes have been hampered by overly-bureaucratic delivery mechanisms, and expressed the hope that donor-support for institutional building and human resource development would bring benefits. Germany expressed a particular concern that many social programmes have failed to build a broader base for pro-poor development through the self-help potential present at the local level. This is perceived to be a problem both in the design of the government's programmes, for example the failure to embrace user fees in the irrigation and power sectors, and in the institutions through which programmes are implemented. In particular, the government's lack of enthusiasm to utilise local non-governmental organisations, user groups and self-help groups leaves it reliant on tradition-bound administrative systems. Other comments included:

Panchayati Raj reforms have been unevenly implemented across states, with the result that the institutional base at the local level varies greatly. The scope for supporting poverty reduction in the neediest of states, such as Bihar, is very limited where corruption is combined with a weak local-level institutional base.

Although there is growing support for a participatory approach within government, too many projects are presented to donors which are still designed and implemented from above. One donor commented: 'The Indian Government thinks that working with the poor is to conceive of a project and then get NGOs to get the people to accept it. We think that the poor have to be there much earlier.'

The GoI is moving towards a more decentralised approach, such as in the District Primary Education Project, but it remains the case that rarely is the diversity of problems and contexts found at the local level incorporated into the planning process in government programmes.

German officials felt that while Central Government is showing greater willingness to support a Self Help approach and to cooperate with NGOs to this end, there remains scepticism and mistrust of this approach and of NGOs as implementing partners among many within the administration. The potential of this approach was also being limited if

NGOs were not engaged within a framework which recognises their particular capabilities and constraints. NGOs are not alternatives to the government system, are relatively few in number, and are not a panacea for caste problems.

There is a strong belief within KfW that macroeconomic and structural reforms, such as the removal of subsidies and expansion of the tax base, are preconditions for effective development and an improved distribution of the ensuing benefits. The continuing flow of foreign investment is seen as providing strong pressure for further moves in this direction, as well as helping to improve the competitiveness of Indian industry, creating more employment in the process. This was echoed by the UK, which also recognised that India, unlike many other developing countries, *has* the capacity to make effective strides towards poverty reduction. A decade ago there was no willingness to look at macroeconomic reform. Now there is. If political will can be mustered for macroeconomic reform, the hope of the UK and others is that it can be mobilised for sector- or state-level reform.

Recipient-donor dialogue on poverty reduction

Context

Dialogue takes three main forms. Firstly, most donors hold annual bilateral aid talks with the Indian government; secondly, through the continuous process of interaction between the donor and senior Department of External Affairs (DEA) officials, within the Ministry of Finance; and finally, through more sector-specific contacts between donor experts and line ministries at central or state level. To this may be added the recent (and limited) donor-state dialogue, covering macroeconomic and state-wide reform issues rather than simply sectoral or project-level matters. The most obvious point to make is that it has been quite rare for the poverty to be discussed in depth as a generic issue through any of these channels, though this may be improving slightly. The second point is that donors universally see themselves as having little leverage given the paucity of their resources relative to those of the government, and in the face of the sheer scale and diversity of poverty in India.

Although the overall recipient-donor relationship is reasonably positive, both identify factors which constrain the effectiveness of dialogue, and thus potentially limit scope for pro-poor changes. One DEA official contrasted the recent high-profile OECD DAC document, *Shaping the 21st Century,* which is full of confidence in recipients to manage their affairs, with the patronising attitude of most donors. This lack of confidence in Indian capacities was, he argued, very detrimental to good relations. Interestingly, his conclusion that India, unlike many other developing countries, has a highly developed administrative system, even though its implementation is sometimes flawed, is one which is shared by some of the European donors. It seems likely that there is some substance behind the feeling that donors may under rate government capacities and push for high levels of donor control as the only means of 'guaranteeing results'. This is may be more true of the more 'hands on' donors such as Denmark and the UK, though some concerns have been expressed about the German and European Commission insistence on providing technical support in the field to projects. Some within DFID themselves speak of the dominance of a culture of micro-management, driven by a belief that change occurs only in response to external pushing and control. There is some awareness of this among senior management and indeed some field management offices have been requested by the Delhi office to adopt a more 'hands off' approach.

Equally, there are concerns expressed on the donor side. Many feel, for instance, that the Department of External Affairs is totally indifferent to dialogue on poverty reduction, seeing its role as restricted to securing donor financing and allocating it as far as possible to meet Indian needs, rather than tackling issues of pro-poor policy reform.

It is likely that state-level dialogue may be more fruitful in terms of the poverty reduction objective. This is partly a question of leverage. At the state level, donor financing, particularly when taken together, often accounts for a very significant share of new investment (plan) expenditure within individual sectors. If donors gave greater priority to arriving at a common position on that sector they could exert collective leverage far beyond that which they currently exercise individually. Indeed, all the bilateral donors cherish the idea of less bureaucratic and centralised dialogue. A concerted effort was made to have the principle of direct donor-state dialogue accepted at the 'India Development Forum' meeting in Tokyo (September 1996), but this was rejected. The government has long preferred to retain central control, partly because of a fear that development aid may become even more lop-sided in its state-wise distribution if donors are free to deal directly with their 'pet' states. However, there are encouraging signs of a greater openness on this issue, partly as a result of the general drift towards greater decentralisation of government.

DFID sees great scope in state level dialogue as an important vehicle for taking the reform agenda forward, in the social sectors and the power sector especially. At a more macro level, DFID has had some initial involvement with the World Bank in discussions with Andhra Pradesh concerning a state level structural adjustment programme. DFID sees this as an opportunity to review with the state government DFID's entire portfolio of projects and then set clearer priorities for the future. The degree to which these priorities would have poverty reduction at their core is not yet clear, however. Nonetheless, increased state level dialogue should make it easier for DFID to forge closer relationship with government and project partners, and to gain a better understanding of the local context and thus improve effectiveness. To the extent that dialogue has taken place in the past, there has been criticism that it has concentrated almost exclusively on government officials, drawing very little on NGO insights (van Diesen, 1998). Even if this is not entirely justified, it is damaging to DFID's attempts to build a broad-based and poverty focused partnership at the state level. Christian Aid's recommendation that greater transparency be pursued, perhaps through a forum which allows Indian NGOs to comment on British aid, appears worthy of consideration, and applies equally to other donors.

Sida has also, like many other donors, been pushing to be able to deal more directly with states. Despite the principle that everything must pass through and be approved by the GoI, it has in practice had meaningful discussions with the Government of Rajasthan. Discussions with the Governments of Tamil Nadu and Orissa have been more limited and less positive. The Dutch also engage in serious state level discussions in Uttar Pradesh and Andhra Pradesh, largely with the Department of Planning (DoP). While the main focus of the DoP is felt to be funding rather than policy discussions, there is an awareness at this level of the importance for poverty reduction of participation of local people in development interventions. The Dutch consider this dialogue, and especially that with the individual line departments responsible for implementation, to be far more important than national level discussions. Their feeling, that it is the personality and effectiveness of the individual concerned which determines progress, is shared by the other donors (and by officials on the government side vis-a-vis the donors).

The European Commission has been hampered by its staffing constraints and its organisational structure. At the moment, dialogue operates at two levels. Firstly, the broad orientations, procedures and political aspects of dialogue are discussed in principle between the EU delegation and the Department of External Affairs. This information is relayed to Brussels, where the final decisions are taken in consultation with the member states through the Asia-Latin America Committee. All technical matters have to be referred back to Brussels, yet despite this the Indian government side is not authorised to undertake discussions directly with Brussels. Many EC officials, in the Delegation and in Brussels, feel that dialogue would be far more effective if the Delegation was empowered and sufficient technical expertise was available at the Delegation-level. The Delegation-level education coordinator, for instance, felt that dialogue was compromised by the excessive reliance on consultants, and the resultant lack of continuity made it more difficult to build up an effective long-term relationship. Playing a real part in the policy dialogue process, she argued, required intensive participation. Clearly, safeguards would be required, since a senior official cautioned that as well as advantages, in-country staff sometimes identified too closely with partner government concerns, and were too ready to compromise on the programmes objectives.

It should be added that lack of continuity is at least as serious a problem within the Indian government. Senior and middle-ranking officials change jobs, often changing departments, within 3 years, and sometimes much more regularly. The internal administrative arrangements appear to reduce the chances of promotion within the same location, resulting in very high levels of disruption. In addition, rural positions are highly unpopular, with money changing hands within the 'transfer industry' to ensure a more desirable (and sometimes lucrative) urban position.

At a somewhat more formal level, the European Community programme is shaped by dialogue through a Joint Commission, held on a roughly annual basis. This is attended by the Director General of DG1b, responsible for the Asia, Latin America and Mediterranean programmes, by the Government of India, Department of External Affairs, and by the EU member states. Broad strategies are discussed and agreed in this forum, and more detailed work is carried out in the Sub-Commission fora on Development and Environment (attended the EC officials and GoI only). Although this does allow senior level officials to meet directly and helps ensure coherence and coordination with the EU bilateral programmes, it remains the case that more regular dialogue is scarcely facilitated by the Commission's organisational structure.

Evidence from the bilateral aid talks

Differing emphasis is placed on this mechanism among the donors examined. Both the Dutch and the Danes consider the annual bilateral talks to be a rather formal affair, largely a presentation of their respective viewpoints, at which confrontation is avoided. Danish talks have reviewed the programme sector by sector and project by project, addressing specific problems rather than larger strategic issues. Germany has perhaps had more success than most in achieving concrete results from its bilateral talks. BMZ and GTZ give great weight to the principle of self-help which they have sought to promote through the Small Project Fund and the Self-Help Fund. The sticking point was the principle that Germany funds be made available directly to NGOs without any formal agreement with ministries. This was ultimately accepted at the 1993 bilateral talks after much discussion and debate, assisted by the close personal relationship existing between the heads of the two delegations. This issue has, however, resurfaced in 1996, when the Indian side expressed their dissatisfaction at their total lack of control over this element of the German bilateral programme, and KfW fears that greater controls on NGOs will soon be imposed.

The UK views the annual aid talks as being less significant than the regular interaction with the Department of External Affairs, although their scope has broadened in the past two years. The record of the most recent talks reveals that some attention was given to the issue of poverty reduction, with the DFID asking what steps the GoI and state governments were planning to talk to meet the OECD DAC target of reducing by half the proportion of people living in poverty. More attention was given, however, to the scope for more direct relationship between DFID and its focus states, which met with an unexpectedly positive response on the Indian side. The original motivation of the DEA for increased openness to state level discussion was to get projects moving faster and to increase disbursement rates, but there are, as mentioned earlier, the beginnings of greater openness to policy dialogue.

European donor country strategies

Any analysis of donor country strategies must recognise at the outset that unless they were prepared recently, they must inevitably fail to reflect the latest donor approaches. As a result, several of the agencies assessed here have moved beyond their position as captured in the latest available strategy paper. This includes the Netherlands, whose 1992-95 paper has yet to be replaced, the EC (latest full strategy is 1994) and the UK, which will replace its 1995 strategy paper in mid-1999. This caveat does not apply to Sida or Danida, which have strategies dating from December 1996 and 1997 respectively.

Table 4.1: Six EU donor country strategies: summary of process and content

	Denmark	*European Community*	*Germany*
Date of preparation	Prepared in 1997.	1994 Cooperation Strategy to the year 2000. A new strategy is currently in preparation (an overview was available).	The strategy document was not made available directly to the researchers; analysis below is based on discussions with agency staff.
1. *Process of strategy formation*	New 1997 strategy was entirely donor-driven, partly response to need for new strategy following India's reintroduction as a programme country, and need to incorporate new policies under 'Strategy 2000.' Dialogue with Indian government at courtesy level.	Both documents sought to reflect the outcomes of Joint Commission Meetings (EC, member states, GoI), other meetings with Indian govt. and with NGOs. New strategy drew on commissioned studies of poverty. Nonetheless, strong top-down element, with govt. receiving document near finalisation stage.	Germany produces a country concept paper summarising the main politicial, economic, social (incl. gender), and environmental situation and the main priorities for German aid. It is primarily drawn up within Germany, with inputs from KfW and GTZ.
2. *Goals, objectives and priorities*	PR has become overarching objective for all assistance. Also important cross-cutting gender and environment objectives. PR not reign supreme in practice; risk of conflict between environmental and PR objectives.	1994 doc: Global aim of 'sustainable economic development and social progress'; but also states centrality of PR by improving: (i) access of most deprived to productive resources; (ii) basic social services. Lists range of other objectives, rural development, key sector reform, employment generation etc. New strategy: clearer focus on poverty reduction through human resource development. Also strong environmental objective.	Poverty reduction is a priority among others (including gender envir. resource protection, education, increased economic competitiveness). Germany claims a shift away from an emphasis on investment in economic growth *per se* towards poverty reduction explicitly. Self-help groups are a frequently stressed priority.
3. *Analysis/ definition of poverty*	Some sector reports prepared by Indian consultants. Also Danida Commissioned a study of its four priority states, analysing in detail economic and social devel-	1994 doc: No definition of the poor, no analysis of nature and causes of poverty. New doc: def refers to gender, location, rural *vs* urban and degree of access to services. Strategy drawn on commissioned studies	No clear definition as such; working with general notions that most rural communities are poor etc. A poverty unit in BMZ is charged with monitoring the poverty focus at the country, programme and project

	opment and concentrating on poverty.	of poverty (mainly by Europeans).	level, and developing a better conceptualisation and definition of poverty (e.g. joint workshop in 1997 with Indian government to discuss poverty reduction)
4. *State selection*	Concentration in Karnataka and Madhya Pradesh (phasing out Tamil Nadu and Orissa). Choice of Karnataka and loss of Orissa suggests objectives other than PR are involved.	No state concentration or selection of areas on basis of poverty level. Criteria for geographical focus cited: where past implementation has been effective; and good local participation. New strategy prioritise areas where political commitment is high, on pragmatic grounds.	Seven states in which most aid is focused (Maharashtra, Rajasthan, Madhya Pradesh, Orissa, Karnataka, West Bengal, Himachal Pradesh), though also projects in other states (e.g. self-help funds) and national programmes.
5. *Operational priorities*	Sector programme support approach, concentrated in 4 sectors: agriculture, drinking water, health, and energy & environment. Also a minor private sector programme aimed at facilitating Indo-Danish business collaboration.	1994 doc: 3 priority areas: agriculture, PR and social development, and rural employment. Some effort to identify the poor (e.g. landless, women, children) in each area, and focus on primary level education. But criteria for project selection make no reference to poverty or the poor. New strategy: human resource development through emph. on basic education and health, also rural employment creation.	Priority sectors in 1997 were rural development and agriculture, health, education, infrastructure (esp. power and transport) and finance/private industry). No formal sector programme approach, but increasing emphasis on sector level analysis, with papers on power and vocational training (in 1997), and papers planned on environment, irrigation, water supply and health.
6. *Comments*	Although PR now has formal priority, the choice of sectors and the emphasis on other objectives suggests some dilution in practice.	1994 doc: Reasonable focus on PR, but weakened by top-down nature, lack of analysis of poverty, descriptive rather than strategic. New strategy: hard to conclude based on overview document only, but new emphasis on sectoral basic education and health interventions at expense of ad hoc rural etc. projects.	Considerable thinking and discussion of poverty assessments and poverty reduction, though varies greatly depending on project and personnel. GTZ appears to take more multi-dimensional approach than KfW. The latter tends to consider a very wide range of interventions at a 'rural' (less than 1m population) level to constitute indirect if not direct poverty reduction.

	Netherlands	*Sweden*	*UK*
	1997 policy plan covering South Asian region & 1997 annual plan, finalised Nov. 96.	1997-2001, finalised in Dec. 1996	1995-98, prepared in 1995; and new 3-year strategy currently being prepared.
1. *Process of strategy formation*	South Asian plan prepared in the Hague in top-down fashion. *Annual plan prepared in India, but without consultation outside the embassy.*	Top-down, with largely formal consultation with Indian government. Involvement of Indian researchers in preparation of state/sector background papers; otherwise little consultation outside embassy.	Previous strategy was top-down involving very few DFID staff. Forthcoming strategy: all DFID staff consulted, some consultation of academics, but consultation with Indian government is coming at the end of the process. Little consultation of Indian civil society, apart from several NGOs.
2. *Goals, objectives and priorities*	Unclear: South Asian plan: little guidance on development co-operation. Annual plan has far less detail than earlier country policy plans or sector plans.	Main objectives: (i) fighting poverty and improving living conditions (esp for women and children); (ii) sustainable use of natural resources & reduction of pollution.	*Current CSP:* goal is defined as 'strengthen (ing) Indian capacity to reduce poverty in a sustainable way'; but diluted by six other objectives (economic ref., enhancing productive capacity, promoting good governance, environment). Linkages between these other objectives and PR not spelt out. *New Strategy:* greater attention to linkages between education, health and other activities and overarching PR goal is likely.
3. *Analysis/ definition of poverty*	Nothing in strategy papers. But studies of poverty indicators of four focus states prepared in mid-1990s: AP, UP, Kerala & Gujarat. Could provide justification for concentrating	The new country strategy was preceded by working papers on various themes and sectors, mostly written by Indian researchers and consultants. Sida prepared a state study of Rajasthan, with detailed analysis of economic, social and political profile.	*Current CSP:* Some analaysis of economic reform process, social sectors, environment and good governance, but without closely relating it to poverty. No detailed analysis of nature and causes of poverty, or socio-economic and political constraints to

	Dutch aid on these states and on the poorest districts within these states. Or, may be used to justify existing practice.		PR. Commitment to targeting the poor, directly & indirectly. *Forthcoming CSP:* state level poverty studies and gender studies being prepared as inputs to CSP, but will only be available as drafts.
4. *State selection*	IOV (Inspectie Ontwikkelings samenwerking te Velde) recommended a concentration on 2 or 3 states, but currently aid remains dispersed among 5 states. UP was to be phased out based on criteria of poverty, continuity, state competence, but rejected by Minister. Currently intention to concentrate on 4 states: AP, UP, Kerala and Gujarat, and to phase out Karnataka.	Future assistance in social sectors to be concentrated in Rajasthan and Tamil Nadu, but other sectors India-wide. Dilution of original embassy objective of concentrating all aid in Rajasthan—among the poorest states. Other sectors may be concentrated in ltd no. of states, but not necessarily the poorest. Though state study prepared, concentration plans watered down and now no attempt to formulate strategies at state level.	*Forthcoming CSP:* strong emphasis on state-level partnership. Entered into dialogue with Orissa, Andhra Pradesh and West Bengal, and may also include Madhya Pradesh. Choice depends on level of poverty, commitment of govt. to PR, and (especially) past historical association. Will continue relationship in specific sectors with other states (Karnataka, Maharashtra) and consider a relationship with very poor states through NGOs (e.g. Bihar and UP).
5. *Operational priorities*	Four themes: (i) societal development (rural water supply & sanitation); (ii) agriculture and development (mainly irrigation, drainage & desalinisation); (iii) environment; (iv) women and development. Two other themes; urban dev. and children (but minor involvement to date). Sectors more the result of chance than strategy.	Concentration on 3 'sectors': social sectors (edu. & health); (ii) energy & environment; (iii) natural resources (soil, forestry, regional water). Also, consultancy fund for exchange of technical & scientific knowledge between India & Sweden (1% of budget 1997, 10% in 2001).	Currently spread broadly- no clear sectoral focus in *current CSP.* The *forthcoming CSP* may seek a greater focus by phasing out support to some sectors, and states that it will aim over time to ensure sectoral focus reflects the priorities of partner states.

6. *Comments*	Current regional and country plans provide no clear statement of strategy or of centrality of the PR objective. No analysis of poverty within current documents, though separate, studies prepared. No guidance on operational priorities.	Link between PR objective is clear for social sector spending, but this is to be reduced from 60% of budget in 1997 to 40% in 2001. Trade-off between environmental and PR objective in the natural resource sector is unclear. Little clear poverty focus in the energy./environment and consultancy fund.	The current CSP clearly states the centrality of PR, though the strategy is less clear. The forthcoming CSP promises to be more consultative, with greater strategic content, greater attention as to how the range of interventions may contribute to a poverty-centred state-level partnership. But consultation on the forthcoming CSP with national government is late, and at state-level has been minimal.

Purpose of donor country strategies

Given the stated centrality of the poverty reduction objective, donor country strategies might be expected to provide a careful analysis of the nature and causes of poverty in India, and to articulate the linkages between the PR objective and the donor's current and planned interventions. The rationale for a particular state and sectoral focus should be clear, and again the links between these and addressing the needs of the poor should be apparent. In addition, the donor's future strategy should be presented, including an assessment of potential opportunities and constraints for effective poverty reduction.

By setting out the goals and strategies of the donor, the country strategy paper (CSP) may potentially fulfil an accountability function. Yet in practice, there were no concrete examples of donors examining performance against the objectives outlined in the strategy papers. For this to be effective the papers would need to set out clear indicators by which poverty performance could be assessed, and who within the agency and government is responsible for collating and analysing such data and at what intervals. In addition, senior agency management would need to allocate the time needed to hold programme managers to account against the performance indicators contained in their strategy documents. Clearly, successful outcomes depend on a partnership between agencies and governmental/non-governmental bodies, but an annual review process of this kind would place the onus on managers to measure success, identify the critical factors influencing outcomes and the measures needed to ensure greater poverty impacts. None of the papers include such indicators, and neither do agencies have such country-level accountability systems in place.

These gaps undoubtedly contribute to a further finding, namely that donor officials rarely referred to the documents, suggesting that they are far less relevant than they might be, and are not seen as providing practical guidance to those charged with implementation. Of course CSPs should not be seen as a once-off process of strategic thinking, and may to some extent be summaries of strategic thinking carried forward on a continuous basis through sector and state-level dialogue with partners. There is some evidence to suggest that although in late 1997 there was little evidence of strategic analysis at the sector and state-level, several agencies were preparing such studies which would be 'live' and relevant and thus remedy weaknesses within country strategies.

The process of strategy formation

Some of the value of the donor country strategy papers lies in the process of preparation itself. If taken seriously, we would expect it to be preceded by extensive consultation and debate within the agency itself and with Indian governmental and non-governmental actors. Donors emphasize the importance of ownership by their partners in government and civil society, and the process of preparing country strategies provides an unparalleled opportunity to build ownership. The process of preparation might also be expected to generate background papers, such as poverty assessments or state and sector analyses.

However, the development of country strategy has been an almost completely donor-driven affair, with minimal consultation outside of donor agencies. The contrast between the reality of a top-down approach with the donors' stated commitment to participatory rather than bureaucratically-driven processes is stark. This applies even to the very recent Danida and Sida strategies. In the case of DFID this lack of a participatory approach applied even to its own staff, one of whom described the process in 1995 as having involved 'a few people in a darkened room'.

The record is not entirely negative, however. The Danes and Swedes did involve some of the Indian research and consultancy community in preparing background sector, state and other studies. These had a significant focus on poverty and provided detailed economic and social development indicators. The process leading up DFID's new country strategy to be published in spring 1999 is also far more participatory than hitherto. New guidance from DFID headquarters on the preparation of CSPs calls for an 'opening up' of the process, tapping into outside knowledge such as local stakeholders (e.g. governments, local NGOs and the private sector), and UK sources (e.g. NGOs, business and academia). This appears to have been partially implemented, with full consultation of DFID staff, some consultation of the NGO and research community in India and in the UK. However, consultation with the Indian government occurred at a relatively late stage, limiting to some extent the scope to develop a strategy based on a partnership of equals. The European Commission states that its strategy has been based on discussion with other member states and with the GoI at an annual Joint Commission meeting and other working groups on development and environment. The Commission has sought to elicit the opinions of a range of NGOs both in India and in Europe. However, the actual strategy document itself is only shared with the GoI at a very late stage in the drafting process and in practice external consultation appears quite restrained. Interestingly, the Commission Delegation itself did not appear to be very familiar with the various Commission strategy documents, including the Council Resolution on Poverty Reduction, casting some doubt on the extent to which general Community policy statements on poverty actually shape the development process at the country level.

The overriding conclusion is that the evidence suggests that donors are missing an opportunity for dialogue and consensus-building with Indian government and non-governmental partners, and thus for making recipient ownership more real, and ensuring congruency between donor priorities and those of their partners. This is a serious shortcoming, given that progress in reducing poverty will depend first and foremost on India's economic development and the actions of its government, and donors might therefore be expected to use every channel to help tilt policy in a pro-poor direction.

Goals, objectives and priorities

The papers examined showed the donors to have a wide range of goals and priorities. The new Danish paper must be seen as a major step forward since poverty reduction is now explicitly stated to be the overarching objective for all assistance under the country frame. In practice, however, the selection of states and sectors indicates that the poverty objective does not reign supreme. The same goes for the UK paper. The central objective of the UK programme is defined as 'strengthen[ing] Indian capacity to reduce poverty in a sustainable way over the medium term'. However, it is rapidly apparent that this is diluted by the requirement to meet the six other objectives of British aid, such as economic reform, enhancing productive capacity, promoting good government and the environment. Very little attempt is made to resolve this apparent contradiction by spelling out linkages between less obviously poverty-oriented activities (e.g. the power or finance sectors).[1] This *may* be resolved in the forthcoming CSP, which, according to a draft outline, will seek to ensure that the UK programme is focused on DFID's overall aim of eliminating poverty, and takes the White Paper's commitment to halving poverty and boosting human development and environmental sustainability as its starting points.

The Swedish strategy sets out two main objectives: (1) fighting poverty and improving living conditions, especially for women and children; (2) contributing to sustainable utilisation of natural resources and limiting pollution. The precise relationship and trade offs between the two are unclear. The European Community's 1994 strategy paper sets out a rather vague global aim of 'sustainable economic development and social progress', but nonetheless also states the centrality of poverty reduction by improving the access of the most deprived to productive resources and to social services. The new strategy will, the Commission states, have a clearer focus on poverty reduction, which is to be achieved through an increased emphasis on human resource development. In practical terms this will be met by increased spending on basic education and basic health care (two ongoing projects account for the vast majority of EC aid at the moment). The new strategy will also emphasize rural employment creation, perhaps by working more closely with lower level Panchayati Raj Institutions, though this is not very clear. Its main poverty reduction objective shares priority, however, with an environmental objective. The goals and objectives of the Dutch programme, although known to be poverty-oriented, are not clear from its South Asia regional plan or its short 1996 annual plan. In the case of Germany, the view of officials was that the most recent country concept paper reveals a shift in emphasis towards a more explicit emphasis on poverty reduction, but that similar emphasis was also given to environment and gender objectives, as well as education and improving economic competitiveness.

Analysis of poverty

Table 4.1 reveals that there has been remarkably little detailed analysis of the nature and causes of poverty in any of the donor strategy papers examined. This was a cause of concern to the past Head of the UK programme to India, who underlined the importance of 'a far more in-depth poverty assessment, which analyses scale, incidence, causes, effects, and the social, economic and political constraints to addressing poverty.' What is particularly surprising is that none of the agencies appear to have made extensive use of World Bank, UNDP and GoI poverty assessment data. Some papers revealed a reasonably in-depth analysis of what the donor saw to be the main breaks on social and economic development while others, such as the EC 1994 document, presented none. The new EC strategy does apparently draw upon a range of commissioned studies, completed by European researchers, of aspects of poverty in India, which represents an important step forward. The Delegation in India did not, however, appear to be familiar with these studies, suggesting that they may not be informing the programme as fully as they might.

The Netherlands' situation gives some cause for concern. It has prepared a draft paper which, in accordance with a new directive, covers the entire South Asian region (i.e. Afghanistan, Bangladesh, Bhutan, India, Maldives, Nepal, Pakistan, and Sri Lanka) – all within 36 pages. The Royal Netherlands Embassy (RNE), not surprisingly, is worried that this will limit the scope and quality of analysis and policy guidance. This applies to the analysis of poverty, as it does to all other aspects examined here. The German paper appears also to have been prepared based on rather general notions of poverty rather than on the basis of in-depth studies.

The recent Swedish strategy paper was preceded by working papers on various themes and sectors as well as a detailed study of Rajasthan economic and political profile, all of which contained careful analyses of poverty. The DFID paper contained a detailed examination of the economic reform process, limited analysis of problems in the social sectors, and some assessment of environmental and good governance issues. The forthcoming UK CSP will for the first time draw on several background analyses of the socio-economic profile of priority states, a profile of gender relations and its role in determining development trajectories. However, these studies will only be available in draft form as inputs to the CSP, and the state level studies will not be in-depth studies.

State Selection

In the face of the six donors universally stated commitment to reaching the poor, it comes as something of a surprise to note that the four western and southern states of Gujarat, Maharashtra, Karnataka and Tamil Nadu, which all enjoy per capita income and other development indicators well above average, loom large in their portfolios (*see also* Table 7.1). State selection by donors reflects a mixture of historical accident, business interests, and the desire to 'back winners' as well as to reach the poor. This may help explain why the current UK CSP provides no well-developed link between its focus states and poverty reduction beyond saying that these states provide a balance between very poor states (like Orissa) and states with a more positive environment for change. In future, the UK will pursue a twin track approach, channelling most of its resources to three (or four) partner states across a range of sectors, but continuing and possibly expanding existing sectoral programmes to non-partner states. Poverty focused aid might be delivered through NGOs to very poor and 'difficult' non-partner states, such as Bihar and Uttar Pradesh. Fortunately for the UK, its desire to forge partnerships which build on past experience is consistent with it poverty focus, since a considerable part of UK aid has, largely by an accident of history, been concentrated in very poor states (e.g. Orissa).

It is worth dwelling for a moment on the process by which focus states are selected, as it illustrates a number of the tensions intrinsic to donor programmes, and the difficult trade offs involved. The Danish case provides an instructive example, which undoubtedly is parallelled to some extent by the other bilaterals considered here. During the 1980s and 1990s, Danish aid was concentrated in four states, Tamil Nadu, Karnataka, Orissa and Madhya Pradesh. The first two are middle-ranking in terms of human development, while the latter two are near the bottom. The Danish embassy had recommended that if the state focus of the programme was to be narrowed down to two, then these should be Orissa and Madhya Pradesh. This was based on the fact that these two states are much poorer than the other two priority states. In Karnataka, per capita income is some 50% higher than in Orissa, and the latter contains India's highest proportion of *'adivasis'* (very poor 'tribals'), who have increasingly became an important target group for Danish aid. A further advantage of choosing Madhya Pradesh and Orissa is that they are contiguous, opening up possibilities of working across the boarder in the poorest regions of both states. The debate was settled by the Minister for Development Cooperation himself, who personally decided that Karnataka should be selected above Orissa. It was subsequently argued that the vigorous implementation of the Panchayati Raj in Karnataka provides a good context for Danish support, which is not without merit. Yet, what is probably far more significant is that Karnataka, and in particular its capital, Bangalore, is a highly dynamic city and the computer software capital of India, presenting far more interesting opportunities to Danish business than does Orissa. A Danish private sector adviser has been stationed in Bangalore, and several Danish firms are either established or on their way.

Sweden's strategy with respect to geographical concentration also indicates the role played by wider factors, including political and business interests, in addition to poverty considerations. The current Swedish strategy represents a significant dilution of the original proposal developed by the development cooperation section of the Swedish embassy. The original proposal envisaged a very significant concentration of all types of future Swedish development assistance to Rajasthan. This made sense both because concentration is likely to improve aid effectiveness, because the experience in this state so far has been good, and because Rajasthan is one of the poorest states in India. From a poverty reduction perspective such a concentration might have provided interesting new opportunities. But in the event the decision taken at Sida headquarters and backed by the Swedish government prescribed a concentration to Rajasthan (and to a lesser extent also Tamil Nadu) only with respect to social sector aid, leaving the freedom to provide other types of assistance to other states. Even within other sectors (energy, environment) the aim will be to concentrate to a small number of states, but not necessarily poor states. It is quite evident that the strategy adopted has compromised on poverty orientation, and it is equally obvious that this will make it easier to look after certain Swedish interests. One point in its favour is that it is more in line with Indian preferences that there should not be too much concentration on particular states by individual donors.

It must be acknowledged that the macro-economic, political and institutional context is markedly less conducive to aid effectiveness in the poorest states such as Bihar, Orissa and others. It is also the case that recent experience from the health sector and other sectors strongly suggests that donor assistance will deliver poor returns on investments aimed at reaching the poor unless there is a genuine commitment of government to extensive reform. But this excuse can be overworked, and it is clear that donors could do more to work more closely with the poorest states to help strengthen the constituency for reform. One approach may be for like-minded donors to try and engage in sector-specific dialogue, and thereby enhance their collective leverage *and* the package of support offered. A nod was made in this direction when the Government of Orissa with DFID support convened a multi-donor meeting in Delhi to discuss the scope for a coordinated response to Orissa's health needs. The follow-up and practical implications of this are as yet unclear.

In the case of the European Community, there is no process of state selection. Aid has been distributed across India, mostly in *ad hoc* projects, rather than according to a strategy informed by an assessment of poverty. The main criteria used has been the level of political support existing within a state for a particular intervention. The Commission has argued that to be other than opportunistic (or pragmatic) in this regard results in too much time being spent on trying to mobilise support before implementation can begin. The Netherlands prepared a study of poverty indicators of four focus states in the 1990s, but it is unclear how instrumental this has been in determining aid distribution since the Minister for Development rejected the IOV recommendation to concentrate aid on two or three states, taking account of poverty status. The German case appears similar to that of the UK, operating in a mix of very poor (Rajasthan, Madhya Pradesh, Orissa) and also those states with better development indicators (Maharashtra, Karnataka, Himachal Pradesh, West Bengal). German support for interventions across all these states together with support at the national programme level, suggests a somewhat confused message regarding the priority accorded to poverty reduction—a charge that could be levelled at all six agencies.

REFERENCE

1. Interestingly, the British document points out that the increasing availability of private finance for investment in commercially viable sectors has helped spur donors, with GoaI approval, to focus more on social sector investments.

5

SECTOR STRATEGIES AND PROJECT PORTFOLIOS

The role of sector strategy papers

A good country strategy paper clarifies the goal of a donor's programme and, hopefully, analyses the country context and the resultant opportunities for the donor to contribute to poverty reduction. Ideally, it will be able to demonstrate the linkages between the donor's operational priorities and its goal (of poverty reduction). However, it cannot enter into detail about the potential contribution of interventions on a sector-by-sector basis to contribute to poverty reduction, how this contribution might be maximised, and what the risks and opportunities are. There is thus a strong argument suggesting a role for meso-level analysis, filling the void between (macro) country level strategy and (micro) project level design documents. This could be done either by sectoral studies or, in the case of India, state strategy papers (see below), or some combination of the two. Concentrating first on the former, the role of sector strategies is to:

— summarise the sector context including the:
— government's priorities within the sector; lessons of experience within the sector and relevant experience gained from other sectors which may be further ahead;
— institutional strengths and weaknesses, including of delivery mechanism;
— clarify the degree of coherence between the government's priorities and those of the donor, and how donor's objectives will contribute towards the goal of poverty reduction; ensure that

these objectives are realistic given the country context;
- identify the scope for viable government-donor and other donor partnerships, for example with civil society or the private sector;
- identify the pros and cons of a sectoral versus a project approach[1] in terms of poverty reduction impact;
- explain ongoing reform processes, the approaches taken by different groups supporting the reforms, and reduce the risk of these groups, whether internal or donor, working at cross-purposes;
- identify intra-sectoral priorities according to their potential impact on poor groups, assess the need for targeting, and mechanisms for this;
- expose the political context, including the respective role of the public and private sector.

Without an analytical step between broad country strategy and project and programme design documents, the risk is that donor interventions will be:

- *ad hoc* and of lower effectiveness than if part of a strategic approach;
- inconsistent with government priorities and thus ultimately unsustainable;
- inadequately linked with the overall poverty reduction goal, resulting in lower impact.

Yet, although most donors recognise the importance of having a strategic sectoral framework for their interventions, the donors' studies either lack sector strategies entirely, have inadequate strategy documents, or provide a framework within each project or programme document.

The donor record

Although Dutch aid to India has been concentrated in particular sectors for many years, there are no specific sector strategy papers as such. Sector policies are dealt with in the embassy's annual plans as well as in the country strategy paper, which emphasizes greater attention to 'software' aspects of participation, health education etc. A similar situation of long-standing sectoral concentration exists for Germany, and it too lacks detailed strategy papers. It has, however, prepared papers for power and vocational training, and is considering or currently preparing papers on environment, irrigation, water supply and health. It also provides a sectoral assessment as part of the project document, as is the case for recent DFID projects (see below).

Denmark has begun a process of transition from project assistance to sector programme aid under its new country strategy. So far, however, it lacks detailed sector strategies for its India programme. Although guidelines developed in Danida's headquarters in 1996 did examine, in general, the potential linkages between sector programmes and poverty reduction, this does not address the many country-specific dimensions listed above. However, Danish consultancy firms have been hired to prepare elements of sector strategies. Sida has not initiated a similar change towards sector strategies, but the new country strategy was preceded by a number of working papers on different themes and sectors, mostly written by Indian researchers and consultants. The overall objective of poverty reduction was addressed in many of these contributions (published in the volume 'Sharing Challenges—The Indo-Swedish Development Cooperation Programme', Ministry of Foreign Affairs, Stockholm, 1997).

In the case of the DFID programme, there has been no formal requirement to produce sector strategies. Short summary strategies exist for all major sectors, but within the space of a couple of pages it is clearly impossible to develop a genuinely strategic framework or a tightly-argued analysis of what the scope for poverty reducing activities may be. These summary strategies reveal a very superficial analysis of poverty, if any, and rarely articulate the potential linkages between activities and poverty reduction. Although such summaries may set a direction by specifying areas for which funding is not available, the practical and operational benefits of these one or two page documents are limited. However, it is true to say that in many cases there exists a range of internal reviews and think pieces, especially but not only in the health sector. Although these do not have the status of strategy papers, in some cases they provide the basis for debate that contributes towards the development of a strategy. In addition, recent project proposals, notably in the urban poverty sector and, to a degree, the health sector, include a wide-ranging review of past experience which is integrated in the proposed project. Thus, to some extent, current strategies are defined in new and recent project documents, though this cannot be held to be a particularly satisfactory alternative.

It is interesting to note that when the DFID Delhi office was asked to provide samples of sector strategies, it did not include a substantial 45 page document entitled *Renewable natural resources strategy for India,* which was developed in London before decentralisation to the field took place. This provides a comprehensive survey of the Indian context, specific problems within the natural resources sector, an analysis of DFID's objectives, the performance of 19 ongoing natural resources projects, and develops a strategy for India centred on poverty reduction and environmental sustainability. Yet the fact that this document was not provided to the researchers nor referred to provides a useful warning that sector strategy development should be seen as a process which does not end with the production of the document.

The Commission has produced two sector strategy papers for education covering issues such as developing institutional, financial and human capacity, sustainability, monitoring and evaluation. Both papers are statements of general principle, rather than relating directly to the context in India. The full text was not available, and while the papers may provide useful guidance to officials they appear unlikely to have the depth necessary to identify constraints and solutions with respect to poor groups in particular.

The case for a more coherent and comprehensive approach to sector strategies among all six donors seems strong. Sector strategies which address the issues identified above could potentially greatly strengthen the strategic approach and effective operationalisation of donor poverty reduction objectives.

Sector-wide approach

As mentioned above, Denmark's new strategy for India envisages a transition from project aid to sectoral support. In principle the strategy is meant to serve the overarching objective of poverty reduction. This has been operationalised through an elaborate policy paper on poverty reduction as well as comprehensive guidelines for sector programme support. It remains to be seen, however, to which extent the sector strategy will actually strengthen the poverty reduction objective. There is a risk that other cross-cutting objectives (gender, environment, democracy and human rights) will erode the poverty focus. Moreover, the increased emphasis on policy dialogue and capacity building in the bureaucracy will make monitoring and evaluation of impact in terms of poverty reduction more difficult. The Swedes favour a concentration in particular sectors, as is clear from the country strategy. However, this does not really amount to a sector programme approach, since it does not appear to draw upon clear sectoral strategies, rather it centres on the search for projects and programmes worthy of Swedish support.

The sector-based approach is increasingly followed by other donors, such as the European Commission and, recently, by the UK. The European Commission's 'Green Paper' has reinforced the commitment to a sector approach within the Community's aid programme. It has raised the question of gradually abandoning the project approach once and for all, and instead trying to strengthen the institutional framework and local capacity in tandem with direct budgetary and sectoral aid. This would be linked with a more realistic and less detailed set of conditionalities, backing a partnership based on policies and strategies rather than on activities and operations. The EC's endorsement of the sector approach is reflected in India in its large scale support of the District Primary Education Programme (DPEP) and of the planned Family Welfare sector reform. It has developed sector strategies for health and for education, and is currently developing a strategy for environment. However, these were provided by Brussels and not by the Delegation, casting some doubt as to how much they are living and practical documents.[2] The Department of Economic Affairs is supportive of this shift in emphasis in the EC programme arguing that the EC's lack of sector experience at the country level means that it is likely to be more effective when collaborating with the government and other donors, who possess greater technical expertise. The Commission's readiness to stay within the government's framework (e.g. in DPEP) and not to push its own agenda is widely appreciated within the government.

Those more directly involved in the Indian programme are strongly supportive of the shift from project to sector. There is a broad recognition that the EC's traditional channel of support, through piecemeal projects, has proved unsustainable, particularly in the rural development sector, which has long been a cornerstone of the EC programme to Asia. The policy decision has been taken only to support programmes with a strong sector reform component,[3] alongside continuing co-financing of international NGOs. This conclusion is likely to meet with approval from member states, though it does not imply that they themselves will abandon project aid, since few of them face the same degree of staffing constraints or ineffective tendering procedures for consultants. In addition, it should be noted that there are not necessarily sufficient numbers of good sector reform type programmes available for funding by donors.

The UK had tentatively begun to provide or to consider providing sectoral support as opposed to project aid in four specific cases in India. DFID's support to the health sector in Orissa, largely by building health clinics, as well as some financing of training and policy issues, was found to be less effective than hoped, with serious problems of sustainability. As a result, the third phase plans to focus on institutional strengthening and improving the policy environment through funding at the sector level. DFID is also contributing to the national Health and Family Welfare sector programme and to the District Primary Education Project which has some of the characteristics of sector aid. Finally, DFID and the Government of Andhra Pradesh are in the closing stages of designing a state-wide urban poverty programme which couples finance for infrastructure with municipal financial reform and a participatory poverty assessment. The hope is that the participatory assessment will allow for more accurate targeting of the poor and vulnerable. Support for decentralisation and reforming the municipal planning, decision making and financial management systems relating to urban poverty reduction activities is intended to enhance the sustainability and breadth of impact compared to the earlier generation of individual slum improvement projects.

The drift towards a sectoral approach has been strongly reinforced by the recent publication of the UK White Paper on International Development. Full partner countries will enjoy not only enhanced levels of resources and a longer-term commitment, but also greater flexibility in the use of those resources. This implies that where the UK has confidence in the policies, budgetary allocation process and in a partner's capacity for effective implementation, it will 'consider moving away from supporting specific projects to providing resources more strategically in support of sector-wide programmes or the economy as a whole' (DFID, 1997: 2.22). Sector aid is likely to be the preferred option, on the UK's part, since it offers a balance between enhanced ownership and control by the partner government, while retaining reasonable accountability with respect to DFID. The White Paper does not spell out the pros and cons of the sector aid instrument in terms of impact on poverty. It is clear, however, that where existing financial, managerial and institutional mechanisms at an all-India or state level are weak, sector reform may be the only way of achieving sustainable benefits, providing there is commitment from the recipient (for example health sector, *see* Chapter 13).

It must be stressed, however, that the sector reform approach also presents risks. Chief among these is that working on upstream issues may lead to a loss of focus on the service users – the poor. The increased emphasis on capacity building is warranted, but it is not yet proven whether this will benefit the sector *per se* or whether it can also strengthen the poverty orientation. Great expectations are vested in strengthening policy dialogue, but in the Indian context it is an open question how effective this dialogue is going to be. The Indian authorities both at the union and state level have clear policy preferences backed by a well-entrenched bureaucracy, and poverty reduction is not necessarily their number one concern. In this context, it is particularly important when setting the reform agenda to trace the links between interventions at different levels of the system and potential benefits for primary stakeholders.

State strategy papers

Strategies may be drawn up at the state level which may also help to bridge the gap between broad strategic statements at the country level and detailed statements at the project and programme levels. A number of the donors studied do in fact produce state level reports which fulfil this function to varying degrees. In the mid-1990s, the Dutch prepared studies of the poverty indicators in four of their focus states, covering AP, UP, Kerala and Gujarat. These papers could be used to provide the justification for concentrating further Dutch aid on these states, or they may simply serve to justify existing practice. At the end of 1997 the UK began preparing profiles of its focus states which are intended to feed into the ongoing process of country strategy preparation. These reports are not expected to provide very detailed analysis of poverty, and will therefore only provide limited guidance on the appropriate sectoral mix and type of interventions likely to generate the greatest poverty impact in each state. They are, however, an advance on the past, when no studies at all were conducted. The European Commission has no strategic state focus, and therefore prepares no state level strategy documents.

Danida in preparation for the new country strategy commissioned a study of the four priority states (Tamil Nadu, Karnataka, Madhya Pradesh and Orissa). This provided a general profile of the states, including numerous tables and figures concerning economic and social development and notably poverty. In the event other factors than poverty played a major role in the decision to concentrate on Karnataka as well as Madhya Pradesh. There has been no attempt to devise state strategies. Sida (i.e. the development section of the embassy in Delhi), in its attempt to concentrate the major part of its future assistance in one state (Rajasthan) commissioned and published a volume, 'Rajasthan: A State Study' (Sida, New Delhi, 1997). It contains a wealth of information about all relevant (and some irrelevant!) aspects of the state's economic, social and political profile. However, ultimately the concentration plans were substantially watered down, and there has been no attempt to formulate strategies at the state level.

Portfolio of projects

It is important to recognise that each donor's current portfolio of interventions necessarily will not perfectly reflect their recently-defined priorities. This is due to portfolio 'overhang', caused by the fact that many large projects agreed when the emphasis on poverty reduction was far less strong, continue to appear on the donors' books. This is illustrated in Table 5.1 which reveals a growth in the share of Danish aid with substantial potential for poverty reduction from less than half of the total programme at the start of the 1990s, to over two-thirds by 1996. Aid to the 'modern sector' (capital intensive assistance often benefiting Danish business interests) has in contrast fallen fairly steadily from over 40% in 1990 to a fifth in 1996.

Table 5.1: Sectoral share of Danish aid disbursements, 1990-96 (%)

	1990	1991	1992	1993	1994	1995	1996
Potential Poverty							
Reducing Sectors:	43.3	49.1	56.9	71.7	60.1	57.8	68.2
Agriculture etc.	8.9	10.1	16.3	25.0	26.1	28.4	21.2
Health	18.2	20.6	23.1	20.7	19.3	22.5	39.7
Water & Sanitation	16.3	18.4	17.5	26.1	14.7	6.9	7.3
Environment	0.0	0.0	3.8	3.3	4.1	5.9	6.0
'Modern sector'	44.3	44.7	33.8	19.0	30.7	27.5	20.5
Total	100	100	100	100	100	100	100

This shift into sectors with greater poverty reducing potential has, to a varying extent, been mirrored by trends in the composition of the other European donor programmes considered here. For example, by all accounts DFID's current portfolio of projects focuses far more on poverty reduction than it did even five years ago. In the 1980s, direct measures to reduce poverty were largely limited to some admittedly large slum improvement projects. Even here, although these did address some of the broader dimensions of poverty, the accent was nonetheless predominantly on infrastructure provision. The lack of emphasis on poverty in the UK's portfolio at that time was partly a reflection of the DFID central policy framework which saw direct poverty reduction as competing with a range of other objectives. One of these was environment, and it can be seen that many of the natural resource projects, some of which are on-going, were designed primarily to meet the environmental objective, with far less thought given as to who would get the benefits. The increasing prominence of poverty as DFID's overarching goal has been reflected in the greater efforts being made currently. The approach is far more sophisticated, and poverty is addressed across a far greater range of interventions, including rural development projects such as two major rain-fed farming projects targeting tribal farmers, and a watershed project. In addition, education, health, and water and sanitation projects are beginning to be designed with poverty concerns as a major component, rather than fixing on issues of efficiency and quality in isolation from equity.

Table 5.2 attempts to assess the balance of direct, indirect and other strategies for poverty reduction as revealed in each agency's portfolio of interventions for India. In discussion with agency officials a judgement was made as to whether each intervention sought to address poverty directly, indirectly or through other mechanisms for which the linkages with poverty reduction are less clear or likely to occur only in the long run.

- Direct PR projects/programmes:
  - — interventions which address PR directly and seek to target the majority of their benefits to the poor/poor groups.

- Indirect PR projects and sector/policy reform interventions:
  - — interventions with a plausible link between the activity and PR (explicit or implicit), which can be expected to bring substantial benefits to poor (though others may benefit);
  - — measures designed to promote pro-poor policy reform or increase institutional capacity to benefit poor groups.

- Other projects/programmes:
  - — interventions which may bring benefits to the poor, but the linkages between the intervention and PR are less clear or likely to occur only in the long run.

There can be no assumption that attempts to benefit the poor through 'direct' measures will necessarily be more effective in promoting poverty reduction than indirect or other approaches. Direct interventions tend to be smaller in scale, with fewer potential beneficiaries, and their effectiveness is likely to be contingent on a supportive policy, economic and political environment. Equally, however, there is considerable evidence that poor groups may face particular constraints which prevent them from sharing fully in the benefits of population-wide interventions. This suggests that direct and indirect measures which pay particular attention to the design and implementation to ensure that poor groups are not marginalised should feature prominently in a poverty-focused country portfolio. Furthermore, while 'other' interventions may contribute towards reducing poverty in the long run, there was little evidence of agencies attempting to quantify such benefits or put in place systems which would allow this in the future.

Table 5.2 shows tremendous variation in the degree to which each agency favours direct, indirect and other approaches to poverty reduction. It is striking that on average fewer than one in six interventions (by value) or 15.9% had a direct poverty focus, with virtually half of all interventions having no particular poverty focus whatsoever. The portfolios for Denmark, KfW, and Sweden had greatest share of interventions with a direct or indirect poverty focus, while the UK had the greatest proportion of direct poverty interventions (31.5%).

The Netherlands considers that its primary contribution to poverty reduction is made through project aid, with the other half of its programme, import support (now debt relief) and budgetary support to government programmes, having little direct impact on the poor. The sectoral composition of the Dutch project portfolio has changed little over the past decade or more, and remains concentrated in land and water, rural drinking water, water transport and environment, though water transport has declined somewhat recently. However, the nature of the projects themselves within the portfolio has evolved considerably, with far greater attention being paid to specific mechanisms for targeting the poor in its drinking water projects. If project aid alone is examined and debt relief/budgetary support excluded, then the share of Dutch assistance which has a direct or indirect poverty focus rises from 43% to 86%.

The German government requires that its entire portfolio of projects possesses a direct or indirect poverty orientation. However, it is clear that these categories are based on a rather loose definition as to what constitutes poverty and thereby what type of intervention is poverty reducing and how. KfW considers its projects to have an indirect poverty orientation if over 50% of the target group can be classed as poor. The assessment of who the poor are is based on income levels together with indicators measuring other dimensions of poverty such as illiteracy and ill-health. To be classed as a direct poverty reduction project, it must go beyond simple redistribution of existing income to the generation of new income via economic growth. This is particularly important at the state and union government levels, where an expansion of the tax base is

Table 5.2: Poverty orientation of donor portfolios (%)

	Denmark	GTZ	KfW	NLs	Sweden	UK	Average
Direct	21.7	7.8	2.4	14.7	17.2	31.5	15.9
Nat Res. & Envir	6.4	1.6	-	11.5	4.0	4.5	
Water	-	-	-	-	-	-	
Urban	-	1.4	-	-	-	11.7	
Education	-	-	-	-	7.0	15.2	
Health	14.4	-	-	3.2	6.2	-	
Modern/Heavy sector	-	-	-	-	-	-	
Other sectors	-	4.8	2.4	0.1	-	-	
Indirect	42.9	10.2	65.1	28.7	50.4	11.7	34.8
Nat Res. & Envir	14.2	6.4	11.8	4.7	24.2	0.2	
Water	18.3	-	23.6	17.1	9.7	-	
Urban	-	-	14.9	-	-	-	
Education	-	0.1	-	-	-	5.4	
Health	10.4	3.7	3.5	0.3	16.5	6.0	
Modern/Heavy sector	-	-	-	-	-	-	
Other sectors	-	-	11.2	6.6	-	0.0	
Other	35.4	82.0	32.5	56.5	32.4	56.9	49.3
Nat Res. & Envir	3.3	13.2	-	1.8	0.8	5.7	
Water	-	-	-	1.2	-	-	
Urban	-	-	-	-	-	-	
Education	-	17.7	-	-	-	1.4	
Health	10.9	-	-	-	-	10.3	
Modern/Heavy sector	21.2	20.3	19.0	2.6	31.2	39.1	
Other sectors	-	30.9	13.5	50.9	0.3	0.4	

Notes: Each agency's current portfolio of interventions was categorised by broad sector and the direct, indirect and other categories defined in the text. The figures indicate the share of commitments within each category as a proportion of total agency commitments in India. The categorisation was based on groups of interventions or 'sectors' in the case of the Netherlands, rather than on an assessment of individual projects. Information was not available to categorise the European Community portfolio. The categorisation necessarily simplifies more complex realities, but represents an attempt to make a broad assessment of the approximate share of direct, indirect and other interventions. The categorisation was discussed with officials within each agency, but does not necessarily represent the agency's formal view. In the case of GTZ, the categorisation used reflects the categories used by the agency itself. Half of the Netherlands' aid to India is provided as debt relief or budgetary support and is included under 'Other', 'Other sectors'.

required to generate additional funds for implementing social sector programmes.

Although KfW classified all its projects as having a direct or indirect poverty orientation, the figures indicated in Table 5.2 reflect an attempt to apply the same criteria as used with respect to the other agencies. This suggests that while only a tiny proportion of KfW's assistance has a direct poverty focus, nearly two-thirds does have a plausible indirect link with poverty reduction. In the case of GTZ, the agency's own definitions were used, revealing that as much as 82% of GTZ's assistance has no particular poverty focus. This reflects the fact that many of the projects undertaken by GTZ are specific training or research projects which do not include the poor as a target group.

The areas of intervention defined in the Sida document reflect the dual poverty and natural resources/environmental objectives. Thus, of the three main sectors selected, social sectors (education and health), energy and environment, and natural resources (soil, forest, water), only the first reveals clear links with the poverty reduction objective. Nonetheless, the social sectors have attracted a very considerable proportion of Swedish aid. Particularly impressive is the 1996 country strategy which envisages that over 60% of the budget will be allocated to the social sectors in 1997, though the planned gradual decrease to 40% over five years weakens the thrust. It is expected that the poverty reduction objective will feature together with its sustainable resource management objective, but it remains to be seen how the trade off between the two will work out. It is clear that the energy and pollution sector will have very little focus on poverty, which is true also of the new and growing consultancy fund and the envisaged 'exchange' of experiences and expertise in technical and scientific matters between the two countries. Thus whole substantial parts of the future programme will have very little relationship with the poverty reduction objective, and these parts of the strategy are those which are partieularly interesting for Swedish business interests and the broader Swedish 'resource base'.

REFERENCES

1. Both sectoral investment programmes (where the government and donors draw up a reform programme funded from a single, joint resource pool), and the sector-wide approach (where the government and donors prepare a reform programme consisting of discrete government and donor interventions, where the funders maintain full accountability and control).

2. The Technical Unit appeared to be unfamiliar with these strategy papers, arguing that it is not necessary to develop separate sector strategies where it is working with other donors. This is arguably only valid in the short term, and a through assessment of the nature of the constraints and opportunities in various sectors would help inform future investment priorities.

3. How this will be implemented in practice remains to be seen, since the Desk Officer for India indicated that sector-type projects may in practivce consist of an agglomeration of individual projects, forming a programme.

6

DONOR ORGANISATION AND COORDINATION

Amongst the six EU donors covered by this study, there are considerable differences in the organisational structure and in the location of personnel. These differences reflect not only the scale of the bilateral aid being provided to India, but more importantly the different perceptions as to how best to achieve the aid framework objectives for which the donor organisation is responsible, first and foremost to their own government. In theory, the signing of the Maastricht Treaty in 1992 brought a new level of agreement in to European Community and member state aid, since this spelt out common objectives of poverty reduction and promotion of democracy and human rights, among others. This, coupled with the fact that virtually all the European donors share environmental and gender equity objectives, would suggest substantial consensus among the EU donors on the goals of their development cooperation programmes.

In reality, this consensus is more fragile than it appears. The Maastricht Treaty has not genuinely provided an effective policy framework for EU development cooperation. In practice, European donor policy makers rarely refer to the Maastricht objectives, still less do their developing country partners. The commonality of objectives owes more to heterogeneous policy influences, ranging from the World Bank, UNDP, the Development Assistance Committee of the OECD, and to the regular interactions between donor officials. This heterogeneity coupled with the lack of an effective accepted policy umbrella undermines the possibility of agreement leading to a greater coherence in aid policy. Thus, when the intermediate and the immediate objectives of the various EU donors begin to be considered, so the picture begins to fragment. While Germany and the Netherlands are willing to press for a considerable level of conditionality in their project aid to India, the two Scandinavian countries studied, Denmark and Sweden, appear as far 'softer' donors, with conditionality limited to specific project level requirements. Similarly, there are marked differences in the weight given to ownership in project implementation and design; in how far one can work with the Indian 'system' and how far it must be changed; in the emphasis placed on structural change and the need to promote collective self-help; and in the priority accorded to budgetary, sectoral, project and technical assistance channels for aid.

The differences in approaches to aid, in the modalities involved, are reflected in the different ways that the 6 donors have structured their organisations and management systems (*see* Table 6.1). In the space of a few pages it is not possible to do justice to the complexities of each donor's operations or to the intentions that lie behind the management systems employed. We should also qualify our work by restating once more that our approach is from the perspective of poverty reduction and that this may lead us to downplay or neglect other important factors and considerations that lie behind donor practices.

Organisational structure and personnel

One of the most notable features of the six donors is the difference in the degree to which they have decentralised their country level operations to date. While decentralisation can take several forms, three of these are of particular relevance to the nature and role of donors in India: first decentralisation whereby the country-level capacity is merely that which is deemed necessary for the daily management of the aid portfolio and for the channelling of information back to the headquarters (HQ) while communicating and implementing policy downwards. The HQ remains the nodal point for decision-making, retaining country and regional capacity as well as being the main location for sectoral expertise. The second form of decentralisation involves the partial division and partial replication of the institutional capacity between the HQ and the country level office in Delhi; for example some sector and country expertise located in Delhi with country, regional and cross-sectoral expertise at the HQ. The formulation of country strategy, sector programmes and decisions as to the composition of the project portfolio remain at the HQ with country-based inputs. The third form of decentralisation involves not only the decentralisation of personnel and institutional capacity to the country office, but also the devolution of decision-making competence with only the overall budget and donor policy framework being decided at the HQ.

Within these three options lie a number of other variations including the decentralisation of sector expertise to the country, based in specialised sector units; the regionalisation of capacity at either HQ or within the region (South Asia); the vertical segmentation of capacity into institutions responsible for financial cooperation on the one hand and technical assistance on the other; or the decentralisation of responsibilities together with the indianisation of country level personnel, to name but a few.

German aid has perhaps the most centralised organisational structure in which the Bundesministerium für Wirtschaftliche Zusammenarbeit und Entwicklung (BMZ—Federal Ministry for Economic Cooperation and Development) is the ministry in charge of German aid, but then divides its aid between Financial Cooperation (FC) and Technical Cooperation (TC), with the Kreditanstalt für Wiederaufbau (KfW) as the institution responsible for FC and Deutsche Gesellschaft für Technische Zusammenarbeit (GTZ) as the institution responsible for TC. While BMZ has a Development Counsellor attached to the embassy in Delhi, KfW and GTZ both have their own separate country level offices in Delhi.

Informally, there is a degree of cooperation between the three country level departments, but formally the lines of accountability are vertical with coordination and overall responsibility for everything from country strategy to project selection lying with the India Section of BMZ in Bonn. KfW is itself highly centralised with only one Project Coordinator in the office in Delhi. All sector and country expertise is located within country and regional units at KfW's HQ in Frankfurt. GTZ is in the process of moving towards a more decentralised organisational structure, but there are only three non-project officers in India at the Delhi office and country and sector expertise is located in a unit at GTZ's HQ in Eschborn. To emphasize the centralised nature of German aid is not to ignore the fact that project officers and other country-based staff are procedurally involved in policy development and project assessment or that management authority in implementation lies in India, however. It is perhaps the tripartite structure of German aid with GTZ and KfW implementing BMZ's country programme that reproduces the central role of Bonn and the German end of the organisational structure.

At the other end of the spectrum is UK aid to India, administered by DFID, which has since January, 1996, been managed by a country aid management office, the British Development Cooperation Office, Delhi (BDCOD). UK aid allocations to India, although considerable, are well below those of Germany. The shift from a London-based Development Division to BDCOD was therefore not so much linked to the scale of the aid programme but more to a perceived need to increase effectiveness and to make it easier to pursue the central objective of poverty reduction according to DFID. It is a move that has been watched with some interest by the other donors, and it should be noted, some envy by other country level offices.

With respect to the other EU donors, Sida, Danida, and DGIS are all closer to the decentralised end of the spectrum. Each possesses a significant country level capacity in terms of personnel and sector-based expertise relative to their scale of donor involvement, but at the same time retaining a strong country and sector capacity at their respective HQs. From January 1997, DGIS devolved decision-making with respect to projects down to the Dutch embassies, with the ambassador as the principal head. The increased country-level autonomy this created was restricted however through a change in the budget structure for development cooperation, from a country specific budget to a thematic or sector-based budget system. This has caused problems at the country-level as funds cannot be moved from one sector budget line to another and changes have subsequently been made in 1998 to try and improve the situation.

Danida has a relatively well developed administrative capacity at the country-level with a relatively large field presence. Development cooperation is in fact the main item on the embassy's agenda with the ambassador closely involved. In addition to the development counsellors at the embassy, Danida has also experimented with special sector units. In the past there have been such units in health and drinking water and at present there is a 'Watershed Development Coordination Unit (WDCU)' located separate from the embassy. This is somewhat similar to the Field Management Offices (FMO) operated under BDCOD. WDCU administers Danida's watershed projects, but has to refer back to the embassy. The division of labour and responsibility between the unit and the embassy has been a problem and a proposed similar health unit has not been established as yet.

In Delhi, Sida is incorporated into the embassy and therefore is under the authority of the ambassador, but in Stockholm it remains a separate entity from the Ministry of Foreign Affairs. Fears were expressed in Sida, Delhi, that the country-level integration might bring other concerns than development to bear upon development assistance. Some connected to Sida's aid assistance in India believe this to have occurred.

The EC remains something of an exception in that it has a remarkably small staff in Delhi, given the scale of its aid in terms of volume. There is a Development Counsellor responsible for India with a staff consisting of two consultants, two local project officers and an Education Adviser. In addition to its responsibilities with respect to the EC commitments to India of some 1 billion ECU, this very small number of staff also has some responsibilities for EC aid to Nepal and Bhutan. Most of the decision-making power resides in Brussels, but the Technical Support Unit in Brussels is also extremely small, with the equivalent of only 1.5 full-time staff working on India. The EC Delegation is also frustrated by the fact that it has no delegated authority to make anything other than small local payments, which reduces disbursement rates and effectiveness. This was disputed by an official in Brussels, who argued that the Delegation may be unaware of the degree of influence that it has, and that although formal decision-making power rests with Brussels, the Delegation is the driving force given its superior information base.

The Department of External Affairs of the Government of India finds it extremely frustrating working with the EC as all negotiations must go through the Delegation in Delhi despite the fact that this is effectively a disempowered body. Even the smallest of issues can take a very long time to resolve causing long delays in disbursements etc. This is in strong contrast to the German system, which despite being centralised, enables Indian officials to be in direct dialogue with counterparts in Bonn. Although an internal reorganisation of the European Community aid programme is underway, and a separate Common Services implementation Directorate has been created, it is uncertain whether this will bring rapid organisational change.

As indicated above, the nature of the decentralisation varies considerably and involves a number of factors including staffing levels, location of country/sector expertise, location and level of decision-making responsibilities particularly with respect to projects, sector programmes and country strategy. Where do the crucial inputs come in? Where are decisions on content etc., made in practice as opposed to formal acceptance? In the following table we have made a preliminary attempt to present the donors' organisational profiles in order to illustrate the different ways that the goal of effective aid operationalisation has been pursued.

It is difficult to make a clear judgement as to the merits and failings of the different organisational structures to be found amongst the donors. Some of the donors can be seen to have taken decisions that facilitate a more effective delivery of aid for poverty reduction in India, the UK's establishment of a DFID aid office in India for example. In other cases, the weight of a historical legacy in which the organisational structure of aid delivery was based upon considerations present in the donor country,

Table 6.1: The organisational structure of the 6 Donors (as on December 1997)

Donor	Number of India staff at HQs[a]	Number of India-based donor staff[a]	Is donor organisation an integral part of embassy?	Main location of sector expertise	Main responsibility for preparation of sector programmes	Main responsibility for project selection	Specialised sector units in India	Aid allocation 1996-7 USD
BMZ (GTZ & KfW)	13	5	No	HQ	HQ	HQ	No	58.8
Danida	2 + 2	6	Yes	Country & HQ	Country & HQ	Country & HQ	1-2	36.8
DFID	0.5	32	No	Country	Country	Country	7	164.8
DGIS		8	Partial	Country	Country & HQ	Country	Yes	35.1
Sida	1	4	Yes	HQ & Country	HQ & Country	HQ & Country	No	27.4
EC	2	5	Yes	HQ	HQ	HQ & Country	1	99.3

Note:

[a] Numbers refer to person years, which may represent the part-time input of several staff. All numbers are best approximations available.

for example KfW in Germany, makes such a reform difficult even if it was felt to be necessary. In such cases, the prioritisation of poverty reduction requires a different form of organisational change.

While accepting that organisational structure cannot be simply interpreted as reflecting the donor's preferred mode for achieving poverty reduction in India, discussions with the donors have nevertheless revealed a number of perceived advantages with both centralised and a decentralised approach to aid in India.

The advantages of having a strong country-based representation with a degree of decentralised authority in project and policy matters were seen to be the following:

— Inter-donor coordination requires a considerable pool of competent well-informed staff if the large number of working groups existing are to be attended in addition to the other administrative work required of country level staff.

- Internal donor sector coordination is not possible on a country level unless there are Chiefs of Sector programmes or their equivalents within a donor organisation at the country office.
- One of the main problems faced by donors is that they are formally required to play a reactive role to projects, responding to project proposals that have already progressed through the initial identification and design phases. Informally country-based staff do play a pro-active role, but would like to have the personnel resources, both in numbers and expertise, to support this role. For example, two-thirds of KfW's projects are described as having emerged from a pro-active engagement by the donor. This is partly due to the problem that some 95% of project proposals that they receive are poorly conceived and designed.[1] To quote one anonymous source: 'They reflect weak policy, poor representation in the design, obscure ideas emanating from the Indian government, with a communication to the State to say that "the Germans have money for such and such.... and a project idea being thrown together accordingly"'. Other donors have expressed similar problems, an example was provided by one of an Indian engineering consultancy firm designing an urban pollution project which required a high level of community involvement in the planning and implementation process. The local community was ridiculously defined by the company as those households within 50 metres of the drainage canal. Country level capacity in the donor organisation is seen as being central to improving the quality of the project proposals received. This is ideally done in collaboration with Indian partners, and thus can contribute to capacity-building.
- Two other areas in which a greater capacity at the country level is seen to be an advantage are: (i) improving the scope for cross-state replicability of projects and programmes by being able to provide technical support to ensure that lesson-learning is effective; and (ii) at the national level by building capacity for the monitoring and assessment of sector programmes.
- Developing sector-wide approaches necessitates working closely with union and state level institutions. It is arguably easier for donors to support policy reform and to build in appropriate indicators or conditions, where they have strong country-based sectoral competence. It is also important that this donor capacity

is seen to be there by the GoI, and DFID argues, for instance, that its increased country-based expertise has enhanced its perceived effectiveness and its negotiating position with the Indian government.

— Linked to this, is the importance of significant country-based capacity if the donor is to go beyond merely providing budget support to line ministries for particular projects. This requires not only technical assistance in the form of project advisers, but close monitoring and feedback mechanisms to help ensure that objectives which are particularly prized by donors are achieved, such as community planning or user groups and cost recovery.

— A strong country-based capacity within the donor organisation is seen by some donors to be an advantage for developing a greater awareness and sensitivity to local contexts and local thinking, as well as for developing close local contacts based upon personal relationships etc. For their part, Indian officials have expressed the view that a number of problems could be avoided if donors were better informed and more atuned to local contexts. Some donors argue that a better understanding of state (and union) level political economy is important if real change is to take place and aid is to bring about a genuine improvement. The UK, for instance, supported primary education in Andhra Pradesh for more than a decade, yet saw the budget share allocated to primary education by the Government of Andhra Pradesh fall. While the aid sustained an important programme, it failed to enhance it for reasons that might have been better explored with the state government at an earlier stage.

— A strong country-based capacity is also important for enabling a more inter-disciplinary approach to development aid in India and on the spot resourcing of needs as they arise. These needs may often be met most effectively by using local experts. The UK[2] recognises this and DGIS, Sida and Danida also appear to, but the effective selection and supervision of such experts tend to require a depth of knowledge which comes from having expertise at the country level.

Countering the arguments for a strong country-based representation for the donor are a number of advantages claimed for a strong HQ-based country capacity and sectoral expertise:

— It facilitates a process of learning by experience across the whole donor programme, and especially at the regional level, since sectoral expertise is often organised in regional units within the HQ. The accumulation of knowledge, with respect to innovative organisational and management practices in programmes and projects, can then be 'sent out' to individual countries when the need arises.

— A related point is that by making the donor HQ the focal point for strategy and policy, it may be easier to ensure that full recognition is given to the most recent thinking on poverty reduction or on methodologies for monitoring and assessment. This will strengthen the link between development theory and practice.

— It brings a greater weight and authority to the decision-making process and, in particular, to the annual bilateral negotiations at union, state, and ministry levels.

— The location of country or regional experts at the HQ together with the presence of a strong technical advisory support for sectoral and cross-sectoral programmes is a more rational and cost effective use of donor resources. It should be noted that DFID acknowledges that there are higher costs with devolution and delegation, but argues that these are justified by increased effectiveness. Increased costs can in part be contained in the long-run by the greater use of Indian staff at the professional level. DGIS estimates that delegation of staff (and responsibilities) to embassy level has increased costs between three and four hundred per cent over the costs of the same at the Hague.

While it is not easy to make a judgement as to which model can best be seen to achieve a more effective poverty reduction in aid, there are several points that would argue strongly in favour of the more decentralised approach. Poverty reduction requires more than the promotion of economic growth through investment in infrastructure, support to the leading sectors in the economy, and the improvement of the social sectors to benefit those disadvantaged groups not directly aided by the first two. Poverty reduction also requires locally researched knowledge of poverty, good targeting of the poor and, not least, the involvement and active participation of the poor themselves. They must be encouraged and supported to enable them to become actors in their own development. This relies on the government and donors working together actively to bring people into the dialogue on development and seeking to link local development with national development. To do this effectively demands greater expertise at the country level and below.

Donors have recently given increased emphasis to sectoral approaches to development. Sector-wide approaches may be defined as 'a medium-term collaborative programme of work concerned with the development of sectoral policies and strategies... the establishment of management systems by governments *and* donors... and institutional reform and capacity building, in line with agreed policies.'[3] This implies an *ongoing* collaboration between government actors and donors, to develop policy frameworks which link strategic analysis with resource allocation decisions, building government capacity to lead the process of sectoral development, the development of appropriate incentives for the public and private sectors, and the development of common management systems which also provide financial accountability. This kind of close collaboration with the government and partner institutions and an understanding of the constraints and the opportunities present again arguably requires a strong country level expertise.

A third factor is the sheer size and institutional structure of India and the demands this places upon a donor. On the one hand it is the need to work at union, state, district and local levels and to be able to negotiate the intricacies of moving across and between the political, administrative and socio-cultural boundaries and spaces that exist. On the other hand, it is the sheer scale of the poverty problem, upwards of 400 million people close to or below the poverty level. It is estimated that if the states of India were taken independently, 6 of them would be in the 20 poorest countries in the world. Given these facts, it is questionable as to whether aid to India can be efficiently and effectively administered from afar and that pragmatic reasons alone may well explain the shift towards decentralisation by some of the EU donors, whether through transferring personnel to India or through the greater use of Indian personnel or both, as well as some devolution of budget responsibilities to country level offices.

One final point to emerge during our study; the Indian comments appear to reflect a preference for the country-based expertise as it aids the daily administrative cooperation between the bilateral parties.

It is clear that there are advantages and disadvantages associated with both the centralised and decentralised approaches. However, from a poverty reduction perspective, if not a general aid-effectiveness standpoint, the advantages cited of a strong country-based representation appear to be considerable. The disadvantages indicated also carry weight: the accumulation of cross-country experience within a decentralised system can be a problem, for example. However, the improved potential for effective coordination, capacity building, replicability, monitoring systems, use of local expertise and increased understanding of the local context cannot be ignored.

Appropriateness of staff resource levels: The case of the European Commission

Clearly, the effectiveness with which aid is used to support poverty reduction depends not simply on the type of donor management system and its degree of decentralisation. The number of donor staff available to manage those aid resources, the range of skills which the agency can draw upon, and the competence of those staff are also important factors. Here, the position of the European Community aid programme should be examined. The European Commission is entrusted by the EU member states with the management and implementation of the European Community aid programme to India. Yet for this task the Commission has the equivalent of only 7 full-time staff to implement its mandate. The EC delegation in India comprises, as shown in Table 6.1, of only 5 staff of which 2 are officials and 3 are locally recruited. Not one of these is an expert in the sectors of health or education, the two largest programmes in the EC portfolio. In contrast to the UK programme, for instance, the Delegation lacks both sectoral and cross-cutting (gender, institutional development, social development) expertise. They are therefore reliant first on technical support from Brussels, and secondly on consultants. However, the EC Technical Unit for the whole of Asia comprises only 12 people, who collectively provide about 1.5 'person equivalents' for the India programme. There is a single specialist on education for all of Asia, and one for health. There are a few experts covering the 'horizontal' issues such as environment, forestry, and women and development, but these can offer only a very limited input into the India programme due to the scope of their remit. In addition, there is a desk officer responsible for India, who takes a lead in strategy development, but whose mandate is to spend at least half of his time on political and trade-related activities as opposed to development cooperation.

The Commission is therefore extremely dependent upon consultants for the design, implementation and monitoring of their programmes. However, the system for tendering for consultants is widely acknowledged to be unsatisfactory. A separate unit, known by some within the Commission as 'the black hole', situated outside of the technical unit and the country desk, is charged with managing the tendering process, with a representative of the technical unit as one of the evaluators. The emphasis is on the transparency of the selection process, resulting in legalistic considerations predominating over technical quality. There is no pre-qualification procedure to ensure a minimum standard of technical excellence, and the pool from which the EC can draw is severely limited by the fact that it pays significantly lower rates than other donors. The importance of ensuring a 'fair' balance of nationality in the allocation of contracts among the member states can be argued to compromise the quality of technical expertise provided. In the health sector, the cost of preparing bids, which may amount to 20,000 ECU, and the lower rates offered have drastically reduced the scope to involve institutes of public health, which may well have highly appropriate expertise for the projects. Several officials commented that the quality of the consultants was in part a matter of chance, and that the procedures for dismissing consultants were very lengthy, resulting in the least-cost option often being to put up with mediocrity.

A final and perhaps the most serious flaw in the procedures is the fact that those technical experts who have been involved in project or programme design are automatically excluded from competing at the implementation phase. This is intended to ensure fair competition, yet it can have negative consequences for effectiveness. An example is the reproductive and child health sector programme, to which the EC has allocated 200 m. ECU. A team of EC consultants spent about 9 months in India working with other donors and the Indian government on the design of the programme. This same team was thereafter unable to tender for the implementation of the programme. Given the EC's limited staff resources at the Delegation and the Brussels level, the ineligibility of the team represented a significant loss of knowledge, established rapport and trust involving the consultants, the government and other donors. In addition, the re-tendering process is slow, resulting in a significant loss of impetus. EC officials are understandably frustrated by procedures which they perceive as undermining their attempts to deliver an effective and poverty-oriented aid programme.

The main burden of responsibility for this appears to lie with the member states. For long they have been sceptical of the Commission's ability to implement its aid programme effectively and have favoured the reliance on consultants. Member states have also failed to support the decentralisation of decision-making authority and personnel to the country level, preferring to retain greater control through their representation on the Brussels-based Councils and Committees. Clearly, with only 12 technical staff covering all of Asia there is no immediate scope for decentralising personnel to the field, and without providing for greater sector expertise at the Delegation level decentralisation of decision-making is also problematic. A significant expansion of staffing levels in Brussels and at the country level is essential if the Commission is to fulfil its mandate effectively.

Policy conditionality with respect to poverty reduction

Again there is considerable variation both in the degree to which EU donors are prepared to attach conditionalities to their aid and as to the type of conditionalities that they are prepared to impose. Whether conditionalities are directed towards achieving poverty reduction or more generally attached to improve the broader development process and the effective utilisation of aid within that is a further difficulty that we face in our study.

For example, sector framework conditionalities designed to introduce cost recovery can be argued as being poverty reducing if they generate greater local ownership, more sustainable projects, and the removal of infrastructural and bureaucratic bottlenecks. They can also be argued as negatively affecting the poor, particularly the poorest of the poor, if such cost recovery becomes a barrier to their participation. This can be as true for the social sector, for example school fees, as it can for the productive sector, for example power charges or irrigation fees.

In the case of German aid, BMZ has not been afraid to impose conditions for the receipt of aid or for the continuation of aid to a project or programme in India. This has particularly been the case with financial cooperation projects carried out under KfW. Here they have very strict guidelines concerning the sectoral framework conditions necessary before a project is accepted. Sectoral reforms are often demanded. This has been the case with projects for river lift irrigation in Orissa, water supply in Rajasthan, power supply in Madhya Pradesh. In several cases disbursement of funds has been delayed or stopped due to a failure to carry through the reforms required. KfW has been described as being tougher than the WB in its sectoral requirements prior to aid disbursement.

In the public goods areas of water supply, sewerage, minor irrigation and waste disposal there has been a growing insistence for consumption-based fees being collected and for the systems to be placed with elected local authorities, i.e. municipalities. For example in the case of support to water supply in West Bengal which began in 1997, KfW insisted upon tariff collection being brought into the existing system and were surprised to find that it was not rejected by the Left Front Government. It should be noted that capital cost recovery has not yet been attempted by BMZ/KfW.

As the above indicates, there has also been an element of conditionality with respect to the selection of institutional delivery system, in particular the use of local NGOs and of the decentralised institutions of local government, where they exist. The agreement of the Indian government to the Self-Help Fund and the Small Project Fund in 1993 almost became a condition for the whole German aid package.

For its part, GTZ is less willing and/or able to make such demands prior to agreeing to a project or disbursing funds. Most of its projects are much smaller than those of KfW, and it lacks the political and economic clout to push through such demands. On occasion, GTZ has been used to provide a technical cooperation project component in support of the sector framework reforms required prior to the disbursement of funds for financial cooperation. The Indian state officials have not always accepted the preliminary technical cooperation input. For example in Himachal Pradesh with the Changar Eco-Development Project, an informal suggestion came from the Indian side that the technical assistance be dropped and that they proceed immediately with the financial support.

Dutch aid appears to follow a similar line with quite strict demands being made as to the organisational and management systems they require to be set in place in order for a project to commence. In some cases this has resulted in long delays between the reaching of a project agreement and the commencement of a project with the concerned state government. In the recent case of a Dutch rural drinking project in Karnataka, the Government of Karnataka regarded the requirements on such matters as personnel recruitment, tendering etc., as unwarranted intrusions into their internal affairs and management systems.

The Dutch have also applied more general conditionalities in the annual negotiations with the Indian government with respect to the overall objectives of Dutch aid and specifically with respect to the proportion that should be devoted directly to poverty reduction.

Danida does not tend to employ policy conditionalities in its development aid and this appears to be appreciated by the Indian counterparts, a joint secretary in one of the central ministries stating: 'Danida never tries to ride roughshod over the recipient'. Conditionality has been imposed occasionally within individual projects however, in Tamil Nadu a condition for Phase III of a health project was that the Panchayati Raj Institutions should be involved, against the wishes of the then AIADMK government. In Karnataka, Phase II of a Integrated Rural Sanitation and Water Project included the condition that cost recovery for operation and maintenance costs be introduced.

Sida must also be considered as employing only 'soft' conditionality. One exception has been in the proposed extension to the Social Forestry Project in Orissa. Here Sida has set down a number of demands that must be met before a project agreement can be reached. There have been a number of problems with this project both in terms of the success in meeting the intermediate objectives with respect to participatory social forestry and in the Sida-Forest Department relationship. For the extension, Sida will support only aid to local institutional capacity building whereas the Ministry for Environment and Forests and the Forest Department in Orissa would prefer finance in the form of budgetary support to continue their programme. It appears unlikely that the programme will be extended.

Projects and programmes funded by the European Community aid programme have involved strong financial conditionality. The clearest example of this came in 1991, when European Community aid was suspended to India. The Commission officials were unhappy that it provided its resources to Central Government as a 100% grant, which was subsequently on-lent to states as 70% grants and 30% loans. The Commission considered that this provided no incentive to states to use these funds for poverty-focused activities, which themselves would not generate a return to facilitate loan repayment. Within a year, the Commission received an undertaking that funds provided in grant form would be provided to states in grant form. A further example is the strong line taken by the Commission with respect to the ongoing Reproductive and Child Health Programme. Here the Commission indicated that it would be prepared to withdraw its support for the programme unless the GoI was prepared to demonstrate that donor funding would be genuinely additional to existing government expenditure[4]. This was successful in obtaining a commitment from the GoI that donor-support for the health sector would result in a real increase in the resources available to the health sector. At the core of its success lay the decision of the donors to work together from the start, to develop a common platform. Without such guarantees, donor resources are fungible and may be used by the GoI for expenditures in other sectors, including defence.

A similar line was taken with respect to the District Primary Education Programme, where a guarantee of additionality and commitment to decentralisation was obtained, and in which the funding is released in tranches dependent on results. A further illustration within DPEP of the effectiveness of donors acting in harmony relates to government agreement to speed up the devolution of power from the centre to the district. In implementing its support for DPEP the European Commission has differed from the bilaterals in not tying its resources to any particular state or districts. This is widely appreciated by the GoI, who agree with the Commission that this serves to reinforce ownership. This relies on both parties having confidence in the policy framework and monitoring mechanisms. While the European Commission is seeking to fund capacity building measures other donors, such as DFID, consider that they can provide financial and technical support most effectively through a closer involvement with two individual states. To this end, DFID have sought to exercise quality control, in partnership with the Government, over district level education plans, to ensure that decentralisation of decision-making to the local level occurs in practice.

A common point in several of the donors has been the use of conditionality in support of the decentralisation of government in India. Examples mentioned above include Danida, BMZ-KfW and the European Commission, but this appears to be a growing factor for all of the EU donors. In so far as Panchayati Raj[5] involves the democratisation of local government and an increase in the accountability of local administration to the elected local authorities, it can be argued that it has a potential pivotal role in furthering poverty reduction, particularly in rural areas. West Bengal has demonstrated that where there is a political will to bring the poor into the process of local development through local government, quite substantial poverty reduction can be achieved. It has been argued by a growing number of academics that the role of Panchayati Raj Institutions in supporting economic growth and in the distribution of its benefits in the State of West Bengal during the 1980s has been one of the principal reasons for the reduction of poverty in the rural areas.[6] For its part, Uttar Pradesh demonstrates the danger of decentralisation serving to enhance the role of local elites with little regard for the poor and poverty reduction.

The other point in common amongst EU donors with respect to poverty reduction, institutional delivery of aid and conditionality, is the growing pressure for bringing institutions of the poor into the implementation of projects. This goes beyond the elected institutions of local government to user committees, forest protection committees, community health and sanitation groups, slum dwellers associations, and similar organisations. Often the conditionality takes the form of requiring awareness creation and group formation as a project component, with local NGOs often being brought in to facilitate this process.

When considering the use of conditionalities by donors, it is important to recognise that there are both ethical and practical problems attached to it. The ethical issues concern the donor-Government of India relationship and the border between encouraging efficiency, introducing innovation, increasing effectiveness on the one hand and challenging the right of the Government of India to decide upon the direction and form of development for which it has been given an electoral mandate to undertake on the other. It is further complicated by the fact that donors also argue that they have an ethical responsibility to their own governments to secure the objectives for which aid has been sanctioned. There is no clear-cut answer to the philosophical and political issues involved. At best, it can be negotiated through the bilateral partnership relationship and the annual bilateral negotiations play a central role here. But the question as to who 'owns' Indian development and thereby the status of the aid offered to facilitate that development will always remain problematical.

The practical problems concern the question of where should conditionality be applied given the complexity of centre-state relationships, problems concerning the location of responsibility for sector policy and programmes, and much more. Even when it is felt that a degree of conditionality is acceptable on the basis of an agreed agenda by both parties (e.g. donor and Government of India), at the level of implementation, for example a State ministry, the agenda can be very different and strong opposition to the conditions required.

Certainly, where conditionality is used to secure additionality, to promote effective decentralisation with the participation of the poor, to secure better targeting and effective utilisation of resources, then the ethical arguments on poverty reduction must be seen to counter those concerning national ownership and accompanying issues of rights.

Coordination

It is striking that on the whole each of the donors appears to pursue its own agenda with very little reference to the other donors in the field. Partly this can be explained by the organisational structure of the different donors, the independent origins of their respective strategies and policies, the shortage of staff at the country level with time to participate in coordination working groups, and the lines of management including accountability and decision-making that structure the donor personnel's routine work.

One might imagine that the European Commission would represent the potential for a more coordinated approach towards aid to India, both in terms of strategy and operationalisation, but the reverse appears to be true. One senior KfW official expressed the view that it would be best for all if the European Commission abandoned its aid role due to its poor performance and that the individual members retain the funds for their own aid budgets. There are quarterly EU donor coordination meetings held, but more than one donor official described them as being, for the most part, a waste of time.

One might also imagine that at an operational level, inter-donor coordination would operate at the level of exchanging information on project activities and similar matters with possible coordination where areas overlapped for example. Again this appears not to be the case. For example, a new DFID supported watershed project in Karnataka will overlap with Phase II of a Danida supported watershed project in Bijapur District of the state yet there has been no attempt at donor coordination.

A member of staff at the Swedish embassy expressed the view that donor coordination is not very necessary in India, in contrast to Africa where foreign aid plays a much greater role. It was argued that as India is so large, the total contribution of aid is so small, and the donors operate in different sectors and states, the risk of duplication is therefore very small. Staff at the Royal Netherlands Embassy expressed similar views with the additional comments that the agencies who should arguably be responsible for encouraging such coordination are either not up to the task (i.e. the European Union) or not particularly interested (i.e. the World Bank).

In some cases, donor coordination has been quite specific. For example, there has been close coordination between KfW and the World Bank on a number of programmes even to the extent of operating as its junior partner. There is general BMZ support for the World Bank's policy dialogue with the GoI and at the sector and project levels, there is close support and coordination between German aid and the World Bank. For example, in 1994/5 similar requests for support to the health sector in West Bengal, and the rehabilitation of hospitals, were received by both the World Bank and BMZ. It was agreed that the World Bank would focus upon the secondary hospitals while BMZ-KfW concentrated on the primary health care provision. Initially there was a geographical division between the two donors as well, a form of parallel financing. However, this was subsequently changed on the BMZ-KfW side as 10-15m DM had too little impact upon the political system. By coming with 60m DM and taking up the primary health sector in the whole state, a far greater reforming impact could be achieved it was felt.

Such examples of close cooperation are not very common, however.

The scepticism expressed time and time again by officials from the EU donors both towards the possibility for closer coordination and towards whatever attempts have been made in this direction is difficult to explain. There does appear to be considerable competition between the different bilateral donors with often negative sentiments expressed about other donors' activities. An official from the World Bank office in Delhi argued that the 'bilaterals are constantly inflating their own importance and criticising whatever the Bank does.' Justified or not, there is much criticism of the World Bank and the European Commission, but it does not help moves towards greater coordination.

The most active agency in the area of donor coordination is UNDP. Since 1994, UNDP's traditional coordination mandate, first articulated in detail in UN General Assembly Resolution 47/199 in 1992, has been further strengthened. In India, UN working groups have provided the basis for the more recent establishment of a number of thematic donor coordination groups (there were 21 such groups in December, 1997). The groups vary in membership size and work agendas and are all convened by different organisations. The criterion for the establishment of a group is interest expressed by the agencies, with UNDP only providing a background secretariat role. While most of the groups are only fora for exchanging views and information, a few collaborative initiatives have emerged.

For the most part, the EU donors appear to favour some degree of coordination, but on an *ad hoc* basis. Where there is a need, let those with similar interests meet, but not on a formal basis with regular meetings etc. While sector focused coordination appears to be more successful, it is unlikely that in the present donor context, poverty reduction could be the focus for any such coordination which is unfortunate.

For its part, the GoI prefers to work with donors on an individual, bilateral basis, understandably so. The idea of donors 'ganging up' on the Indian government is not a popular one.

Donor coordination is particularly important at the sector programme level. Coordination and cooperation ensures donor consensus around a policy reform agenda and allows different donor strengths, financial and technical, to be drawn upon most effectively. If donors are to make good on a commitment to ensure that macro and meso (sector) reforms take full account of the needs of the poor, they need to be singing from the same hymn book as far as possible. It is therefore heartening that there have been a number of good examples of effective coordination, notably in the Reproductive and Child Health Programme and also the District Primary Education Project. The European Commission played an important role in obtaining donor consensus that the Reproductive and Child Health Programme should only be supported if the additionality of funds could be demonstrated by the GoI. The Commission and the UK aid programme cooperated effectively, with an enlightened willingness on the part of both to benefit from the Commission financial 'clout' and the UK's greater health expertise.

The effectiveness of coordination is dependent on government capacity and determination at least as much as donor commitment. Arguably, of the two examples given above, coordination was more effective, at least at the policy formulation stage, in the education sector than in the health sector. This partly reflected the determination of the Deputy Secretary within the Ministry of Education to lead on policy development and programme implementation drawing on donor expertise and resources where *he* felt he needed them. The donors were referred to as 'external agents', whose contribution would be within a framework developed and owned by the GoI. In the health sector, although donor coordination was effective, Indian government capacity and coherence within the Ministry of Health and Family Welfare was lower. The result, some donor and government officials have argued, is that donor profile and influence was raised at the expense of that of the government, and that ownership was lower. This may well change and develop, however, and there has certainly been substantial and effective cooperation between both parties.

At project level the record on coordination has not been particularly impressive, but this is perhaps to be expected in that projects remain the domain of specific donors. Perhaps more surprising, however, is the lack of coordination involving the sharing of information between donors. Apart from fairly superficial exchanges concerning their respective activities, there appears to be little or no exchange of more detailed information such as that contained in state level poverty or gender assessments, or in the state or sector profiles and papers that are often prepared by individual donors.

REFERENCES

1. A Commission official also indicated that the quality of projects proposed by the GoI was often quite low, with donors scrambling over each other to fund the better ones. However, it was often preferred to agree to fund a less-than-ideal project and try to improve upon it, since projects initiated by the donor could take a very long time to receive official sanction.

2. The UK has a policy of promoting the greater use of Indian staff at the expert as well as the administrative level. This is designed to draw upon local knowledge, such as through its imaginative secondment of a GoI employee as an Institutional Development Adviser, as well as to reduce costs (total employment costs of UK staff are about 10 times those of local staff). Currently, the UK aid office has 3 Indian staff at the adviser level, and a further 11 at the professional level. There is a training programme in place to upgrade the skills of existing and new Indian staff.

3. Andrew Cassels, 1997, A Guide to Sector-wide Approaches for Health Development: concepts, issues and working arrangements', WHO, Danida, DFID, European Commission.

4. Interestingly, although World Bank staff accepted the validity of this approach, the Bank's legal department argued that it was not in a position to impose conditions on budgetary allocation decisions taken by a parliament.

5. Panchayati Raj is the name given to the programme for the decentralisation of government in India. It received a considerable boost when the GoI passed the 73rd and 74th Constitutional Amendments, in early 1993. These require that all Indian states implement Panchayati Raj and thereby decentralise government down to district, block and village levels with similar institutional structures in municipalities. The state governments are also required to appoint a Local State Finance Commission to develop proposals for the financing of local government.

6. See for example J. Dréze & A. Sen India: Economic Development and Social Opportunity, OUP, 1995, S. Bose, B., Harriss-White & B. Rogaly (ed) Sonar Bangla: Agricultural Growth and Agrarian Structure in Contemporary West Bengal and Bangladesh, Sage, 1999.

7

OPERATIONALISATION OF AID FOR POVERTY REDUCTION

The foregoing chapter examined some of the more general aspects of the EU donors operationalisation of their aid programmes for poverty reduction. There are a number of more specific dimensions that also need to be taken up in this assessment, aspects dealing more specifically with the donors' engagement with the poor in the operationalisation of their aid assistance.

Institutional dimensions of poverty reduction

For all six donors, participation by the beneficiaries has emerged as a key aspect in the attempt to address the institutional dimensions of donor-financed poverty reduction programmes and projects. From an initial move towards engaging with the poor through consultation, problem identification, project evaluation and assessment, participation has now become a priority aim in local institution building and in institutional capacity raising generally. Today the ideal is to achieve participation within all phases of the project cycle and participation is deemed to be central to the ownership and thereby sustainability of projects, and ultimately to the process of sustainable poverty reduction. Participation has also become central to other cross-cutting imperatives including the environment and natural resource management, gender, and human rights and good governance.

To a greater or lesser extent therefore, all six donors have sought to bring the beneficiaries into a far more prominent role within their sector programmes and the specific projects. This has taken a variety of forms;

in the case of KfW there has been an increasing pressure placed upon state governments and the departments concerned to bring beneficiaries into projects through economic mechanisms, for example the introduction of user fees to cover recurrent costs in irrigation in Orissa. The argument being that not only will this aid the financial sustainability of the project, but that it will also facilitate the formation of local user committees through the strong sense of ownership coming from the payment of such fees.

Elsewhere, the focus has been more directly upon the formation and strengthening local institutions through often quite complex interventions. Danida in the second phase of the Karnataka Watershed Development Project has developed an 11 stage approach to ensure a continual involvement of the beneficiaries in the project with the accompanying capacity building that accompanies the institutionalisation of such procedures within a project. Similar efforts have been made by DFID in a recent watershed project.

In quite a number of instances, the generation and strengthening of local institutions within a project draws upon the particular skills that Indian NGOs are seen to possess in this area. For example, the introduction of the two Indian NGOs, SEWA and SPARC, by DFID into the Gomti River Pollution Project located in Lucknow reflected the specific need to generate local community-based organisations capable of presenting their needs and interests both into the project through community planning, but also in a wider engagement with the municipality.

The implementation of Panchayati Raj has proved to be of growing importance for some of the donors. In those states in which it has been or is currently being implemented[1] donors are looking to see how far the reforms have gone and to what extent they provide an improved institutional basis at the local level for project implementation. But there are also exceptions here; Sida for one has not sought to involve Panchayati Raj Institutions in its projects. This might partly be explained by the weakness of these institutions in the states where Sida has its projects, notably Rajasthan, Orissa and Tamil Nadu, but there are no considerations with respect to their potential role in the future of Sida projects either. Financial weakness and local elite-domination appear to be the other explanations available for Sida's position, but it runs counter to thinking elsewhere amongst the EU donors.

Targeting

On state selection

The selection of recipient states within India is one of the first stages involved in the process of targeting. This selection is based upon many considerations amongst the six donors, but a trade-off that has concerned a number of donors in making their selection is that between the level of poverty present in a State and the institutional capacity present that determines how far the poor can in practice be reached. Reference has already been made to Danida's narrowing of its state focus to only Madhya Pradesh and Karnataka. An Important argument for continuing support to Karnataka rather than to the State of Orissa, one of the poorest states, was that Panchayati Raj in Karnataka presented a much better institutional basis at the local level for carrying through successful projects.

In preparing its most recent India country strategy, Sida commissioned a report in which the poverty of certain states was set alongside the institutional 'condition' of those states, and specifically the extent to which Panchayati Raj has been implemented. Elsewhere, a similar concern as to the institutional capacity of states, not least with respect to the issue of 'corruption' has played an important role in state selection. The issues involved in Danida's and Sida's selection of Indian states are discussed at greater length by Folke (Folke, 1998a, 1998b).

In the case of DGIS, the decision to keep the State of Karnataka in the Dutch portfolio for the time being was due to the direct intervention of Jan Pronk when the state was about to be dropped, and the role of ministers in other donors' selection of states in India has been known to be an important factor.

DFID have traditionally worked closely with a number of states, largely because of historical associations. It has recently decided to formalise its state focus by developing special partnership with three or four states, which are likely to be Orissa, Andhra Pradesh, West Bengal, and possibly Madhya Pradesh. The state selection is based on the two-fold criteria of commitment to poverty reduction and to sound economic policies, including redirecting budgetary resources away from inefficient subsidies and towards pro-poor social sector spending. All of these, apart from West Bengal, fall into the bottom half of Table 7.1, ranking states by level of human development. Such criteria were not applied in the past where, for example, the UK's environmental objective led to large scale support to the forestry sector in Himachal Pradesh.

Table 7.1: Disaggregated Human Development Index for India and Donor States

State	Life expectancy 1990-2	Adult literacy rate (%) 1991	Real GDP per capita (1993 PPP$) 1992	HDI value	HDI ranking	Donors
Kerala	72	86	1,017	0.597	1	nl
Punjab	66	52	2,124	0.516	2	
Maharashtra	64	60	1,802	0.513	3	d, uk
Haryana	63	49	1,915	0.476	4	
Gujrat	60	57	1,416	0.458	5	nl
West Bengal	61	57	1,186	0.452	6	d, uk
Himachal Pradesh	64	51	1,180	0.447	7	d
Karnataka	62	52	1,224	0.442	8	d, dk, uk, nl
Tamil Nadu	62	51	1,119	0.432	9	s, dk
Andhra Pradesh	60	40	1,227	0.393	10	uk, nl
Assam	54	49	932	0.374	11	
Orissa	55	46	896	0.368	12	d, s, dk, uk
Bihar	59	39	640	0.3504	13	s
Rajasthan	58	36	961	0.3503	14	d, s
Uttar Pradesh	56	38	884	0.343	15	nl
Madhya Pradesh	54	41	898	0.341	16	d, dk

Primary source: Mahbub ul Haq, *Human Development in South Asia,* 1997, p.116.

Notes: Denmark is to reduce its state focus support to Karnataka and Madhya Pradesh in future. DGIS has proposed to phase Karnataka out, but it remains for the time being. Sida has no focus states as such, but the states indicated have been the focus for social sector and forestry projects. Elsewhere there have been major power projects etc. In future, Sida plans to concentrate social sector projects in Rajasthan and Tamil Nadu. Other projects will be throughout India. The EC has no priority states.

The trade-off between the level of poverty and the possibility of reaching and aiding the poor in different states does raise the difficult question as to whether the poor, in say the State of Bihar are being abandoned through little fault of their own.

In the following table, we present the level of poverty and five of the donors' involvement in aid where they have a state focus. The table is based upon the UNDP's Human Development Indices as used in the 1996 Human Development Report (UNDP, 1996), with deviations in some of the components of the indices due to lack of data (Haq,

1997:116). The last column is based upon the information collected from donors for this study, but it is constructed by the authors and not the donors.

The European Community aid programme has never had a strategic and poverty-based geographical rationale. Where particular states were favoured, this was more to do with which state the particular GoI DEA official responsible for EC aid came from, or the personal preferences of EC Delhi-based staff. The relatively recent shift to a more sectoral approach has not changed this, since the concern has been to ensure that sector reform generates benefits across a range of states. Although the majority of the Commission's programmes operate at the state level, the Commission has not found it easy to work with state governments, principally because it has needed to go through central government first, which builds in delays.

On the selection of localities

If the selection of states is primarily a donor prerogative, the selection of districts or localities within a state is much more influenced by the state governments through the negotiations between the state government and the donor, but the donor nevertheless retains a strong role. An example is provided by the selection of Chengelpattu District for the first phase of the Sida supported Integrated Child Development Services. The Government of Tamil Nadu had suggested Pudukottai District which is much poorer than Chengelpattu District, the former being located next to the city of Madras/Chennai. Sida preferred Chengelpattu primarily for reasons of administrative convenience; in rationalising its choice it pointed to the large scheduled caste population present in the district. Chengelpattu District was eventually agreed upon as the focus for the first phase while Pudukottai was included in the second phase.

Danida was opposed to the inclusion of the relatively developed Uttara Kannada District in Phase I of the Karnataka Watershed Development Project, but it was demanded by the state government. Again in Phase III of the Tamil Nadu Health Care Project, while there was consensus on the selection of the poor and backward district of Dharmapuri, the state government insisted on including the two relatively well-endowed Districts of Thanjavur and Nagappattinam in the Cauvery delta.

DFID officials have been self-critical over the district focus of a long-standing health and family welfare project in Orissa. Although the districts chosen included poor ones, others were better off and chosen partly out of administrative convenience and partly out of a desire to achieve good results.

Targeting the poor at the local level

Moving beyond the targeting through the selection of states and districts/ localities, it is when one begins to examine the EU donors= targeting of the poor at the local level that the weakness, verging on the absence, of the poverty reduction objective in their aid approach begins to truly manifest itself.

For the EC, 'almost anything you do in India would lead to poverty reduction' was the statement of one official and similar, though perhaps not quite so simplistic, statements emerged from most of the EU donor agencies. While this might be true at an extremely general level of abstraction, it was to be hoped that at least at the level of project design, a more sophisticated approach towards targeting the poor would emerge. While there were many exceptions, the overall picture is that the poor are poorly targeted even at this level, however.

Danida supported projects do not specifically target the poor. In agriculture, health, and drinking water projects, for example, the target group is the community within a particular locality. In some watershed and social forestry projects a greater effort is made to reach small or marginal landowners and farmers, and secondary components are often attached for economically disadvantaged groups such as women, youth, or landless, but little systematic thinking lies behind such efforts.

With Sida the picture is very much the same although there is a particular emphasis upon women and children running through a number of their projects. In the case of DGIS, poverty and the poor at the local level are approached in terms of the state's own official categorisations as to what constitutes poverty and as to which groups are predominantly poor: scheduled castes, scheduled tribes, landless and women. There is little attempt to go beyond these fixed categories or to reflect more recent thinking on poverty and identification of the poor.

The German government requires that all projects possess a direct or an indirect poverty orientation. However, it is clear that the poverty categories used, direct or indirect, are based upon a loose definition as to what constitutes poverty and thereby who are the poor to be targeted. For KfW, if 50% of the target group can be identified as being poor, then the project is deemed to have a direct poverty orientation, and the assessment of poverty is based upon income levels together with poverty indicators linked to such factors as literacy and health. BMZ is currently working towards a more refined approach in which a range of dimensions ranging from direct self-help through to indirect poverty orientation feature (a 2 page form is being developed with a check list for assessing project proposals).

In the case of GTZ, most of the projects are acknowledged as not being directly targeted at the poor. Of the limited number that are claimed to be directly targeted towards the poor, again as with KfW, the concept of poverty and the identification of the poor is based upon a broad general definition with little or no attempt to develop or utilise indicators that might separate between the different forms of poverty to be found at the local level. The one possible exception is the Self-Help Fund with its attempt to work closely with NGOs in identifying the nature of poverty and the problems of the poor through needs assessment and contextual analysis.

To some extent it is important to accept that social sector projects implemented through government departments do embrace a broader concept of poverty and that the nature of the intervention—primary health care, primary education, drinking water and sanitation etc., can only be directed at a community within a locality and that targeting can only be refined within such programmes through secondary components, for example, free school books to female pupils, free school meals to encourage the poor to send their children to school, and similar components.

On the productive side, the problem is that the beneficiaries are reached through a particular asset or resource. For example irrigation water goes to land rather than to people, agricultural technology requires land to utilise it, tree plantations similarly require access to land. When such projects are described as being targeted at the poor, this is only true in so far as the poor have access to the assets through which the benefits introduced by the project are transmitted or mediated.

If donors fail to carry out their pre-project appraisals with a more sophisticated assessment of the poverty condition locally, and if they continue to approach poverty in somewhat simplistic terms of limited variable causality (e.g. irrigation will reduce poverty), then the targeting of the poor in their projects will continue to be one of the greatest weaknesses in the overall role of EU aid for poverty reduction.

Gender in poverty reduction

Gender is an important cross-cutting issue for all of the EU donors, but some appear to have greater success in pursuing their gender objectives than others. Gender is also coterminous with poverty in many contexts; not all women are poor, but where there are poor people, the women are amongst the poorest.

Danida and Sida have both sought to go beyond targeting women through secondary components within projects and directed projects specifically at women in poor areas. DFID argue that they do not favour 'bolting on' women in development components to their projects, but seek to 'mainstream' gender concerns into the design and implementation of all its projects and programmes. To this end, DFID draw upon four social development advisers in its main office, and several more in sectoral field management offices. This aspiration is no doubt more closely met in the most recent projects and programmes, but it is clear that earlier projects were less integrated in their approach.

In general, the overall tendency among most EU donors is to stress the gender dimension in country strategy papers, to encourage its consideration in the preparation and selection of projects, but for women to be subsequently slipped into the secondary component category. Project after project covered in the sector studies reveals this tendency. The European Community aid programme has some rather limited access to gender expertise in Brussels, but seeks to consult its gender expert for Asia during the project design phase. It has no specialist gender expertise or social development expertise in its Delegation in Delhi.

Certain sectors possess a stronger gender dimension than others, it should be noted. Forestry is one sector in which the gender division of labour is quite specific, with women often having primary responsibility for minor forest product such as silk cocoons, medical plants, decorative plants, firewood etc. Yet the social forestry projects, which have been supported by the donors almost invariably, focus upon the timber side of forestry even when based upon local community-based organisations. Furthermore, the community-based organisations, e.g. Forest Protection Committees, are often constituted with only one member from the household, namely the man. Secondary components to the projects include vocational training programmes, for example teaching women to use sewing machines (Danida supported Agro-Forestry project in Karnataka).

While there are some examples of relatively successful projects involving women (*see* Chapter 15) it has to be concluded that the overall tendency is for women to have secondary component status in practice. Such components are not sufficient if there is to be a gender dimension to a project and if it is to be linked to the needs of poor women.

Ownership *versus* 'hands on' management

For many years, the Indian Central Government view of technical assistance in aid was not a particularly positive one and obstacles were, and sometimes still are, frequently placed in the way of donors providing technical advisers to support the projects that they are financing. The argument from the Indian side is essentially that they possess the ability to carry through projects with their own management systems and that the role of the donors should be to provide financial support to the programmes and projects implemented by the Indian authorities.

From the donor side, the general concern is with achieving the most effective utilisation of the funds allocated. While they do not wish to dispute the GoI's ownership of the programmes and projects which they, the donors, support, they do wish to be involved in some aspects of their management, not least because one of the aims of the aid support is to improve the institutional capacity of the partner institutions. It is undeniable that it also reflects a concern to ensure that funds are correctly used and thus to provide accountability to donor parliaments.

In addition to the issue of ownership between donor and the GoI, there is a second issue that is perhaps more directly related to the poverty reducing impact of aid, namely the issue of local ownership. In the case of projects directed at the poor, in many cases the local ownership of key components is central to the success and sustainability. Examples would be projects in drinking water and sanitation, social forestry, watershed management, slum improvement, all of which frequently involve the creation of local user groups or community-based organisations as an integral part of the project. This is far from straightforward. DFID originally tried to set up community organisations in slum areas outside of the existing political structures, believing them to be biased in favour of elite groups. However, it found that these were unsustainable, and that greater local ownership was achieved by working with existing groups, even though the poor did not necessarily enjoy the influence that their numbers should dictate.

With respect to the overall trade-off between Indian ownership and 'hands on' management, the EU donors for the most part do not view it to be a problem. In so far as they press for the inclusion of technical assistance in their aid programmes, it is usually justified in terms of factors such as the desire to include partner institution capacity building, the introduction of innovative approaches, and the need to meet more stringent requirements for monitoring and assessment from the donors' side. On the whole, the GoI still appears to be reluctant to accept these arguments and to permit the level of technical assistance that the donors desire within the programme agreements. Less resistance tends to be met at the level of ministries or state governments where there is often a willingness to accept technical advisers. At state government level, the conflicts tend to emerge when donors seek to go beyond the advisory role to change or modify the management systems in place, or when an excessive amount of the project's budget appears to go back to the donors in one way or another.

Some officials within DFID have, however, recognised that trade-offs may occur. Several spoke of what they perceived as DFID's tendency to 'micro-manage' projects. This can result, it was stated, in DFID sometimes being overly prescriptive regarding the type of outputs they wish to see achieved or the precise manner in which they are to be achieved. It was also argued, quite reasonably, that the degree of 'hands on' involvement by DFID should depend on the degree to which an intervention is innovative or experimental. As mentioned above, the UK is seeking to develop closer state-level partnerships, and this may involve establishing state-level UK aid offices, perhaps closing (or integrating into DFID main office) the current sectoral field management offices, which are mainly based in Delhi. It is hard to see how an effective partnership can be established at a state-level without the permanent location of donor staff at that level.

Previous reference has been made to the tensions that have arisen between the Dutch and the State Government of Karnataka with respect to a drinking water project. It has taken ten years for the project to proceed from the initial agreement to the first stage of implementation, specifically because of the government's resistance to the Dutch approach to the project's management. Again in Karnataka, there has been considerable criticism from the Indian authorities as to the amount of funds within the Western Ghats Forestry Project, funded by DFID, allocated to external consultancies and research. The tendency for DFID is in fact to have a far greater involvement in the management of projects than the other EU donors with the possible exception of Danida, which has a relatively high number of field officers attached to projects.

Where the donor staff is quite small and there are few field staff attached to projects, hands off management is practised out of necessity. This applies to the European Commission, which has little choice but to adopt a more hands off approach by its officials. It has, however, sought to maintain accountability and a technical input through the use of European (and local) technical assistance. This has been the subject of lengthy negotiations with the Department of External Affairs from 1994.

The Department considers it to be a diversion of aid funds away from beneficiaries in favour of European consultancies and possibly diminishing its control over the programmes. A compromise was eventually agreed, whereby a European technical assistant would work with an Indian Director of separate Project Management Units, but the expert will be attached for three years rather than for the whole length of the project. While this approach may reflect problems encountered in the past,[2] it risks creating donor-financed enclaves which may achieve results, and it will be difficult to reproduce elsewhere within the government system.

Clearly the issue of ownership and 'hands on management' is strongly influenced by the donor approach towards development, top-down implementation of blueprint models tends very much to require technical assistance, if it is the donor's model that is. DFID would appear to have recognised this problem and wants to move towards a less direct management involvement with its projects. However, many of the older projects remain blueprint type projects with clear objectives and indicators to reveal how far these have been reached. Field Management Units responsible for these projects are quite resistant to the reduced managerial involvement, not least because they want to see their projects to achieve the aims as they were originally set out.

The changes towards a more process-oriented management together with the growing role of Panchayati Raj Institutions in many of the social sector programmes, will perhaps aid the move towards a less direct managerial role on the part of donor field staff. Danida believes that the transition to a sector programme support approach will strengthen ownership on the Indian side and reduce the direct managerial role of Danish technical advisers. Whether it is possible to work towards a managerial and organisational capacity building role for technical advisers wherein their role is to support rather than to manage waits to be seen. One Danish official commented that the positive side of aid in India, in contrast to Africa, was that Indians believe that they can manage themselves, but the danger was that they went too far and believed they had nothing to learn from foreigners. To build a supportive relationship between the technical adviser and his/her counterparts in the partner institution is not easy. Yet the sustainability and replicability of the project, its innovative approach, and much more depends very much upon the nature of that relationship.

The German view is that the organisation and management systems in place on the Indian side tend to be bureaucratic and entrenched in their ways. In addition, their role in administering development programmes is all too often undermined by politicians pursuing short-term political gains. They point in particular to weaknesses in the areas of poverty reduction and environmental and resource protection where the institutional actors are found to be particularly weak. When these are combined with poor sector conditions and problems in the decision-making structures of the government partner institutions, KfW believes there to be a powerful case for greater 'hands on' management. This links in closely with the strong tendency for KfW to demand quite stringent sector framework conditionalities.

For the Dutch aid programme, the aim of strengthening ownership and the practice of 'hands on' management go hand in hand. Within specific projects such as the drinking water interventions, there has been a strong tendency since the mid-1980s to promote local ownership by introducing so-called 'software' aspects into the projects in the hope that it will provide the local communities with a feeling of responsibility to use, operate and maintain the provided facilities. PRIs have been involved in playing an important role in this development. At the same time, the Dutch have demanded that relatively strong monitoring systems be established with a heavy involvement from Dutch consultancy firms.

The Indian government has long opposed the number of Dutch advisers attached to such projects and it was only in the late 1980s that there has been a shift in the government's position. In the pursuit of local ownership and greater poverty reduction therefore, the Dutch currently have the non-technical parts of a number of these projects headed by employees from Dutch consultancy firms, for example, in the Bangalore Urban Poverty Programme and the Netherlands Assistance Project Office in Hyderabad. At the same time, the Dutch programme in India has been strengthened during the 1980s with a number of sector specialists with the aim of enhancing the sector projects. Again the initial reaction of the Indian government was to reject the need for external expertise in areas where they felt that they already were competent. According to the 1997 annual plan of the Royal Netherlands Embassy, India has now expressed the desire for technical assistance, particularly in the area of environmental technology. It is perhaps a little ironic that the pursuit of greater local ownership requires a greater Dutch presence.

However, the Dutch experience exemplifies the three-way balance needed between challenges to Indian ownership, donor desire for effective aid utilisation, and the issue of local ownership linked to poverty reduction. The achievement of a balance between these three concerns rests upon the main parties concerned and these are primarily the GoI and the donors. The interests of the poor for whom poverty reduction is of the greatest concern are, unfortunately, not represented as such in this process.

Several government officials argued that they believed that externally aided projects, on balance, systematically differed from local ones in terms of the extent to which beneficiary participation was anticipated. One official in Orissa underlined that rural development projects involving donors tended to involve farmers in their implementation to a far higher degree. This contributed to effectiveness since it responded to the reality that the government lacked the capacity to manage everything effectively. Secondly, it made ownership more tangible, so that beneficiaries were also direct contributors, and that any assets created were theirs and not the government's or the donor's. Similarly, at national government level, a significant number of officials testified to their perception that levels of participation and ownership among project beneficiaries had increased over time, and that donor's had had an important role in fostering this.

Commitment to innovation

The quantity of aid provided by donors to India is relatively quite minor when set against the overall development expenditure of the GoI. However, one of the more important points made by EU donors with respect to their aid to India is that its importance lies not so much in the quantity of aid delivered, but in its quality. Here, innovation plays an important role.

All of the EU donors claim that their support is important for the innovative approaches to development that they bring. It is quite difficult to find the evidence to support the strength of this belief, however. In the past two or three years, DFID has supported a series of highly experimental pilot projects. These include projects in the health sector, others in natural resources such as the KAWAD watershed project and the Western India Rainfed Farming project. Each of these has involved a considerable investment in time and energy on the part of DFID, one and a half years in the case of the watershed project, which will only prove to be worthwhile if such projects are scaled up and/or replicated at a later stage. Such an investment is thereby justified on the basis that its innovative nature will prove to be a success and establish a model for subsequent projects, whether funded by donors or, preferably, the GoI. DFID believes that its investment in participation in these two projects, along with efforts by other EU donors, has had a substantial positive impact on the development of National Watershed Development

Guidelines, which should affect the design and implementation of future investments in this sector wherever they are located.

The Netherlands has also sought to pursue innovation and prides itself on having led the way in some areas with respect to participation and the development of a more integrated approach in projects. The Mahila Samakhya Programme is an example of a project regarded by both the Dutch and the Indian government as being both highly innovative and successful. But again, it is recognised by the Dutch that innovation depends very much upon the staff involved and the attitude of government officials involved at state and central levels. The EC has also stressed this dimension very much with respect to its perceived successes and failures in watershed projects in Uttar Pradesh.

Long delays in sanctioning and the release of disbursements and partnership problems generally can seriously reduce the impact of an innovative approach. Most recently, the country-level staff based at the Dutch embassy have begun to express the feeling that the focus of their aid should be away from specific projects and aimed more towards the transfer of knowledge and the improvement of the government institutions involved in the delivery of development programmes. Innovation should thereby come more directly from institutional capacity building rather than by demonstration through projects.

Danida is another EU donor that sees itself as innovative, and in the areas of gender specific approaches and participatory methods it argues that it has made significant contributions in developing approaches in training programmes for farm women for example, or to the community-based maintenance of hand pumps.

Whether innovation is linked to better poverty reduction is another matter. While it can be argued that a more participatory approach to management and the organisational structure of projects can be poverty reducing in that the poor targeted can better influence the design, implementation and assessment of projects, innovation in areas such as cost recovery is more debatable. Innovation is easier where it is working to change existing institutions and their management and organisational systems. If these are not particularly pro-poor in the first place, it may well be that there will be no poverty reducing impact. To begin from the standpoint of a needs analysis of the poor and the design of a project and a management and organisation system designed to carry through such a project would be too radical for most of the existing partner institutions on the government side. At present, to bring government officials into direct contact with the poor is regarded as a major innovation in a project.

If innovation is to be directed towards better poverty reduction, it is probably going to require the heavy investment of time and labour on the scale that DFID has recently invested in health and watershed. Few of the other EU donors have the capacity to undertake this at the moment. This is certainly true of the European Community aid programme, whose lack of any particular emphasis on innovation no doubt reflects in part very real staffing constraints.[3] Its recent shift towards a more sector-based approach implies supporting reform processes and thus innovation. In this regard, the European Commission (and member state support is vital here) might do well to concentrate on reforming its own systems, notably its legalistic consultancy tendering system, which remains a source of tremendous frustration for its development officials.

NGOs

For all of the EU donors investigated, local NGOs are primarily the responsibility of other, northern NGOs and are not of significance in bilateral aid. Having said that, it should be noted that some EU donors, notably DFID, are increasingly prepared to make use of local Indian NGOs in order to enhance the participatory and institutional capacity building dimensions of quite a few of their more recent projects. This in itself is a recognition that local NGOs do have certain comparative advantages over government institutions, particularly when it comes to working with local communities. This can also be seen to support the poverty reduction objective if the project is targeting the poor. A good example of this is DFID's extensive use of local NGOs in the health sector through 'managed networks'.

Direct bilateral support to Indian NGOs remains very much the exception. From the Indian government side, bilateral aid should be government to government, thereby excluding NGOs. For their part, donors require a degree of security for their funding often involving the guaranteeing of aid funds raising the difficult question as to who will guarantee funds provided to Indian NGOs. Most direct funding has therefore been on the basis of small one-off grants made from funds available to the ambassadors of most of the EU countries.

One solution adopted and then dropped by the Dutch, and more recently used by the Danish, has been to channel funds through CAPART, the Council for the Advancement of People's Action and Rural Technology. However, the poverty reduction impact of the projects supported in this way has not been seen to be very good.

GTZ-SHF (Self-Help Fund) has taken the broader BMZ emphasis

on pursuing a self-help approach towards development and specifically towards poverty reduction. It is currently working directly with some 35 or so local NGOs on a bilateral funding basis. This was achieved after considerable pressure was asserted on the Indian authorities in the 1993 annual negotiations. The Self-Help Fund, and to a lesser extent the Small Project Fund, are both aimed at trying to utilise the specific advantages that local NGOs are seen to have with respect to poverty reduction. The former of the two funds aims quite specifically to develop a partner relationship with the local NGOs that takes up many of the issues involved in the operationalisation of poverty reduction in aid—local ownership, innovation in management and organisational structure, improved monitoring and assessment and feedback into the project process, and a multi-dimensional approach towards conceptualising poverty and designing projects accordingly.

The European Community Aid Programme has a discrete NGO component operating in the area of HIV/AIDS, democracy and drugs. The budget line finances international NGOs, rather than Indian NGOs, though the two may work together. NGOs are selected at the European Commission Headquarters in Brussels, which also plays a role, together with the Delegation, in commenting on the design of NGO projects and trying to ensure that they are participatory. The Delegation in India tries to provide a limited monitoring function. In addition, a similar, though variable, amount of funding is provided to international NGOs from the main technical cooperation budget line. The effectiveness of the EC's NGO financing, EC officials argue, depends primarily on the level of commitment to poverty reduction of particular NGOs. However, even where commitment is high, the poorest rarely benefit. Taking the natural resources sector, most NGOs are accustomed to participate in irrigation and agricultural extension, yet the poorest usually have no or limited access to the land, water or other inputs required to participate effectively. This has contributed to the shift in the EC programme away from natural resources and towards the social sector, where NGOs are also being used.

Whether the GTZ-SHF can offer an example to others as to how to operationalise NGOs in poverty reduction with aid support, is yet to be seen. The project has only been operational for three years. Certainly, the experience of DFID with local NGOs in projects such the Gomti River Pollution Project, and the experiences to date from the SHF, would suggest that NGOs can and do have an important contribution to make.

Monitoring and evaluation

Monitoring and evaluation has always been of central importance for the donors and considerable emphasis is put upon developing and utilising new methods: Logical Framework Analysis, ZOPP etc. and the monitoring and assessment of the poverty impact of projects has increasingly begun to emerge in line with the listing of poverty as an overall priority objective of donors' aid.

The UK Country Strategy Paper for India devotes a section to discussing the importance of developing an improved poverty assessment and of committing resources to undertake research on this. Research has already begun in the areas of urban poverty and more recently health. Elsewhere, DFID have been working with the Andhra Pradesh government to develop quantitative and qualitative indicators, including participatory indicators, in order to better assess the impact of the DPEP programme. One of the aims is to demystify the evaluation process so that it can better enable a greater 'hands off' management involvement on the part of the DFID Delhi office.

Danida argues that its substantial field presence provides an important contribution to its monitoring and assessment capacity with respect to its projects. As with all of the EU donors, periodic reviews and independent evaluations are carried out in most cases. However in some areas, the monitoring and assessment appears to slip away. Danida has not evaluated any of its watershed projects as yet.

Monitoring and evaluation is emphasized a great deal in German aid. For example, the implementation of sectoral reforms is closely monitored and feedback provides the basis for subsequent release/denial of funds/further funds. Similarly, there is a very clear system of monitoring within GTZ projects, particularly those involving NGOs where monitoring is built into the partnership relationship as well as being part of GTZ's own process of assessment. Here it is to be noted that there has been an attempt to move away from a strict indicator-based monitoring system and assessment system towards a more 'process-oriented' approach. The main tool used in identifying the objectives to be reached, overall, intermediate, immediate etc. being ZOPP.

GTZ describes itself as bearing 'joint responsibility with the partner country's agencies for a project's success', and one key component in the monitoring and assessment that this is seen to require is the Project Progress Review (PPR)—an in depth and systematic examination of each project by external examiners. In addition to this, there is an annual cross-section analysis, which assesses a range of project activities which can feed back to the individual projects in the forms of better monitoring and valuable information for strategic control and institutional learning. These processes amount to a parallel system of external and internal monitoring of the project, externally this is phase by phase and case-by-case primarily under BMZ; internally through annual progress reports, Project Progress Review (and monitoring) and Project Completion Reports and Reviews.

The European Community aid programme has been rather hamstrung in its capacity to monitor and evaluate projects effectively. Each project is allocated to one of the 5 officials in the European Union Delegation in Delhi. This means that officials only have time to attend the six-monthly steering group meetings, involving EC consultants and government officials, and are thus highly reliant on the quality of the monitoring provided by their consultants attached to projects. Full-scale evaluations of EC projects are very rare. However, the accumulated experience of EC officials has led them to conclude that its past approach, funding a large number of projects in a rather *ad hoc* and non-strategic way, is not proving effective. It has therefore, as mentioned earlier, decided to concentrate on sector-wide programmes in which case its own individual capacity to monitor and evaluation is relatively unimportant. Instead, it seeks to support national monitoring and evaluation systems within the government administration. Some EC officials have been self-critical in pointing to the lack of a systematic exercise to determine where the agency's comparative advantage lies or might lie in future. Learning across countries is absent, and even learning within a country may be lacking. It should be added that this analysis also applies to other donors. This lack exacerbates the lack of institutional memory within the Community aid programme.

For all of the EU donors, the quality of many of the assessments made rests upon the quality of the information gathered at the outset; this applies as much to quantifiable indicators as to process-based indicators. It must be said that there is a remarkable absence of benchmark surveys and general collection of data prior to the implementation of projects.

A second area of notable neglect is in the post-project assessment. There appears to be absolutely no attempt to return after 5 years or so to assess the longer term impact of a project once it has finished.

Thirdly, with respect to the assessment of the poverty reduction impact of a project, the assessment can only be as good as the concept of poverty utilised provides for. Given the general failure of the EU donors to move towards a more sophisticated, multi-dimensional concept of poverty, the donors' ability to assess the poverty reduction impact is severely circumscribed.

It is interesting to note the investment in research with respect to poverty issues that DFID is proposing to undertake in this light. If some of the more recent thinking on poverty can be developed into operational indicators for measuring poverty, then the role of impact and assessment could be greatly enhanced with respect to poverty reduction.[4]

There is, however, a cost involved with effective monitoring and assessment in that if it is to be used to support improved aid interventions, not least better poverty reduction, then it can introduce delays into the project cycle. When there is pressure for money to be spent, to reduce the funds awaiting disbursement in the pipeline, then the importance of monitoring and assessment can be downgraded. At present, monitoring and assessment remains primarily a donor driven affair; it is still quite unusual for joint assessments to be made with the GoI. It might well be that it has been too donor driven and been labeled as the donor's responsibility. If there could begin to be greater Indian ownership of monitoring and assessment, this might well help improve the situation. This has occurred in the DPEP programme, where an effective joint supervision mission system exists. However, even here there have been problems, and several of the states have felt that excessive monitoring has been time-consuming. Although the predominant problem is a lack of monitoring, the dangers of over-monitoring must also be recognised.

REFERENCES

1. While all states are constitutionally required to implement Panchayati Raj, in some states, the political will is clearly lacking. In the some cases significant advances have been made or are underway, for example West Bengal, Madhya Pradesh, Kerala, and Karnataka.
2. This arrangement is specifically designed to achieve a faster disbursement of funds, which the Commission considers to have been delayed by 'heavy Indian bureaucracy', although some officials acknowledge that the need to refer back to Brussels also builds in delays.
3. The Commission Delegation considers its expertise to lie in the renewable natural resources sector and in promoting participation at the grassroots level, particularly through NGOs. While the latter is likely to continue, the recent emphasis on sectoral approaches is unlikely to draw upon its experience in the natural resources area.
4. UNDP's Human Development Report 1997 has taken up this directly in its four dimensional definition of poverty and its subsequent development of the Human Poverty Index.

8

CASE STUDIES OF SPECIFIC INTERVENTIONS

Overview

Sectors and projects

As mentioned in the introduction to this report a major part of the study has consisted of assessments of the effectiveness in terms of poverty reduction (in the wide sense) of selected donor-supported interventions in nine different sectors: watershed, irrigation, forestry, drinking water, primary health, primary education, women's training, urban housing and 'NGO sector' (self-help projects). Clearly it is problematic to call all these 'sectors' (e.g. women's training or the 'NGO sector'), but we have taken a pragmatic approach and identified groups of projects in the donor portfolios that are comparable and as a matter of convenience called them sectors. In each sector we have selected 3-5 interventions supported by one or the other EU-donor - Denmark (Danida), European Commission (EC), Germany (KfW and GTZ), The Netherlands (DGIS), Sweden (Sida) and United Kingdom (ODA/DFID)—and assessed them from a poverty perspective.

This has been an exercise in purposive sampling. For each of the donors studied we have tried to select interventions (projects or programmes) that are relevant in a poverty context in such a way that there is a fair coverage of the donor, but the coverage has not been equally extensive for all the donors. In order to make the study manageable it has been necessary to confine the study to interventions in five states, namely Uttar Pradesh, Orissa, Andhra Pradesh, Karnataka and Tamil Nadu. The six donors studied support interventions in many other states, but these are the states where there is maximum concentration and overlap among the donors. The state context is in itself an important dimension in the functioning of foreign aid and in the five states we have conducted Numerous interviews and studied documentary material to shed light on this. It is significant that our selection of states includes two very poor northern states and three Southern states which are somewhere in the middle among Indian states in terms of per capita income.

In three cases we have departed from this and included interventions in other states in order to cover donors and a particular sector. Two deal with primary education, namely the District Primary Education Programme in Madhya Pradesh (with EC funding) and Lok Jumbish in Rajasthan (with Sida funding). The third is an urban housing scheme in Kerala (with KfW funding). But the constraint in terms of states has entailed that some donors are more well-represented than others. We are convinced, however, that taken together the 33 projects and programmes studied (in nine sectors and five states) give a good picture of the most poverty-oriented parts of the portfolios of the six donors..In the selection of interventions there has been some dialogue between us and the donors, but the final choice has been ours. Table 8.1 gives an overview of the projects and programmes taken up in this study.

Parts of the programmes of the donors studied are directed towards promoting economic growth more generally, financing imports, supporting the development of the 'modern sector' or assisting large infrastructural projects, for instance in the power sector. It may of course be argued that even these types of interventions contribute to poverty reduction—at least in the long run. We do not want to engage in the debate over this. Although it is obvious that economic growth and infrastructural development etc. have implications for poverty reduction it is equally clear that the relations between these are extremely complex and difficult to document. In agreement with the donors we have concentrated our study to those parts of their programmes which are most likely to have a more direct impact on the livelihoods of the poor.

Study approach

Regarding selection of interventions (whether projects or programmes) —apart from trying to ensure a fair degree of representativity—we have sought to include both projects that have been completed, projects that have been under implementation for some years and projects of recent origin. Evidently any assessment of impact requires that a project has been under implementation for some years. On the other hand we have found it necessary and interesting to include also some recent projects

Table 8.1: Overview of projects taken up in this study

	Project	Donor	State	Project period	Total grant/ loan*	Stated Principal Objectives**	Main activities	Target groups
	(1)	(2)	(3)	(4)	(5)	(6)	(7)	(8)
					Watershed Development Projects			
1.	KWDP	Danida	Karn.	1990-1997	DKK 48.8	Sustainable watershed development, improved agriculture	Soil and water conservation	(Small and marginal) farmers
2.	DVP	EU	UP	1993-2001	n.av.	Sustainable watershed development, improved agriculture	Soil and water conservation, irrigation, non-land based activities	Farmers, women
3.	KIWMP	KfW	Karn.	1994-2000	ECU 23.7	Sustainable watershed development, improved agriculture	Soil and water conservation	Farmers
4.	KAWAD	DFID	Karn.	1997-?	£ 14.9	Poverty reduction, sustainable watershed development	Soil and water conservation human resource development	Poor farmers, women
						Irrigation		
5.	TIPP-II	DGIS	Karn.	1996-?	n.av.	1. Reduction of water usage levels in the top reach without reduction in income to farmers; 2. Increase in availability of irrigation water at tail end; and 3. Increase in agricultural and agricultural related incomes for farm households	Training and organisation of farmers (e.g. formation of Water Users Associations), maintenance of field channels and drainages, other development activities.	Farming communities, with special attention to tail end farmers, agricultural labourers.

(Contd.)

Table 8.1: *(Contd.)*

	(1)	(2)	(3)	(4)	(5)	(6)	(7)	(8)
6.	OLIP	KfW	Orissa	n.av.	n.av.	1. To design and install lift irrigation facilities in order to increase cropping intensity and crop yields, 2. To reduce farming risks by providing water for irrigation; and 3. To provide food security and increase farm incomes.	Formation of Water Users Associations, construction of irrigation facilities	Small and marginal farmers
7.	TRP	EU	TN	1984-	n.av.	To develop a sustainable, economically viable strategy for tank modernisation	Restructuring of tank bunds, sluices, and main irrigation and drainage channels, surplus arrangements and improvements to supply channels, lining and construction of ancilliary works, construction of field channels, training project staff and farmer leaders	(Small) farmers
						Forestry		
8.	JFMP	DFID	Karn.	1992-98	£ 18.1	1. To rehabilitate and protect the major environmental resources; 2. To assure the sustainability of the living standards of those people dependent on the forest; and 3. To assure the sustained yield of all categories of produce proper to the natural forest.	Institutional development in Karnataka Forestry Department, research, training and organisation	Villages in forest areas

(Contd.)

Table 8.1: *(Contd.)*

	(1)	(2)	(3)	(4)	(5)	(6)	(7)	(8)
9.	BAIF	Danida	Karn.	1990-97	DKK 19.5	1. To secure the allotment of land or trees to 1,000 landless families; 2. To increase the income of the target population; 3. To reduce the dependency of project participants on existing forest resources; 4. To diminish the dependency of the target group on casual wage labour or out-migration; 5. To demonstrate the feasibility of intensive afforestation and agro-forestry models.	Soil conservation, training and awareness building, motivation, research trials of improved techniques for agro-forestry	Scheduled castes, scheduled tribes and other weaker sections having marginal landholdings, Government of Karnataka, NGOs.
10.	SFP	Sida	Orissa	1983-96	SKK 282.5	1. To create sustainable forest resources; 2. To involve people fully as individuals and communities; 3.To meet people's needs for products such as fuel, fodder, small timber and minor forest products, 4. To (re-afforest degraded land and improve village environment	1. Establishment of village woodlots; 2. Reforestation and rehabilitation of village forest; 3. Development of farm forestry; and 4. Support to Forest Farming for Rural Poor (FFRP)	Entire community in project area, landless, poor and marginal farmers (Phase 1 had a female and poor focus)
						Drinking Water and Sanitation		
11.	SP-VI	DGIS	UP	1987-	Rs. 331.584	To achieve saturation in the supply of drinking water facilities in rural areas.	Water supply, sanitation (toilets), hygine education, community, participation, training of handpump caretakers, drainage works.	Entire population in project area

(Contd.)

Table 8.1: *(Contd.)*

(1)	(2)	(3)	(4)	(5)	(6)	(7)	(8)
12. SP-VIII	DGIS	UP	1995-	Rs. 617.237	To achieve saturation in the supply of drinking water facilities among rural areas through community participation, training and maintenance	Water supply, sanitation (toilets), hygine education, community participation, training of handpump caretakers, corrective interventions	Entire population in project area
13. IRS&WS	Danida	Karn.	1989-2000	Rs. 139.591	To achieve improved health standards through the integration of improved and sustained rural drinking water supply and sanitation conditions with community participation and training	Water supply, sanitation, health and hygiene education institutional toilets, social forestry, community participation..	Entire population in project area
14. IRWSS	DGIS	Karn.	1993-	Rs. 771-968	To achieve better living conditions among the rural areas through the integration of provision of the safe and accessible water with the development of sustainable community organisation, environmental sanitation and education, and promotion of proper use of facilities	Water supply, sanitation, household, toilets, health education, environment care, community participation, construction of anganwadis, washing slabs, cattle troughs, drains etc.	Entire population in project area
Health and Family Welfare							
15. ADP	DFID	Orissa	1979-1997	£ 232.3	To expand the system of primary health care downwards to the village level by constructing health sub-centres	Construction of village-based health sub-centres, training, health and welfare education	Health workers, doctors and entire population in project'area

(Contd.)

Table 8.1: *(Contd.)*

(1)		(2)	(3)	(4)	(5)	(6)	(7)	(8)
16.	ADP	Danida	TN	1981-2000	DKK 343	Improving the health infrastructure with particular attention to maternal and child health	Construction of health sub-centres, human resource development, IEC and AIDS programmes, setting up a health information system	Health workers, doctors, and entire population in project area
17.	ICDS	Sida	TN	1989-98	SKK 180	To improve the health and nutritional status of children under 6 years of age, to encourage school enrolment, reduce school drop outs and to enhance the mothers awareness and ability to provide proper care for their children	Recruitment and training of Anganwadi workers, awareness building, provision of food, literacy training	Mothers, children, health workers
						Primary Education		
18.	DPEP	EU	MP	1995-	Rs. 6.850	1. Universal enrolment; 2. Reducing drop out rates to less than 10%; 3. Improvement in learner achievement and 4. Reducing inequities of all types of less than 5%. Added focus on gender issues and tribals.	Building schools, local area planning, school mapping, microplanning, in-service training of teachers, establishing Village Education Councils	Children (particularly girls), educational functionaries, teachers, parents, tribals.
19.	DPEP	DFID	AP	1996-	Rs. 2.400	1. Universal enrolment; 2. Reducing drop out rates to less than 10%; 3. Improvement in learner achievement; and 4. reducing inequities of all types of less than 5%.	Building schools, local area planning, school mapping, microplanning, in-service training of teachers, establishing Village Education Councils	Children (particularly girls), educational functionaries, teachers, parents,

(Contd.)

Table 8.1: *(Contd.)*

(1)		(2)	(3)	(4)	(5)	(6)	(7)	(8)
20.	LJ	Sida	Raj.	1992-	Rs. 960	To provide elementary education to all children covered under the project blocks, improve the quality of education, empowerment of women to make education an instrument of women's equality, and effectively involve people in planning and management of education.	Training to develop local capacity to plan and implement programmes, provision of infrastructural facilities, school mapping and micro-planning exercises, establishing Village Education Councils and Women Groups.	Children and women.
						Women Training		
21.	WYTEP	Danida	Karn.	1982-	DKK 108.5	1. To increase agricultural production; 2. To strengthen self-confidence of women and improve their social status	Agricultural training and extension services to selected women farmers so that they can disseminate skills to other women farmers.	Small and marginal women farmers
22.	TEWA	Danida	Orissa	1987-2000	DKK 38.5	To increase agricultural production with emphasis on food security	Agricultural training and extension services to selected women farmers so that they can disseminate skills to other women farmers	Small and marginal women farmers
23.	MS	DGIS	UP	1988-1997	Dfl. 30.0	To provide educational opportunities for women in rural areas in a way which contributes to their development and empowerment	Skill-based training and training aimed at imparting a new set of values and attitudes; Formation of women's groups	Poor women

(Contd.)

Table 8.1: *(Contd.)*

(1)		(2)	(3)	(4)	(5)	(6)	(7)	(8)
						Urban Slums		
24.	BUPP	DGIS	Karn.	1993-	n.av.	To develop and test a model of sustainable comprehensive urban poverty alleviation based on the concept of enduring and effective community participation	Formation of Slum Development Teams, employment generation via promoting micro credit, habitat and infrastructure improvement	Slum-population NGOs government
25.	HDFC	KfW	-	n.av.	n.av.	To improve housing and living environment for the poor in the urban and rural sector	Building of house, complementary infrastructure development, promotion of building centres	Urban (and rural) poor
26.	VSIP	DFID	AP	1988-1996	n.av.	1. To increase standards of health, education and community life via an improved physical infrastructure and an enhanced level of services; 2. To increase economic productivity; and 3. To provide incentives for self-help improvements of housing	City-wide upgrading including the provision of basic amenities and related health, education and community development inputs, and housing; Organising community in local groups which can manage the facilities created and be responsible for cost recovery.	Slum-population

(Contd.)

Table 8.1: *(Contd.)*

(1)		(2)	(3)	(4)	(5)	(6)	(7)	(8)
27.	CHIS-II	DFID	AP	1996-1998	n.av.	To create conditions for sustainable poverty reduction and improvements in the quality of life of the target families.	Integrated project covering such activities as environmental improvements, health and education activities, economic support programmes and creation of community-based organisations.	Slum-population
28.	HUDCO	KfW	Kerala	n.av.	n.av.	1. To provide cost effective, innovative and affordable technology transfer and training at the grass-roots; 2. To reach decentralised production of materials and components.	Building of housing centres, training, building of low-cost houses	NGOs, urban and rural poor
						NGO Sector		
29.	NIRP-HAD	Danida	UP	n.av.	n.av	Providing economic infrastructure to the poor so that human development occurs	1. Providing economic infrastructure such as agricultural extension, irrigation, livestock development; 2. Providing infrastructure of human development	Small and marginal farmers belonging to depressed castes
30.	PHCC	Danida	TN	n.av.	n.av.	Protecting the deteriorating natural resources	1. Alternative practices in agriculture and forest lands; 2. Suitable technologies for natural resource management; 3. Plantation of trees and perennial crops in dry lands; 4. Creating local expertise	Small farmers owning 2 to 5 hectares of land

(Contd.)

Table 8.1: *(Contd.)*

	(1)	(2)	(3)	(4)	(5)	(6)	(7)	(8)
31.	RDO	GTZ	TN	n.av.	n.av.	Facilitating self-help promotion	1. Enabling people to possess the land; 2. Planting perennial crops on lands controlled by the poor for the stable income flow; 3. education of children	Deprived sections of the community
32.	SHARE	GTZ	TN	n.av.	n.av	Total empowerment of the poor through income generating programmes	1. Enabling the poor to undertake income generating activities through skill upgrading, marketing and raw material support; 2. Providing education and support services for the poor and their children	Poor and marginalised women
33.	Homo Sapiens	GTZ	AP	n.av.	n.av.	Not applicable as project under formulation	Not applicable as project under formulation	Tribals with a focus on women

Notes

* In million currency

** Objectives of the latest phase, unless otherwise stated

n.av. Not Available

Donors

DFID	Department for International Development (United Kingdom)
Danida	Danish International Development Assistance (Denmark)
DGIS	Directorate General for Development Cooperation (the Netherlands)
GTZ	Gemeinschaft für Technische Zusammenarbeit (Germany)
KfW	Kreditanstalt für Wiederaufbau (Germany)
Sida	Swedish International Development Assistance (Sweden)

Projects

KWDP	Karnataka Watershed Development Project
DVP	Doon Valley Integrated Watershed Management Project
KIWMP	Karnataka Integrated Watershed Management Project
KAWAD	Karnataka Watershed Development Project
TIPP-II	Tungabhadra Irrigation Pilot Project-II
OLIP	Orissa Lift Irrigation Project

States°

Karn.	Karnataka
UP	Uttar Pradesh
AP	Andhra Pradesh
TN	Tamil Nadu
Raj.	Rajasthan

Currencies

£	British Pounds
Dfl.	Dutch Guilders
DKK	Danish Kronen
DEM	Deutschmark (German Marks)
ECU	European Currency Unit
Rs.	Indian Rupees
SKK	Swedish Kronen

Projects

TRP	Tank Rehabilitation Project
JFMP	Joint Forest Management and Planning
SFP	Social Forestry Project
SP-VI	Sub-Project VI
SP-VIII	Sub-Project VIII
IRS&WS	Integrated Rural Sanitation and Water Supply Project
IRWSS	Integrated Rural Water Supply & Sanitation Project
ADP	Area Development Programme
ICDS	Integrated Child Development Scheme
DPEP	District Primary Education Programme
LJ	Lok Jumbish
WYTEP	Women and Youth Training and Extension Project
TEWA	Training and Extension for Women in Agriculture
MS	Mahila Samakya
BUPP	Bangalore Urban Poverty Programme
HDFC	Housing Development Finance Corporation
VSIP	Visakhapatnam Slum Improvement
CHIS II	Chinagadili Habitat Improvement Scheme Phase II
HUDCO	Housing and Urban Development Corporation
NIRPHAD	Naujil Integrated Project for Health and Development
PHCC	Palani Hills Conservation Council
RDO	Rural Development Organisation
SHARE	Self Help Association for Rural Education and Employment

because they reflect current donor (and Indian) policies and approaches.

As mentioned in the introduction nine of our Indian colleagues have been responsible for the assessments of 3-4 projects in a particular sector. They have been furnished with documentary evidence in the form of project documents, review and evaluation reports etc. and they have carried out field studies, spending about a week (incl. travel) on each project (3-10 days). Needless to say this is not enough for in-depth impact studies, but it is sufficient for an assessment.

In a methodology-cum-planning workshop (in Delhi in January 1997) we established a common approach. The projects and programmes studied cover a great variety in terms of sectors, size, scope and modalities. Some of them are quite localised, while others cover many districts and a large number of villages. This means that the approach has varied from case to case. Field work in localised projects has been carried out within 3 days whereas it has required up to 10 days for some of the complex projects covering a vast area.

Generally speaking information has been obtained by interviewing the following types of persons:

1. Project personnel (managers at various levels, field staff etc.). These have also furnished written documentation on process, outputs and impact.
2. Responsible persons in local government and administration (e.g. panchayat members, BDO officers or local officers under respective line ministry).
3. Key persons, independent of the project (e.g. belonging to NGOs, professionals, teachers).
4. Beneficiaries. Men and women from different castes/ethnic groups. Poor, average and well-to-do.
5. Non-beneficiaries. Persons in a similar situation as the beneficiaries, but outside the project's target group.

Project personnel and beneficiaries have been covered in all cases, the other categories to the extent possible.

Within the time frame available representative sampling by way of random or random stratified sampling has clearly been impossible. The feasible alternative has been to carry out 'purposive sampling'. This has involved several steps. First there has been a selection of significant components of the project to be covered. The ambition has not been to cover the broad range of activities, but only those that weigh heavily in the project and/or are particularly interesting from a poverty perspective.

Secondly, within each of these components one or more project localities have been selected. Where there are many such localities this has been done by random sampling or purposive selection according to relevant criteria. Thirdly, within each of the localities a number of beneficiaries (and ideally also non-beneficiaries) have been selected - either at random or purposively to cover gender, socio-economic status etc. This procedure of course includes arbitrary elements, but it should be adequate for an assessment.

The assessment of the effectiveness of a particular intervention in terms of poverty reduction has been based on our conceptualisation of the four dimensions of poverty and poverty reduction, viz. livelihoods (improvement-impoverishment), resources (access-exclusion), knowledge (expansion-reduction) and rights (participation-alienation).

The studies of the selected interventions have resulted in nine 'sector reports', written by our Indian collaborators and varying in size from about 30 to more than 100 pages. These are in themselves an important outcome of the research project. The following chapters on the nine sectors are based on these sector reports, but they are also informed by the authors' brief visits to some of the projects, our own reading of documentary evidence and our previous knowledge about the sectors.

9

WATERSHED DEVELOPMENT PROJECTS

Introduction

Since the mid-80s several Indian government programmes have employed a watershed approach to improve natural resource management in rainfed agriculture. Under the Seventh Five Year Plan a National Watershed Development Programme for Rainfed Agriculture was launched, later changed into a National Watershed development Programme for Rainfed Areas, i.e. including treatment of non-arable lands. The aim is threefold, better conservation of natural resources—soil, water, vegetation—increased agricultural productivity and improved procurement of fuelwood, timber and fodder. An important objective is *in situ* moisture conservation. The programme covers both privately owned, government and communal lands. The main watershed development activities are split between the Ministry of Agriculture and the Ministry of Rural Areas and Employment; the latter puts great emphasis on the employment generation involved in the activities. In focusing on regions dominated by rainfed agriculture the programmes also address equity concerns, since these areas have a greater proportion of poor people. This is particularly true of the watershed development schemes which are linked to the Drought Prone Areas Programme.

A number of foreign donors have supported these endeavours, usually by establishing projects in collaboration with state government institutions. The World Bank took a lead in the 80s, followed by the European Commission and several bilateral donors, including Germany, U.K. and Denmark. In the first generation of watershed development projects priority was given to the conservation objectives. Gradually more importance has been attached to their potential contribution to PR. The European donors involved are among those who have led the way in this direction. They all perceive these projects as highly relevant for poverty reduction.

Selected projects

Four projects, assisted by EU, Denmark, Germany and U.K., have been assessed as part of this study. For a full account of this we refer to Ninan, 1998. The four projects are the following:

1. Karnataka Watershed Development Project (KWDP), implemented by the Department of Agriculture under the Karnataka State Government with support from Danida. First phase of the project has been carried out in the years 1990-97 and the project has moved into the second phase, planned for 1997-2004. First phase has covered 106 villages in Dharwad, Belgaum and Uttara Kannada districts, mostly on the Deccan plateau, but also including "Malnad" villages in the Western Ghats and spanning agro-climatic regions ranging from semi-arid to humid. In second phase the project is shifted to Bijapur and Gulbarga districts which are considerably more dry than the regions covered so far. First phase has covered an area of 41,000 ha, second phase will cover 42,000 ha. The budget for first phase has been 48.8 mill. DKK, for second phase 46.7 mill. DKK, all financed by the donor.
2. Doon Valley Integrated Watershed Management Project (DVP), implemented by the Watershed Management Directorate, Uttarakhand Development Department under the Government of Uttar Pradesh with aid from the European Commission (EC). The project period is 1993-2001 (9 years). The project is targeted to cover 250 villages and 185,000 ha in Dehra Dun and Tehri-Garwal districts in the Himalayan/Siwalik foothills. The budget is 23.7 mill. ECU. The donor's share is 95% and the remaining 5% is financed by the Uttar Pradesh State Government.
3. Karnataka Integrated Watershed Management Project (KIWMP), implemented by the Dryland Development Board under Karnataka State Government with assistance from Kreditanstalt für Wiederaufbau (KfW). The project period is 1994-2000, but actual commencement was in February/August 1996. The project is targeted to cover 54,000 ha and 215 villages

in Kolar, Mandya and Hassan districts, located in the semi-arid parts of the Deccan plateau. The budget is 24 mill. DM. The donor's share is 84% and the State Government will contribute the remaining 16%.

4. Karnataka Watershed Development Project (KAWAD), with aid from ODA/DFID , to be implemented by Karnataka Watershed Development Society which will be set up as an autonomous body by Government of Karnataka. The project is in the final phases of negotiation. It is planned to have a first phase of 5½ years and a second phase of 6½-9½ years. It will cover 55,000 ha in Chitradurga, Bellary and Bijapur districts, located in the semi-arid parts of the Deccan plateau. The budget is £14.9 mill., entirely financed by the donor.

The projects have been purposely selected to represent watershed projects assisted by the donors in question. Some of the donors, notably Danida, support a number of such projects in different states. It was felt important that the small sample studied should include both completed projects (KWDP/Dan., phase I), well established projects (DVP/EC) and projects of recent origin (KWDP/Dan., phase II, KIWMP/KfW and KAWAD/ODA).

Geographical location

An important feature of the projects, evidently, is their location. Phase I of KWDP/Dan. was located in a transitional zone—from semi-arid to humid and partly hilly—in the Northwestern part of Karnataka in a region which by and large is quite developed. This apparently was to "play it safe", and the inclusion of a favoured, humid district also was owing to pressure from a leading government bureaucrat. In phase II the project will shift to two drier, poorer and more remote districts. This will tend to strengthen the poverty orientation. With hindsight it would clearly have been preferable if already phase I had been implemented in these districts. DVP/EC is implemented in Doon Valley (and an adjoining part of Tehri Garwal) in the Himalayan/Siwalik foothills in a hilly zone with a fragile ecology (erosion), but quite developed in many respects. Actually Dehra Dun district has one of the highest per capita incomes in Uttar Pradesh. The project, however, focuses on the upper, relatively remote slopes of the valley where people are considerably poorer than further down in the valley. KIWMP/KfW is located in the dry parts of three districts in the relatively developed Southern part of Karnataka. Finally, KAWAD/ODA will be implemented in fairly remote, dry and drought prone districts in Northeastern Karnataka. Since the watershed projects are essentially a land-based activity it is quite obvious that location in a dry and remote region increases the likelihood of benefiting really poor people. On the other hand it is administratively more difficult and cumbersome to work in such regions.

Project components

All the projects have planting activities and soil and water conservation measures as their core components. In KWDP/Dan., phase. I, the emphasis was on soil and water conservation, especially through tree planting, construction of check dams, bench terracing and contour bunding. Planning was in terms of physical and financial targets and there was no involvement of the potential beneficiaries. A number of the check dams subsequently were damaged because of weaknesses in construction and many farmers removed the contour bunds which crossed their fields. The functioning checkdams were mostly in the lower parts of the watershed and benefiting downstream farmers who tend to be better off than those upstream. After a mid-term review the project was reoriented with less emphasis on construction of costly physical structures such as check dams and bench terraces. Moreover, prompted by the donor, a more participatory approach was adopted, and this will be considerably strengthened in phase II.

DVP/EC employs a holistic approach to the conservation and development needs and problems of the area, and in practice it falls somewhere in between a traditional watershed project and an integrated rural development project. The project activities include social forestry, soil conservation, horticulture, livestock, minor irrigation, agriculture, energy conservation and community participation. The project document allocated 47% of the budget to social forestry, followed by 14% to community participation and 10% each to minor irrigation and livestock. But in the period 1993-97 only 33% of the expenditure has been on social forestry as against 21% on minor irrigation and only 5% on community participation. The discrepancy between planned and actual outlays on social forestry and minor irrigation reveals the (influential) villagers' preference for irrigation benefiting their private lands compared to afforestation on common lands.

Both social forestry and non-land based activities (e.g. energy conservation) have a potential to benefit also the landless poor who are in general the poorest of the poor. Non-land based activities likewise play a significant, but secondary role in KWDP/Dan., phase II, and KAWAD/ODA, whereas no such component is planned for KWIMP/KfW. In KWDP/Dan., phase II, a livestock component is planned and women and landless agricultural labourers will be a "special target group for biomass based income generating activities". KAWAD/ODA similarly will direct such activities at economically weak groups and in particular women.

Poverty concept

Poverty in all the projects is primarily seen in economic terms as low income and lack of employment opportunities. But in most cases other dimensions are also taken into account such as inadequate drinking water facilities, shortage of fuel and fodder and food insecurity. In some cases drudgery in women's work, the long hours spent on fetching water, fuel and fodder, is also considered.

Targeting

Only the most recent project (KAWAD/ODA) has PR as primary objective. The selection of watersheds to be treated under this project emphasizes the poverty orientation in so far as about 70% of the population is stated to be below the poverty line and the SC/ST population over 40%. Socio-economic criteria (e.g. per capita income, percentage of small and marginal farmers) have played a certain role in selection of the watersheds under the other projects, least so in KIWMP/KfW, but by and large the main emphasis has been on agro-climatic characteristics (degradation, rainfall, slope etc.). Similarly in these projects the environmental objectives (conservation, eco-restoration) tend to be prioritised, but in all the projects there is a concern that the poor should get their share of project benefits.

Under KWDP/Dan., phase I, a special effort has been taken to ensure that small and marginal farmers get their share of the benefits. In the phase II project document, however, the target group is defined as "all rural farming households in selected watersheds", explicitly including the well to do. In view of the donor's primary overall objective of contributing to PR this is quite remarkable. But as already mentioned a minor component will support non-land based activities targeted at landless and poor women.

In the project document of DVP/EC there was no component aimed at poor landless agricultural labourers, but during implementation they have been targeted for participation in income generating activities (mushroom cultivation, bee keping, poultry keeping, sericulture, forest nursery raising and knitting). Horticulture and livestock components were similarly included during implementation, both of substantial relevance for the poor. Further it is ensured that poor, especially SCs and STs are among the recipients of a variety of other inputs provided by the project (e.g. pressure cookers, chaff cutters).

Finally, the project document of KIWMP/KfW specifies that a number of measures must be taken in order to ensure that some of the benefits reach the economically disadvantaged: "One of the obligations of the implementation agreement shall be to ensure that economically weaker members of the watershed population (especially women, landless, small and marginal farmers) be enabled to equally utilise the resources of the watershed, e.g. fodder grasses and firewood. The Programme Executing Agency ... shall especially ensure that these members be preferred in the distribution of paid manual opportunities (watershed treatment works) and by obtaining loans out of the Sangha funds for production purpose. The respective Watershed Implementation Team and NGO shall provide social education for the Sanghas with the aim of protecting the interests of the economically and socially weaker members in the internal decision making process and shall ensure that they be given a sustained and equitable access to the resources of the watershed and to the assets created by it".

Participation

In all the projects under implementation the potential beneficiaries have had no initial influence on project identification and design, but all projects try to employ participatory methods in implementation. This in some cases includes the use of Participatory Rural Appraisals (PRAs) and related methods which—notably in DVP/EC—have resulted in amendments of the project plans. And in all the projects a number of committees are formed at various levels and for different purposes, but with the common aim of involving the beneficiaries directly in project activities and particularly the maintenance of assets created.

KWDP/Dan., phase I, was initially implemented in typical top down fashion, but after a mid-term review a participatory approach was introduced. However, it took considerable time (two years) to reach the implementation stage under the new approach, partly because of lack of the appropriate qualifications and outright resistance among the bureaucrats. In phase II of this project (in a different area) a very elaborate and impressive planning of people's participation is envisaged, embodying eleven stages (!), including an initial PRA and ending with withdrawal and follow-up. Based on the experiences from phase I the first year of the second phase will be used for community organisation and planning. KAWAD/ODA likewise puts a lot of emphasis on participation and makes it a condition for carrying out physical activities.

Most of the projects to some extent use the assistance of NGOs in mobilisation and training. This is most pronounced in KIWMP/KfW where several NGOs will play a relatively large role in motivating villagers, assisting in organising committees and undertaking training activities. This has been pushed by the donor and reluctantly accepted by the State Government authorities. Some NGOs wanted to take directly part in implementation of the watershed development works, but this has been rejected by the government side. However, the KAWAD/ODA project on a trial basis plans to make an NGO the implementing agency in one watershed.

The participatory approach—especially the use of PRAs and the formation of village level committees—has contributed to make the projects more relevant to the villagers felt needs. But there are several problems involved in this. First, the crucial watershed or village committees tend to be dominated by the better off (male) farmers, usually from the dominant caste. Naturally they use their influence to ensure that their peers are able to corner most of the benefits. Secondly, the participation of farmers in decision making has an understandable tendency to prioritise short-term gains over long-term benefits and private gains over benefits to the community. Thirdly, even so these committees are still weak and project management as such continues to be essentially top down in all the projects.

In order to ensure that the poor get their share of benefits it is necessary to move beyond the formation of watershed or village committees and support the organisation of more homogeneous groups of poor, e.g. landless agricultural labourers, SCs/STs, hamlet dwellers etc. Such groups can function as users groups under a particular project component or as self-help groups with a wider agenda, often incorporating savings and credit activities. Such groups can also provide a backing of poor representatives on the village committees and thus improve the chances of their participation being more than a token presence.

Gender

Soil and water conservation, which is central in most watershed projects, is largely the men's domain, although the benefits of course accrue to the whole family. But other activities have a potential to involve and benefit women more directly. The collection of fuel and fodder, for instance, is the responsibility of women. Planting activities that improve fuel and fodder availability will benefit women as well as the family. For the women it is important that their heavy work burden is reduced.

Under KWDP/Dan., phase I, a special effort has been made to mobilise the women. The Watershed Development Committees include women members although the target of 25% has not been reached. However, the female presence in the WDCs tends to be token. More important, the project has supported the formation of women's self-help groups, Mahila Sanghas. These are engaged in a variety of activities; from the project they have received vegetable seeds as well as training in various fields, and each Mahila Sangha has been given 1,000 Rs. A number of families have received smokeless chullahs (stoves) from the project, but in many cases these are not working. Usually the Mahila Sanghas also function as savings and rotating credit groups. Many women have expressed that the project has given them more self confidence and contributed to their empowerment.

DVP/EC puts a lot of emphasis on formation of women's self-help groups. Young university-educated female motivators, assisted by trained village women, build rapport and raise awareness in the villages and assist in the organisation of groups. The women's groups function as savings and rotating credit groups, each woman saving on average 10 Rs. per month and loans being given at 2-4% interest per month. The money is used for income generating activities like mushroom growing, poultry keeping, bee keeping, sericulture, forest nursery raising and knitting (and to some extent for covering costs associated with marriage, illness etc.). Mushroom growing for some women has been highly remunerative. The project also addresses the needs of women in their role as managers of crops, livestock and common resources (firewood, fodder, water). Moreover a number of families have received biogas plants, pressure cookers and kerosene stoves. There is no doubt that apart from the material benefits the women have gained a feeling of empowerment. The flip side of this is that some of these activities have increased the already heavy work load of the women.

Also in the KIWDP/KfW women's groups are formed, but at least in some villages the watershed/village committees were found to consist of men only. The absence of female members in these committees seems to be at variance with the proclaimed wish to ensure that women are benefited by the project. The KAWAD/ODA, in contrast, plans to have a strong gender dimension. It includes organising women's groups, credit programmes, income generating activities and the involvement of women in planning as well as implementation of watershed development plans.

Sustainability and replicability

In watershed development projects sustainability has a number of connotations. By definition such projects should contribute to environmental sustainability and there is no doubt that this is the case with the projects studied here, notably in terms of improving *in situ* moisture conservation. The extent and quality of this contribution of course vary from project to project and from component to component, depending among other things on the technical solutions in the soil and water conservation works. In addition to environmental sustainability there are concerns regarding technological, economic and institutional sustainability and these also have consequences for replicability.

In KWDP/Dan., phase I, as already mentioned, there was an emphasis on construction of costly physical structures like terraces and checkdams, some of which subsequently broke down. The changed approach in phase II will in itself ensure better sustainability as well as replicability. An important feature of the project in the first year was that the benefits generally were given to the villagers free of cost. After the reorganisation the project has tried to introduce an element of cost recovery, but this has proved to be difficult. In 1997 a study is planned which shall propose the relevant level and modalities of contribution from the villagers in this project (phase II) as well as the other Danida-supported watershed projects.

Also in DVP/EC most of the inputs are provided free of cost. This has enabled the village committees to accumulate funds by charging the individual beneficiaries a fraction of the value of various inputs. But it is also a major problem. It has contributed to the 'dependency syndrome', an expectation that generous donors will somehow provide the necessary means and solve the problems. In some cases (e.g. chaff cutters) it has led to disuse of equipment that turned out to be inappropriate or irrelevant. Moreover, the high level of subsidisation implies that the project is difficult to replicate, and for this reason it has been criticised by leading government representatives.

Under KAWAD/ODA regarding cost sharing a level of 15-25% is foreseen, higher in private lands than in common lands. But this is easier to put on paper than to implement in practice. The modalities, however, have to be decided by the community. It is proposed that communities get 100% of the benefits in common lands and that poor people get preferential access to such benefits. The Watershed Development Committees are supposed to maintain assets created in common lands. A development fund is proposed for this purpose, partly based on cost contributions as well as part of the usufructs from common lands.

Economic and institutional sustainability are important dimensions of sustainability as well as replicability. The viability of the various watershed and village committees and users groups, set up under the projects, is thus crucial. Although it is too early to judge, a few observations may be in order. In KWDP/Dan., phase I, there is a grave risk that these committees may not survive when the project withdraws (phase II has been shifted to another area). There has only been a few years to organise the committees and they have not been able to accumulate funds (for maintenance etc.) on any significant scale. The prospects are somewhat better for the village committees set up under the DVP/EC; some of them have accumulated considerable funds (up to 100,000 Rs.) and there is more time left to strengthen them institutionally.

The planned outlay per ha in KAWAD/ODA is considerably higher than in other watershed projects - about 8,000 Rs. per ha against 2,500 Rs. -5,000 Rs. in most projects. An unusually large amount –3% of the budget in phase I and 16% for the entire project—is allocated to human resource development. Most of this money will be spent at training activities at the community level (assisted by NGOs). This will not only strengthen implementation, but can also contribute to better sustainability. The drawback in this, obviously, is that higher costs will reduce the prospects of this approach being replicated on a large scale.

An institutional issue with a bearing on sustainability concerns the involvement of Panchayati Raj Institutions (PRIs) in project implementation. It is noteworthy that none of the three projects under implementation tries to involve the PRIs, in spite of the fact that two of these are located in Karnataka where PRIs have been functioning quite well since the mid-80s. The planned KAWAD/ODA project in contrast will involve the PRIs in a major way, both at the district level and at the watershed and sub-watershed levels. It is interesting that KWDP/Dan., phase II, which will be implemented in the same part of Karnataka, does not plan to involve the PRIs. Where PRIs are not involved there may be a potential conflict between the watershed and village committees organised under a project and the Gram Panchayats.

Monitoring and evaluation

None of the projects studied has been formally evaluated so far, but it is only KWDP/Dan., phase I, which is completed. No benchmark surveys have been carried out in the projects that are under implementation, but in KWDP/Dan., phase II it is planned to make socio-economic profiles of all project villages and collect economic baseline data to be used for later impact assessment. Most of the monitoring in the projects deals with physical outputs, whereas there is little monitoring of process or poverty reach. However, KWDP/Dan., phase II, plans an elaborate monitoring and evaluation system covering both progress (quantitative), process and impact. An important feature is that participatory monitoring and evaluation will be built into the system. So far this is all on paper, but if put into practice it will be a major step forward in monitoring and evaluation.

Impact in terms of poverty reduction

Two of the projects studied—KIWMP/KfW and KAWAD/ODA—are so new that it is impossible to assess any impact. The same applies to KWDP/Dan., phase II. So the following is confined to KWDP/Dan., phase I, and DVP/EC. It has to be remembered that poverty reduction has not been the main objective of any of these, and both projects have certainly contributed to their main eco-restoration objective. They have also led to improvements in crop yields and better availability of fodder as well as a number of secondary benefits from income generation activities and distributed implements and utensils. But the following assessment largely deals with impact in terms of poverty reduction.

In the case of KWDP/Dan., phase I, after two years a sample survey was conducted which proved that most of the benefits had been cornered by persons outside the target group. Whereas the project documents stipulated that a special effort should be made to reach small and marginal farmers, constituting 65% of the watershed communities, it became clear that in practice big farmers were the primary beneficiaries, generally receiving 50-80% of the project benefits. Later, however, the distribution of benefits has been better.

A peculiar problem stems from the fact that watersheds and village boundaries often do not coincide. The first phase of KWDP/Dan. has been implemented strictly on a watershed basis with the consequence that in 61 out of the 106 villages covered only part of the village has been included under the project because the rest falls outside the watershed boundary. In many villages it has created resentment and tension that part of the village thus has been excluded from the project benefits. In order to overcome this problem Danida has suggested that in phase two of the project entire villages are included even if parts extend beyond the watershed boundary. However, this has met resistance on the government side because it blurs the watershed approach.

On the whole KWDP/Dan., phase I, has only reached and benefited the poor to a limited extent. The selection of relatively favoured areas for its implementation in itself has increased the likelihood of benefits accruing to more well to do farmers. No doubt, a growing share of both planting activities and soil and water conservation works has been directed towards small and marginal farmers, but relatively speaking better off farmers have appropriated the major benefits. It has been a problem throughout the project that most of the activities have been carried out on privately owned lands. The landless agricultural labourers —and more generally the Scheduled Castes and Tribes—have by and large been bypassed by the project, except in terms of getting some temporary employment. The formation of women's groups has resulted in some small tangible results as well as contributed to a feeling of empowerment, but this component has been relatively marginal in the project.

However, from a poverty reduction perspective the shift of phase II to two drier, poorer and more remote districts must be seen as a step forward. With hindsight it would clearly have been preferable if already phase I had been implemented in these districts. In phase II the participatory approach in the project will be substantially strengthened (a conditionality set up by Danida). It is likely that the new approach will result in more relevant and sustainable project benefits. But given the power structure in the villages this does not ensure that these benefits under phase II reach the poor to any greater extent than under phase I. The project component dealing with biomass-based income generating activities for women and landless will obviously benefit the poor, and formation of self-help groups around this component can help in making the activities viable and sustainable. But this is a minor activity in relation to the entire project.

In the DVP/EC it is clear that some of the major components of the project, notably irrigation and soil conservation, have benefited mainly farmers who are slightly better off. Social forestry has a potential to benefit also, or even primarily, poorer sections, including the landless and SCs/STs, but it depends on the way these common resources are managed. At present it is too early to assess. Users' groups could play a major role in this. The various income generating activities supported by the project have mostly been taken up by women's groups. Apart from the material benefits this has also contributed to empowerment.

In the project document there was no component aimed at the poor landless agricultural labourers. Many of these belong to the SCs and STs. But they figure prominently among those involved in income generating activities. They are also among the recipients of the range of inputs provided by the project: biogas plants, pressure cookers, chaff cutters, kerosene stoves etc. The costly biogas plants have only benefited the well to do farmers since a complement of at least four cattle is necessary prerequisite for the operation of the plant. But poor landless workers have received a share of the other implements and utensils. However, an impact assessment in 1996, based on a sample of villages, showed that the proportion of such inputs obtained by SCs/STs was in most cases somewhat below their proportion of the population. The most important benefit for the landless in general is the temporary employment in the planting, irrigation and soil conservation schemes.

Although it is too early to say anything about the impact of KIWMP/ KfW, one observation may be in order. Seen from a poverty reduction perspective it is a problem that landless people are left out of the Watershed Development Committeess and that no non-land based activities are planned. It is positive that the project aims to reach economically weaker sections in different ways, but it remains to be seen to which extent and how this is accomplished in practice. It is stipulated that half-yearly progress reports will include monitoring the measures taken to fulfil this aim. But in spite of such useful mechanisms it will be difficult to avoid that the major benefits are captured by the landowners, given the project's overall design.

Conclusions and suggestions

— Until now the major benefits from the watershed development projects have accrued to the landowners, and the slightly bigger farmers have received a disproportionately great share. This is both because they own more land and because, generally, they are more powerful and use their power to take care of their own interests.

— All the projects studied, however, in various ways try to ensure that some of the benefits are directed towards the economically weaker sections (marginal farmers, landless labourers, SCs/STs, women, etc.). This is accomplished to some extent, varying from project to project.

— Since watershed development projects are land-based activities it is difficult to avoid that the landowners become the major beneficiaries. Nevertheless, there are a number of ways to ensure that watershed development projects address both environmental, productivity and equity concerns and notably contribute to poverty reduction:

- Poverty reduction should be set up as (one of) the primary objective(s).
- The emphasis should be shifted—at least partly—from land-based to biomass-based activities and from privately owned lands to common lands. The poor should get equal or (preferably) preferential access to the usufructs from common lands.
- Treatment of the watersheds should always start from above, both owing to ecological considerations and because more poor people tend to live here.
- In selection of watersheds for treatment emphasis should be put on the prevalence of poverty in addition to ecological factors.
- The soil and water conservation works on private lands should at least give the small and marginal farmers their proportionate share and they could be partly or wholly exempted from payment for inputs.
- Watershed development projects should have a component of non land-based activities, specifically targeted at the poor.
- The poor should have preferential access to the employment created under the watershed schemes.

— Although it is logical to implement the watershed development projects strictly on a watershed (and sub- and micro-watershed) basis this may create tensions where parts of the villages are being left out. As far as possible the projects should include whole villages, even where this is in conflict with the watershed boundaries.

— All projects are using participatory methods to a greater or smaller extent. However, participation so far has been largely limited to the implementation phase. Even here it is a matter for discussion how real the participation is. It will take a long time to make the watershed and village committees effective partners in decision-making.

— While participatory approaches are clearly necessary they are not without problems. The watershed and village committees tend to be dominated by better-off (male) farmers, usually from the dominant caste. In order to reach the poor it is necessary to take participation one step further and support the organisation of more homogeneous groups of poor people (self-help groups).

— All projects try to ensure that women are involved and receive some of the benefits. In the two projects, that have been under implementation for some years, women's committees have been organised and women have received both (secondary) material benefits and gained in self-confidence.

— So far most of the projects have provided the inputs free of cost. This is clearly a problem for replicability and it also contributes to the 'dependency syndrome'. In the future those who can afford it should contribute to sharing the costs. However, it is of vital importance that a differentiated system of cost sharing is developed and that the poor are generally exempted from payment.

— Until now none of the projects under implementation has involved Panchayati Raj Institutions (PRIs) in this. In the future this may create conflicts between the committees organised under a project and the Gram Panchayats. It is interesting that two new projects in the same part of Karnataka employ completely different approaches to this, one by involving and the other by not involving the PRIs.

— There is little donor coordination—or learning from each other—in the sector. Three of the projects studied are located in Karnataka; it is conspicuous how different they are in approach. Two are even planned in the same region and there has so far been no attempts at coordination.

— Most of the monitoring in the projects deals with physical outputs. There should be more monitoring of process and poverty reach. There is a lack of benchmark surveys and indicators. One of the new projects plans to include participatory monitoring and evaluation. This should be taken up by others.

10

IRRIGATION PROJECTS

Introduction

Over the last few decades, India has achieved major increases in agricultural production. The famines, which haunted the country in, for instance, the 1960s seem to be something of the past. Major efforts in the field of irrigation contributed heavily to this agricultural success story although only a third of the agricultural land in India was irrigated in the early 1990s. Irrigation has been the key-note of agricultural development since the inception of planning and thus the key-note in increasing agricultural production. The development of irrigation has also been aimed at creating employment directly through the undertaking of irrigation projects and indirectly through increased agricultural production. Irrigation can thus be regarded as part of the fight against economic poverty.

The irrigation sector, however, is beset with a large number of problems (Mitra 1996). Firstly, there are those problems connected with the construction phase like cost and time overruns, faulty design, rehabilitation of the project-affected people, and environmental degradation. Secondly, there are those problems arising after construction. Grouped together under operation and maintenance, these problems include under-utilisation of irrigation capacity (potential), iniquity in irrigation, lack of dependability of irrigation, indifferent quality of irrigation, wastage of irrigation water, water logging, soil salinity and alkalinity, sustainability of irrigated farming, and financial losses and pricing of water. Particularly the latter issue is regarded as central and of such overriding consideration that all the other problems stated seem to be largely the fallout of the problem of financing irrigation management.

Maintenance of irrigation facilities is taken up as one of the central components of irrigation development in the Sixth Five Year Plan. It took, however, up to the Seventh Plan for responsibility for maintenance to no longer be consigned to the state governments and financed by irrigation charges from the beneficiaries. More direct involvement of farmers in groups organised to take responsibility for the proper functioning of major/medium irrigation schemes is only proposed in the late 1980s/early 1990s. The goal of such participation is quite clear: enhancing the responsibility of the users and simultaneously reduce the pressure on government funds for operation and maintenance and, in the process, ensure better utilisation of the created facilities. According to the Eighth Plan, there has been little user participation in the past mainly because the large irrigation systems have been completely state managed and the Plan calls for a strengthening of efforts to involve farmers in the operation and maintenance of irrigation schemes. With regard to minor irrigation schemes, the Plan calls for intensification of traditional local systems for construction, maintenance and management.

Exact data on development assistance for irrigation are not available after 1981. M. Lipton and J. Toye (1990: 57) observe that aid-flow data are not presented separately for irrigation but nevertheless appear to constitute a large component of the aid flow. Of the total Official Development Finance (ODF) provided by bilateral and multilateral donors to India, a total of 24% went to agriculture (encompassing irrigation) in 1986. This figure was down to 13% in 1987 and to 3% in 1988. Since 1989, donor interest in agriculture in India has shown signs of recovery. In 1992, 14% of ODF to India was provided for activities in the field of agriculture. With regard to irrigation, donors 'have preferred to invest in new irrigation schemes rather than to provide financing for the improvement of existing schemes' (OECD 1986: 220). Furthermore, donors have showed a strong preference for large-scale projects in the field of irrigation (Hoebink 1995b: 21).

Selected Projects

Three irrigation projects funded by European donors have been assessed as part of this study (Reddy, 1997):

1. The Dutch funded Tungabhadra Irrigation Pilot Project (TIPP-II) in Karnataka. TIPP-II started in 1996 in continuation of the first phase (which officially ended already in 1989) and has to be

regarded as an experimental project in a part of the command area of Tungabhadra River. The main objectives of this project are threefold: (1) reduction of water usage levels in the top reach without reduction in income to farmers; (2) increase in availability of irrigation water at the tail end; and (3) increase in agricultural and agricultural related incomes for farm households.

2. The German funded Orissa Lift Irrigation Project (OLIP). The Orissa Lift Irrigation Corporation is the only implementing organisation of this minor irrigation project in the districts of Balasore, Cuttack and Puri. The main objectives of the project are: (1) to design and install lift irrigation facilities (i.e., 500 tube wells and 150 creek/river lift projects) in order to increase the cropping intensity and consequently crop yields; (2) reduce farming risks by providing water for irrigation in times of water shortage or drought; and (3) to provide food security and increase farm incomes, particularly for small and marginal farmers.
3. The EC funded Tank Rehabilitation Project (TRP) in Tamil Nadu. The TRP presently is in its third phase (Phase 1 was from July 1984 to September 1991, Phase 2 was from October 1991 to December 1995 and Phase 3, officially Phase 2 Extension, started in January 1996). The main objective of the project has changed over the years and at present is to develop a sustainable, economically viable strategy for tank modernisation, which will provide the basis for extending the programme to all tanks.

Location

In order to understand the specific features of the projects it is necessary, like with the watershed projects, to pay attention to the location of the projects and the specific problems that play a role in these locations. This particularly holds for TIPP-II that, in contrast to TRP and OLIP, is being implemented in a part (Distributary 36) of the Tungabadhra Reservoir (TBS) in Karnataka. As such, it aims at correcting some of the negative outcomes of this major inter-state irrigation project. The aim of the TBS was to supply irrigation water for protective irrigation in an area, which was known for its frequent drought conditions. To date the project has not been able to achieve the target defined at the time of planning. Even within the developed command area, the problem of receiving water at the tail end is very high. Moreover, the entire project suffers from salinity and water logging.

One of the social problems that is highly consequential to the problems is the 'problem of settlers'. With a predominance of black cotton soils and no history of irrigation, the local farmers were reluctant to use water for irrigation. They gave away their land on lease or sold it to those farmers who migrated from Andhra Pradesh. This trend is seen even today. Consequently, the farmers are categorised as the local and the migrant. Out of the two, it is the migrants who due to their housing either in a compact area called 'camps' or in isolated houses built within the land leased in or purchased are easily recognisable. Further, the entrepreneurial abilities of the migrant farmers has placed them economically far above the local population. With this, the farmers in the command area are categorised as the local farmers and the migrant Andhra farmers. Local farmers live in the villages, which are normally located at the tail end of the distributary or the canal and continue to own and cultivate in the non-irrigated areas. However, of late, there is a realisation of the benefits of irrigation and there is a demand for irrigation.

The process of owning land acts as an element that creates poverty condition within the command area. For the process of owning land the migrants adopt the procedure of leasing in by paying heavy advances to the landowner. Normally, unable to pay back the advance taken the landowner sells the land. Consequently, the locals who own land not only loose the land that is leased out but also get into the circle of getting poorer day by day.

The nature of owning land and the salinity has contributed in one way to the formation and expansion of poverty in the command area. Heavy irrigation by the migrants has resulted in salinity in the top reaches. This has resulted in relative poverty at the tail end. Further, within the top reach, the need for labourers, especially the cheap and trusted, has made these migrant farmers to encourage migrant labourers. These migrant labourers getting gradually tied up to the 'advances' has to settle down. Such an act of settling down of labourers adds to the pressure that is already present and growing. Compared to the labourers from the area, the migrant labourers are forced into higher degrees of poverty right from the type of house they have to live in and also denied of certain basic facilities. Such a level of poverty can be found in almost all the villages in the top reach where the migrant labourers have settled down.

Compared to the top reach, in the tail end the nature of poverty especially in the project area is determined by the same factors such as migrant farmer from Andhra Pradesh. The inability of the local farming community to lift water from the Krishna river and in bringing in the water to the earmarked command area has resulted in leasing out of the land to the enterprising farmers from Andhra Pradesh. The additional factor is the inability of the administrators to supply water to the ear marked area.

The three districts included in the Orissa Lift Irrigation Project are the coastal districts served with delta of several large and small rivers. Consequently, there is abundant groundwater and surface flow available for lift irrigation. One of the advantages is that in some of the coastal districts, the backwaters do offer a chance for lift irrigation as they maunder through creeks that are natural or man made. Despite this, many of the areas that are relatively uplands and those that are at the tail end of the project fail to receive water for irrigation. In such areas, paddy crop is cultivated as rainfed crop. Consequently, the yields are low and the possibility to grow beyond a single crop is also limited by the non-availability of water for irrigation. The selected districts are in flood prone region, which is both beneficial as well as a constraint to raise more than a single crop. Many a times, the crops are lost due to flooding over a period of time. Consequent to such limitations placed by the nature, seasonal migration is very high in most of the areas. In places such as Aul, most of the youth migrate in summer months to Calcutta in search of employment.

Project activities

The TRP and OLIP project both are minor irrigation projects with a large construction or rehabilitation part. The TRP, for instance, includes such activities as (1) restructuring of tank bunds, sluices, surplus arrangements and improvements to supply channels; (2) restructuring of the main irrigation and drainage channels, lining of the main irrigation channels, and construction of ancillary works such as additional control structures and cart track crossings; (3) on farm developmental works including construction of field channels to facilitate direct supply to individual holdings, lining of field chánnels to 2 ha limit additional control structure to facilitate introduction of rotational water supply, construction of ancillary works such as structures for cattle crossings, but also (4) training of project staff and farmer leaders in improved system operations and better water management techniques and adoption of improved agricultural practices; and (5) project monitoring and evaluation. Emphasis in the second phase and, particularly, in the extended second phase shifted towards developing good social organisations and to training of farmers in water management practices based around the traditional systems evolved by the farmers themselves for their particular tank.

The drive towards greater involvement of farmers in the TRP is also clear from the OLIP in Orissa. Within this project specific attention is given to Water Users Associations (WUAs) thereby creating a space for the farmers to air their opinions on the water management, supply timings or operation of the pump, cropping pattern, etc. These WUAs are to take over management of the irrigation facilities. The TIPP-II project is, in contrast, not geared at construction of irrigation facilities but at a better management of the existing major irrigation canal with the aim to divide the water more equally between farmers at the top reach and at the tail end. Training of farmers therefore forms a major component of project activities, as does organisation of farmers. Within TIPP-II it is realised that there are various developmental issues pertaining to the villages and camps the target group lives in. Tackling the irrigation water issue alone will not help in bringing about community participation and it alone cannot solve all the factors that are causing various problems in the project area.

Poverty concept and targeting

Looking at the objectives of the three projects it is clear that none of the projects actually and formally specifies poverty reduction as their objective. Nonetheless, the projects do target specific groups that in general are considered as belonging to the poorer sections. In the Orissa Lift Irrigation Project, for instance, small and marginal farmers are supposed to be the principal beneficiaries. TIPP-II, although embracing all farmers within the project area, specifically aims at reaching women and the (poorer) farmers at the tail end. In the Tamil Nadu Tank Rehabilitation Project, the majority of tank users are small and marginal farmers. By providing the possibilities for other development activities not related to participation, the TIPP-II has a broader conceptualisation of poverty, as do TRP and OLIP.

The fact that those poorer sections of the population are principally targeted in the projects does not automatically mean that these sections also are the principal beneficiaries. Within the OLIP, for instance, small and marginal farmers are targeted. The main indicator for selecting beneficiaries is thus the size of the land. Besides, KfW also took over the general indicator used by OLIP that 60% of the beneficiaries have to be those whose annual income is less than Rs 6,400 (i.e., below the poverty line). The Block Development Officer in OLIP should be checking upon the total holdings of the intended beneficiary to see whether or not he qualifies as small or marginal farmer. In reality, this checking is not strictly practised and most of the times only the holding at the point of the intended well is taken into account.

TIPP-II officially has no mandate to work for the poor. Nevertheless, in the process, the project has a lot to do with the poor. The poor are identified basically as those who live in the villages at the tail end of the distributary and those that have no irrigation source. Few indicators have been developed to identify the poor: those who leased out their land, those who work as agricultural labourers and those families in which the women work as agricultural labourers. Apart from the above the project has also identified the labourers who have migrated into the project area as poor. Most of them would have drawn their wages in advance and to repay the advance, they work for lower wages under inhabitable housing conditions.

Like TIPP-II, the TRP does not have a mandate to include the poor. However, the authorities as well as the consultants claim that the project is serving the poor, as the land held in the command areas is, particularly in the extended phase, less than 2.5 acres. The process of identification of the beneficiaries has thus to be taken as the process of identification of poor. This process is simplified by taking the documents maintained by the village accountant. Normally, for every tank there is a register maintained on the area irrigated and its boundaries. A register will also provide a list of owners. Basically, all those whose names are mentioned in the register are included as beneficiary. The list is updated in a meeting of the beneficiaries.

With regard to the question of addressing the poor in the TRP it is important to make a distinction between direct and indirect beneficiaries. The direct beneficiaries are the ones who draw water from the tank after the rehabilitation and the indirect beneficiaries are those who get benefited by the use of additional water available for irrigation or by the activities that are carried out to rehabilitate the tank. The direct beneficiaries are in way fixed for each tank as the numbers of people who can draw water from the tank for irrigation are decided by the land ownership within the command area. The majority of the beneficiaries within the command area own less than 2 acres. However, it has to be noted that this holding is pertaining to the command area of the tank taken up for the rehabilitation only and not the total holding.

Participation

Despite the participatory approach adopted in all three projects, none of them actually involved intended beneficiaries in the design of the project. The projects are, thus, initiated as top-down projects. Participation of the beneficiaries starts at the implementation phase and is mainly given shape through setting up Water Users Associations. In OLIP, the formation of such WUAs is conditional. Eventually, these WUAs are to take over the management of the wells constructed under the project. The major problem in this specific project is that these WUAs lack organisational and institutional training and guidance. This indicates that the ability (or: inability) of the beneficiaries to bring changes in the water distribution or cropping pattern is not visualised within the project.

The formation of WUAs and them taking over the management is one of the major differences between the normal OLIP approach and the one adopted in the KfW funded project. Consequently, there are efforts to bring together the beneficiaries under the institutional framework. These efforts are made more to fulfil the conditionality than with enthusiasm and realisation. To add a realistic approach the need for a sociologist is not felt. Therefore, after the organisation is formed the beneficiaries are left without any training or guidance.

Within TIPP-II, the formation of WUAs is instrumental to bring modifications in the distribution system, maintenance of field channels and drainages and starting other, irrigation related or not, development activities. Institutionally, TIPP-II aims at developing partnerships between the technocrats manning the system and the beneficiaries. The WUAs are supposed to be one of the ways to reach such partnership. Moreover, organisation of poor women is undertaken. In the tail end village Uphal, for instance, the women of the poorer families are organised and have been successful in some ways already. An attempt has been made to bring them together with the men and particularly those farmers who have come from Andhra Pradesh and who are comparatively richer.

The TRP has in the past come across several technical constraints, such as the fact that the sinking of wells in the command area which reduced the supply of water from the tank. Social constraints such as the falling apart of the traditional organisation for water distribution and absentee landlordism, however, are now regarded as more important. To overcome the shortcomings of Phase I, more attention was geared at social objectives and farmers' participation. It was thought that with the reduction in the total investment on OFD, and by raising the contribution of the beneficiaries, the beneficiary would gain a right to decide the pattern of investment. To bring about greater participation of beneficiaries in Phase II, Farmers Associations were planned with a separate budget allocation to recruit community organisers to work at the grass-root level.

One of the consultants was to be the social organiser.

The nature of the Farmers Associations to be developed is left totally to the discretion of the farming community, so that they can plan it either for the specific purpose or for a wide ranging issues prevailing in the village. Once the FA gains the needed legal recognition, it is asked to form the committees and sub-committees to for overseeing the progress in the work. Thus the progress in the Phase II has an emphasis for the participatory approach. In each of the selected tank, a community organiser is posted. The duties of such posted officials are to guide the FAs through various activities and also to act as a bridge between the association and concerned officials. The community organiser also helps the association to acquire the skills required to place their comments on the work performed through a methodology that avoids the conflict between the officials and the association.

Gender

Particularly within TIPP-II attention is paid to gender issues and the involvement of women. In order to understand this it is important to pay attention to understand the implications of the extension of irrigational facilities and its availability on women. Those women, who live in the villages at the tail end have to face shortage of drinking water, fodder and also has to walk for several kilometres for work. The women who work as agricultural labourer has to compete with the migrant labour also. This conflict is utilised by the migrant-landlords to hire in the women from the villages at differential wages. The farming community on the basis of work efficiency of the migrant worker rationalises this.

Those women who live at the top reach also suffer due to the shortage of potable water. In Hanuman Nagar camp the problem is of this nature. Extension of cultivation to the entire area around the village has an implication on the availability of fuel wood in the top reach. The rain season make the women to undergo nightmares as the communication facilities breakdown. It will be difficult to reach up to the stores for provision or for the store that distributes the food grains under public distribution system. This problem is also applicable to almost all the villages. Health facilities are lacking and not approachable in the rainy months.

Within TIPP-II, the role of women in each and every intervention is underlined through a special gender study. The idea is to identify the problems and help the women to resolve them through participation. In this direction already women are made to realise their importance and are motivated experimentally in the village Uppal to form a women's group. An important aspect to be noted is the opportunities being explored to create alternative sources of income through alternative employment opportunities, e.g. dairying.

Impact on poverty

Viewed from a poverty perspective, the projects principally aim at increasing the livelihoods (e.g., income, employment) of the beneficiaries. With regard to OLIP it can be stated that after the construction of the irrigation wells farmers are able to raise two to three crops per year where previously one crop was normal. Taking two paddy crops (the principal produce) and one vegetable crop in between as point of departure, it should be possible for farmers to move above the poverty line. An assumed crop per acre of 30 bags of 78 kilos each and a minimal price of Rs. 450 per quintal would provide for an assured gross income of Rs. 10,530 per crop of paddy. Two crops would add up to Rs. 21,060. Deducting investments of Rs. 13,700 (including Rs. 700 for water charges for the two crops) leaves Rs. 7,360 net income alone for two paddy crops. Adding to this an approximate net income of Rs. 1,400 from the vegetable crop would mean a total net income of Rs. 8,760. Even without the vegetable crop farmers would come above the poverty line of Rs. 6,500. Unfortunately, these figures are calculated for an acreage of 1, while certainly not all farmers have that much land. As such, it shows that the ability of the farmer to move above the poverty line through the utilisation of an irrigation well depends on the total holding.

In the OLIP area, however, visual signs of the impact of the project on the livelihoods of the farming community can be seen. In the area closer to Cuttack, the ability of the farmers to raise two to three crops has a visual impact on the structure of the houses and also in their life style. In most of the villages, the life style is moving closer to the urban areas, at least with respect to the recreation media. The need for schooling has been felt and can be seen in the number of private schools operated in the area. In the Aul area, which was very backward and had seen heavy migration in the past, the youth feel confident that they need migrate and it has been reduced drastically over the years. Only very few who have respectable income through migration, migrate and those who used to migrate earlier in search of casual labour have almost stopped migrating. Here also, as reported by the school teacher, there is a considerable increase in the enrolment of students. As an answer to a specific question, the teacher was of the opinion that the number of children enrolled by the agricultural labourers is on the increase as the area with two irrigational facilities is increasing.

Positive signs were also the fact that complains about the water charges levied were rare. At the same time, it is clear that the charges are far less than the one charged by the private parties who supply water through a diesel pump. For the services of these private parties, the farmers have to pay around Rs.900 per crop. In the project, these costs are Rs. 350 per acre per crop. Moreover, the scheme is, comparatively, a scheme where the management is in the hands of the beneficiaries and they have the freedom to determine the timings and the quantum required. The fact that the area to be irrigated is small and the landowners more or less are related to one another, the management and operation appears to be possible.

The TIPP-II is so new that an assessment of the impact is difficult. Nevertheless, there are some indications, particularly as a result of organisation. The organisation led by the women at the tail end can be seen in their attempts to address the basic needs of the village. The organisation was able to compel the Command Area Development Agency to contribute to the costs for laying a road of 6 km to link up the village to the main road. The organisation was also successful in making the officials to change the supply of water and to get an additional teacher for the school. More in general, an important impact is that for the first time the poor could get organised and sit together and discuss and find solutions to their own problems.

Conclusions

— Looking at the objectives of the three projects it is clear that none of the projects actually and formally specifies poverty reduction as their objective. Nonetheless, the projects do target specific groups which in general are considered as belonging to the poorer sections: small and marginal farmers in the Orissa Lift Irrigation Project and the Tamil Nadu Tank Rehabilitation Project, and women and the (poorer) farmers at the tail end in TIPP-II.

— By providing the possibilities for other development activities not related to irrigation, the TIPP-II has a broader conceptualisation of poverty than do TRP and OLIP.

— The fact that poorer sections of the population are principally targeted in the projects does not automatically mean that these sections also are the principal beneficiaries.

— Despite the participatory approach adopted in all three projects, none of them actually involved intended beneficiaries in the design of the project. The projects are, thus, initiated as top-down projects.

— Participation of the beneficiaries starts at the implementation phase and is mainly given shape through setting up Water Users Associations. One of the major problems with these Water Users Associations is the lack of organisational and institutional training and guidance.

— TIPP-II is the only project in which specific attention is paid to gender issues and the involvement of women. Special gender studies are undertaken to identify the problems and help the women to resolve them through participation. In this direction already women are made to realise their importance and are motivated experimentally in the village Uppal to form a women's group. An important aspect to be noted is the opportunities being explored to create alternative sources of income through alternative employment opportunities.

— The OLIP is by now the only project that shows clear indications that irrigation has contributed to improve the livelihoods (e.g. income, employment) of the beneficiaries. After the construction of the lift installations farmers are able to raise two to three crops per year where previously one crop was normal. Moreover, visual signs of the impact of the project on the livelihoods of the farming community can be seen: better housing, more demand for schooling, less migration.

— The OLIP project also shows that charging levies for irrigation water certainly is possible. Complaints about the water charges levied were rare.

11

FORESTRY PROJECTS

Introduction

The utilisation of forest products have long been regarded as an important set of resources in the development of a country. For many years the conventional development wisdom held that the maximum contribution from these resources could be achieved through the state's administrative management. Poverty reduction was embodied in the revenue contribution from forestry and the more general economic growth that this supported. It was indirect and possessed little or no connection to the poverty condition of the local forest communities.

More recently, forests have come to be viewed as more complex entities and with a range of development potentials. In particular the relationship of the local community to the forest and its role in the management of forests has come to dominate contemporary thinking. This has had quite profound consequences for the way in which poverty reduction is approached within the more general discussion as to how best to manage forests.

Today social forestry occupies a dominant position on the forestry agenda. The local community's relationship to the local forest has become a central factor in the design and implementation of forestry products and poverty reduction within the local community has an important status in forestry programmes.

Forestry in India after Independence continues to remain the responsibility of the Forestry Department. After Independence, forestry policy remained very much along the lines established under British rule based upon expert management and protection of the forests. Local communities were more often than not regarded as a cause for deforestation.

The National Forest Policy of 1988 reflected a major shift in Indian forestry policy by bring the local communities into the management and ecological conservation of forests. The needs of industry ceased to be the primary concern. By mid 1996, excluding the north eastern hill states of India, facilitating orders for Joint Forest Management (JFM) have been passed in all of India's states except for Kerala and Tamil Nadu, and Forest Protection Committees (FPCs) being established involving the local villagers, the Forestry Department and the local government councils (Panchayati Raj institutions—PRIs).

Social forestry has therefore become an integral part of Indian forestry policy at least on paper. However, in addition to the problems of implementing the new policies with a Forestry Department that has traditionally practised a very different approach to forestry management, the Indian government's own view of social forestry is a somewhat limited one. It tends to view it as a means to 'green' the countryside and restore the forest cover; to tackle the fuelwood crisis in both rural and urban areas; to better avail and distribute the benefits of forest production; and to expand public works and employment schemes. Consequently, a good deal of criticism has emerged from NGOs, academics and others who feel that it remains a government programme rather than a people-based programme.

For their part, donors have sought both to support the process of change underway in forest management and the movement towards social

Table 11.1: Principal Ongoing EU Donor Forestry Projects

EU Donor	State	Project	Total Grant
Danida	Karnataka	BAIF Agro-forestry Project	19.5 m DKK
DFID	Karnataka	Western Ghats Forestry Project, incl. the joint Forest Planning & Management Project	18.1 m £
DFID	Uttar Pradesh	Forestry Project-Pilot Phase	1.7 m £
Sida	Orissa (end 96-poss. ext.)	Social Forestry Project	282.5 m SEK
Sida	Tamil Nadu (end 96)	Social Forestry Project	278.3 m SEK
Sida	Bihar (end 96)	Social Forestry	127 m SEK
DGIS	All India	Not known	Not Known
European Commission	Haryana	Afforestation & Agro-Forestry Project	23 m Ecu

forestry, but also to introduce innovative practices and forms of organisation and management to the forestry sector. These have met with varying degrees of success and the problems that have arisen have led to a good deal of criticism being directed at the Forestry Department by the donors and *vice versa.*

Apart from the EU donor forestry projects listed in Table 11.1, a number of watershed projects funded by the EU donors have important forestry components, for example, watershed projects funded by BMZ (KfW) and EC fall into this category. Otherwise, there are a number of forestry projects funded by the World Bank, USAID, World Food Programme, amongst others.

Selected projects

Three forestry projects were selected for a specific assessment of the experience of EU aid for poverty reduction in the sector. For a full account we refer to Kripa (1997) :

1. The ODA/DFID funded project on Joint Forest Management and Planning (JFMP), part of the larger Western Ghats Forestry Project in the State of Karnataka, also funded by ODA/DFID.
2. The BAIF Agro-Forestry Project funded by Danida through CAPART in the State of Karnataka.
3. The Social Forestry Project funded by Sida in the State of Orissa.

Conceptualisation of poverty

All three projects reflect the growing interest in poverty reduction as an important objective in forest policy. Having said that, the concept of poverty remains implicit rather explicit in the projects' documentation and in their implementation. In this they closely reflect the nature of the change in overall Indian forestry policy; a shift towards participation and community involvement as a means of securing community involvement in the management of forests, but a continuing lack of any more profound conceptual re-evaluation of the communities' poverty needs and as to how these are influenced by their relationship to the forests via access, ownership, etc. Given the amount of research and work currently being undertaken around these issues, it reveals a major lacuna in donor and government thinking. At best, it can be excused due to the time it takes to develop new projects and to begin implementation. The Sida project began in 1983 with the current extension of Phase 2 beginning in 1992. The ODA-JFMP and the Phase 2 of BAIF-AF began in 1991 and 1995 respectively with identification and design prior to these dates. Yet while allowing for the time lags between conceptualisation and implementation, there should be a willingness to learn and a degree of flexibility built into the project process that permits the introduction and utilisation of better approaches to the poverty issue.

ODA-JFMP appears to have no specific focus upon poverty nor does there appear to be any attempt to conceptually locate poverty in the thinking around the project. The project is directed at the village as a community with benefits being shared equally within the community. There has been little or no attempt to assess the different relationships to the forest and forest production within the community, the different dependencies involved, or how these might be addressed within the project. At best poverty is conceptualised in simple single variable terms. The original stated target group of the project was identified as being 'poor people, women, trials and other disadvantaged forest dependent groups.' Subsequently, project documentation refers to the project's 'stakeholders', covering a range of occupations and groups of which those originally identified constitute a section. ODA appears to have compounded the problem of a poor poverty orientation by introducing the stakeholder concept into the project's conceptual framework in the second phase. If the original conceptual framework for the project possessed little thinking on poverty, at least the targeting was framed in terms of poverty. Seemingly this has disappeared as the project progressed leaving the focus on the environmental concerns.

The BAIF Agro-Forestry Project funded by Danida does focus specifically upon the poor, e.g. as SCs and STs, but it excludes the landless, i.e. the poorest of the poor. However, in its thinking on poverty, the BAIF-AF project appears to be as weak as the ODA-JFMP project. Again there has been little attempt to conceive of poverty as multi-dimensional; this is reflected in the lack of thinking as to how those benefited by the tree planting might best utilise the assets generated, it is also revealed in the lack of though given as to how the beneficiaries might diversify their livelihood strategies through involvement in labour markets, markets for minor forest products, and so on.

The Sida project on paper appears to have moved towards a more multi-dimensional understanding of poverty in its linking of forestry with other activities directed at asset creation for the poor. It also seeks to combine a community approach on some components with an individual approach in others. Where it appears to have failed in its approach to poverty is in bringing the poor into the process of conceptual thinking and the process of analyzing poverty. For example, the project's plantation approach appears to ignore traditional participatory approaches towards forest management in which the poor actively participated and benefited. While micro-planning is undertaken, it is top down and first carried out well into the design stage of the project.

All three projects implicitly embody the objective of improving the beneficiaries rights and, to a limited extent, the improvement of their knowledge base with respect to the forest and minor forest products. It would be nice to think that these reflected careful poverty analyses of the situations, but in the absence of documentary evidence, it is more likely that they are standard project elements, presented as basic aims on paper, but with little real substance.

Targeting

In most instances forests in India are also areas of poverty, where the majority of the population are not only economically poor but suffer from social discrimination and political marginalisation due to their 'tribal' status. Often they migrated to these areas as they were excluded from settling in more prosperous agricultural regions. The forests provided a variety of means for subsistence until the importance of timber and the need for its scientific management increasingly led to a denial of access to forest lands as came under central government control during colonial rule. The continuation after independence of these policies means that targeting the poor can be achieved merely through taking the local population as the target group. Certainly in the projects studied, the donors appear to have accepted this principle, in line with the Indian government. The problem is that it treats the community as being economically and socially homogeneous.

In the ODA-JFMP project there is no attempt to identify the poor within the project area. In this sense it can be said that the identification and targeting of the poor lies simply in the selection of the sector (forestry) the location (Western Ghats) and through the zonal approach adopted to identify the specific locations within the Western Ghats. Only those degraded areas of forest close to settlements are selected. Given that the project began to be implemented in late 1992, this would appear to be more a state of the play approach towards poverty reduction rather than state of the art.

The BAIF-AF Project has a greater degree of targeting built into the design of the project with a list of those below the target line drawn up for the government's Integrated Rural Development Programme being combined with the list of those who have been allotted C & D waste lands by the government. In this way there is a degree of targeting through a combination of sector together with location (unproductive land and high outward migration), household (landless recently allotted land by Government), and women (via self-help groups). In practice, the targeting was seriously undermined by the fact that no landless received the land allocations promised by the Government (for 'technical' reasons) and the 1,000 landless families originally included in the target group thereby fell out of the project. This has left the target group as being the those with land in the village community, specifically farmers and a number of sub-components involving women and youths.

The Sida project appears to have suffered similar problems. Here both the community and the individual are the targets of the two components, village woodlots and Forest Forming for the Rural Poor (FFRP). On closer examination of some of the project villages it was clear that it has been men who have benefited from the cash incomes generated from tree cultivation and women who have suffered through the loss of access to local firewood. The FFRP component was directed at the poor specifically, but it was a only on a small experimental basis and it required that the individual poor be issued with a 'patta' given him/her usufruct rights over tress, but not land. Again there were technical problems in having the pattas issued. In an new proposal for extending the project, the FFRP component has been dropped.

Gender

Forestry should be a sector in which a clear gender approach could be a developed for the benefit of women. Traditionally there have been quite clear lines of gender demarcation with respect to forests and the collection and utilisation of forest products. The danger in the changing approach towards forest management as adopted by the government and implemented through the Forest Department is that it continues to emphasise the output of timber and that the financial returns. The new development is that 25 per cent of the net value of this now comes to Forest Protection Committees which are predominantly monopolised by men. An innovative approach towards social forestry should be able to secure not only a greater return to the community, i.e. the FPC, but to ensure that women benefit at least equally from the changes. In practice, the donors appear to have failed.

There is little in any of the projects approaches or in their various components that can be said to be gender specific. In the case of the BAIF-AF Project, there is no FPC formation involved and the focus on individual households has left women more often than not responsible for caring for the tree plants and using considerable time for this. As to whether this is a positive development from a gender perspective is certainly questionable. It is often at the expense of alternative paid employment during the summer months. The same project does have a component for self help groups for women and youth which are linked to savings groups and training in embroidery for example. In some instances women have benefited from these, but often it is men who borrow via women from the savings groups and the lack of proper marketing facilities has undermined the impact of the embroidery training programme. The BAIF project has minor forest products as a part of its focus and that these are in themselves quite gender specific, being often the preserve of women, and women met during the field research pointed to the fruit and other items collected both from the forest and the plantations.

The ODA/DFID project does not appear particularly gender sensitive. For example, the fact that only one member from each household can be a member of the VACS, significantly excludes women, particularly as it is the VFC member who is formally entitled to a share of the benefits that accrue (25%) when forest products are sold. Two seats are reserved for women on the executive committee which meets once a month and is the main decision-making body. Just as the poor are covered in so far as they fall inside the target group, so it is with women. There appears to be little by way of a deliberate policy to include them.

The Sida project in its first phase had a specific objective for securing women's employment in addition to a general emphasis upon minor forest products and other activities in which women are traditionally involved. However in the second phase this specific objective was dropped and the general focus of the project shifted somewhat more towards tree growing and agro-silviculture. This was a reflected in criticisms from NGOs that the project focused more upon the production of trees which eventually supported the needs of the paper industry rather than upon social forestry which was the original objective. In so doing, it ignored the strong tradition of community forest protection present in Orissa. In several locations women argued that now they had to go much further to obtain firewood as the (male) protection squads prevented them finding local supplies; they had never been taught how to use the Astra stoves provided in order to counter this problem, and there was not enough 'thin' wood locally available for running these stoves in any case. In reality, the community targeted in the approach was a male community. A final gender insensitivity is found in the gradual loss of secondary vegetable cultivation as the tree roots spread in the land used for the woodlots.

In gender awareness, it must be said that the BAIF-AF project appears to be stronger than the ODA-JFMP and Sida projects. The most apparent factor that can explain this is the type of partner institution involved, a NGO in the case of BAIF and the Forest Department in the case of the other two. Local NGOs are involved in some localities under the ODA-JFPM project, but in a relatively minor way. In the case of the Sida project, NGOs have been extremely critical of the whole approach adopted including the lack of a clear gender perspective.

Participation

The original ODA/DFID funded Western Ghats Forestry Project received considerable criticism for its failure to pursue people's participation as a clear and primary objective. With the JFMP Project, it has been stated that participation in line with the 1988 National Forest Policy and the involvement of NGOs were elements tagged to the ODA/DFID funding. Furthermore, that the Village Forest Committee (VFC) concept in the JFMP project was achieved by local NGOs liaising with U.K. based NGOs and in jointly pushing ODA into including it in the project document.

The Forestry Department argues that the Sida project has been implemented by way of a highly decentralised approach. First potential villages were identified and short listed, the interests of the villagers were then assessed, and only if the villagers themselves were interested in the project was the project introduced through informal meetings. NGOs dispute the participatory nature of this approach, claiming that the micro planning was a Forest Department exercise rather than a joint venture. It would certainly appear that only rather specific needs are being met within what is claimed to be a community oriented approach. On the other hand the villagers do feel that they now participate with the Forestry Department in the management of the trees. The question is whether or not previously they participated in the voluntary protection of the local forests, but in conflict with the Forestry Department. The difference might be that now it is a collaboration in growing and selling the trees to the paper department whereas previously the two parties pursued different objectives in forestry. Certainly, when asked, the villagers said that participation is better and that village unity is greater. One wonders whether this is more of 'we' have a better relationship with 'them', i.e.

the Forestry Department. Women appeared the least positive concerning the question of participation.

The project implemented by BAIF might be expected to be the most participatory given that it is an NGO implementing it. It appears to have brought villagers into the implementing stage at a relatively early stage through micro-planning. These were drawn up at individual household levels which appear to have been successful in allowing opinions and problems to be more fully discussed than is the case in general open meetings. It has also encouraged greater involvement within the wider framework of the project at the village level and greater village unity has been one of the results noted in some of the locations visited. BAIF also appeared to have allowed a longer period for establishing the project which has permitted greater participation to be achieved in the planning stage.

Generally, it would appear that participation is quite good in the donor interventions investigated, but this is to be expected in that the overall policy towards forestry in India places considerable stress upon community participation. The donors appeared to have demonstrated that such an approach can be developed in practice if adequate support and assistance is provided. The weaknesses of the projects are in bringing the participation into the project identification and design stages and not developing it in the implementation stage; secondly, in developing better participatory mechanisms and practices that can bring the poor, women and the more marginalised sections into the process; and thirdly, in achieving a better set of mechanisms by which participation in the assessment of projects can feed back into the ongoing implementation of the projects.

Sustainability

The sustainability of all of the projects is questionable. At the level of group formation and local institution building, there have been successes in building up the Forest Protection Committees or their equivalents in the Sida and BAIF-AF projects, but these are also reproduced through the requirements imposed upon the Forestry Departments in the concerned states by Joint Forest Management.

According to BAIF, the beneficiaries of the BAIF-AF project should begin to see a reduction in their poverty by the fifth or sixth year of the project as the plantations mature, thereby suggesting that a degree of economic sustainability can be achieved within the time frame imposed upon the project.

The Sida project appears less sustainable in economic terms and it appears to have missed an opportunity in the area of institutional sustainability. The local village institutions are project based creations and not rooted in the more traditional village systems for management of local forests for which Orissa is well known. As for the economic sustainability, the securing of financial returns to the individual households via the FFRP component have been downgraded or dropped, and the woodlots, while functioning in many instances and giving a cash income and some firewood, are likely to experience a possible decline as the project slips back into the more general implementation of JFM in the State and cease to receive the support provided from the project, particularly in the form of technical assistance.

The ODA-JFMP project has not only 25 per cent of net income from timber sales going to individuals, but also 25 per cent going into a Village Forest Development Fund which should provide for greater economic viability of the committees and their work in the future. As with all forestry however, it takes time to realise these benefits, approximately 10 years before trees can begin to be felled.

An important point to note with the ODA-JFMP and Sida projects is that by generating local level institutions they have served to legitimise the people's involvement in the projects and in their formal relationship to the Forest Department, something, which the BAIF-AF project has not yet achieved.

Replicability

The potential for replicability for the projects varies considerably. Perhaps the most replicable in the current context is the BAIF-AF project. A German NGO is funding BAIF and MYRADA, another NGO operating in Karnataka, to replicate the project in other villagers in Karnataka. In addition the Government of Karnataka is looking at agro-forestry blocks as training models for both officers and farmers as the project model has a watershed component in it. One of the important reasons for this possibility is that the model has links to the Forestry Department, but is not actually embodied within it. In the short term this means that the rather more inflexible structures and procedures of the Forest Department do not so directly hinder the project in the shorter term and at the local level. In the longer term, however, it would be more desirable for such projects with an explicit poverty reduction objective to be located within the Forestry Department. This would have significant economic advantages with respect to the possible extent of the programme.

The failure of the Sida project in Orissa to be extended illustrates the situation. Sida, according to the Forest Department has proposed a new organisational structure for the project that would effectively entail a demotion for a significant number of local Forest Department personnel. This is not possible. There are undoubtedly other problems leading to the current failure to reach agreement for the new phase, but it demonstrates the problem of bureaucratic inflexibility quite well.

A second factor that makes the BAIF-AF project more replicable is its focus upon individual farmers' lands. In the other two instances, the projects are dependent upon the availability of land such as degraded forest lands or revenue department waste lands. This makes the implementation of such a project very difficult without the close support of government departments.

On the other hand, the BAIF-AF project is dependent upon external donor funds if it is to be replicated elsewhere. It also requires the creation of a new organisation with staff and resources in each location it enters with the financial and organisational costs that this requires. Given that considerable resources have been provided for all three projects the BAIF-AF project covering a total of 906 families in 25 villages or hamlets with a cost of 19.5 million DKK (approx. 100 million Rs.) over 7 years raises serious questions concerning its cost effectiveness. This is to be compared with the 452 million Rs. budget for the ODA-JFMP over five years which covers 294 villages and their VPCs, or the 14,981 villages covered by the Sida project costing 640 million Rs. for the extension phase.

Monitoring and evaluation systems

In the case of the ODA-JFMP project, the ODA has appointed a Project Process Support Team to liaise with the Karnataka Forest Department in identifying group process indicators to assess the effect to JFMP at the village level. The focus on qualitative, villager-based assessments rather than empirical measures is undoubtedly a progressive step as it counters to some extent to base assessments on areas under plantation, VACS created, gobar gas and Astra stoves distributed, and similar indicators of impact and success. One example of this process oriented approach and feedback is that the Forest Department is now considering including non-timber forest products in the benefits to the VACS.

Compared to the other two projects ODA-JFMP is more flexible due to this process approach which is designed to build in 'flexibility' and 'review'. In the case of the other two it would appear that they have not been particularly successful in responding to the unfolding situation as the projects proceeded, for example the setback in the BAIF-AF project caused by the failure of land to be granted to landless households or the problems with gaining usufruct right over trees in the Sida project. Similarly, these two projects have failed take action in the area of marketing of forest products once these are being generated.

Conclusions and suggestions

- Forestry is a sector in which thinking and policy are undergoing fairly rapid processes of change. There are undoubtedly strong arguments that the contemporary emphasis on social forestry is conducive to the pursuit of poverty reduction as a primary objective in aid. The Indian government at national and state levels is pressing for Joint Forestry Management (JFM) and in some states this is being followed through successfully. The donors are therefore correct to place emphasis upon this sector.
- However, there is a clear need for donors to develop a better conceptual approach when incorporating poverty into their forestry sector programmes. To date the conceptualisation of poverty at project level appears simplistic, weak, and even non-existent. This might partly be explained by the long duration of forestry projects, with formulation predating more recent thinking. The institutional framework for forestry in India must also be partly held responsible with a history of management that has hindered or obstructed a more sophisticated approach towards poverty reduction.
- In the area of forestry interventions, there are significant differences between the project documents and their statements on goals, objectives etc, and what actually occurs during the implementation. Objectives and priorities in country and sector programmes often disappear at the point of project implementation.
- There is also a lack of conceptual coordination between the partner institutions involved in a project and sometimes this also extends to the components of a project. An NGO project that fails to incorporate and build upon the Forest Protection Committees required under the JFM policy is intrinsically weakened from the outset. In the case of BAIF, the government intervention in JFM came later, but there could have been greater flexibility on the NGOs part to link into and build upon the

government programme. Similarly, a component to aid women's utilisation of Non-Forest Timber Products is of little use if there is no marketing component that will enable them to secure the increased entitlements (value) that the NTFPs might realise e.g. the Sida and BAIF-AF projects. At the very least, greater participation by the potential beneficiaries/poor in all of the project's phases should be encouraged to minimise such failings. There was no such participation in the identification and planning side in the projects studied despite claims to the contrary.

— Comparison of the three projects suggests that sustainability replicability and long-term local ownership in social forestry projects are best pursued through working towards better designed projects in which the forestry department remains the principal partner rather than opting for a different institutional means of intervention. While projects are meant to originate from the Forestry Department or a local NGO, in practice donors can and do act pro-actively to support project identification and design. It should therefore be possible for the donors to have a far greater impact on the poverty orientation in terms of conceptualisation and operationalisation than they do at the moment. If poverty reduction is to remain a priority, donors must play an innovative role in this way.

12

RURAL DRINKING WATER AND SANITATION PROJECTS

Introduction

Strictly speaking, drinking water and sanitation is part of what has been labelled basic needs by the ILO back in the 1970s. As such, it classifies as part of what has been marked 'livelihoods' in Section 3. Considering, however, the fact that the provision of safe drinking water and proper sanitation is ultimately aimed at improving the health situation of people it is to be regarded as an essential element in the fight against poverty. In this regard, and when talking about the contribution of water supply and sanitation to poverty reduction, targeting of the beneficiaries becomes extremely important in order to provide for an equitable access of the poor to the facilities.

Drinking water supply has been part of Indian government policy already since Independence. At Central Government level an increasing budget has been made available for the sector over the years. Particularly in the 1980s (i.e., the International Drinking Water Supply and Sanitation Decade) funding increased considerably. Simultaneously, attention to policy development within the rural water supply sector also gained in importance. Prior to the Decade attention was mainly aimed at technical hurdles in providing drinking water, whereas in the 1980s attention shifted slowly to operation and maintenance (O&M) issues. This went hand in hand with increased attention to such issues as health education, involvement of the villagers in O&M and an integrated approach to the problem. Slowly also sanitation, which was neglected previously, got more attention in Indian policy. Nevertheless, at the end of the Decade in 1990, still 25% of Indians had no access to safe drinking water and a staggering 97% had no access to sanitation (mainly seen as latrines).

The most important central programmes initiated in the field of drinking water and sanitation are the Accelerated Rural Water Supply Programme (ARWSP) and the Central Sanitation Programme (CSP). Drinking water is also an important part of the Minimum Needs Programme. At state-level, and it should be noted that the states carry the chief responsibility for providing safe drinking water and sanitation, there are numerous other programmes. The main implementing agencies for RWS/S are the State Water Boards such as Jal Nigam in Uttar Pradesh. These agencies principally are staffed with engineers. At central level there is also the Rajiv Gandhi Drinking Water Mission which has been set up in 1986 in order to provide scientific and cost effective content to the ARWSP. The 'Technology Mission', as it is also known, is responsible for technical and policy improvements and co-ordination, and has been functioning as the main dialogue partner with the external assistance agencies. Presently, the Mission is also highly involved in promoting a more participatory approach to rural water supply in the states.

Within drinking water supply it is important to make a distinction between piped water supply and hand pumps. The latter are preferred nowadays by the Indian government mainly because of bad experiences with operation and maintenance of large scale piped water supply schemes. Nevertheless, this does not mean that piped water schemes are not constructed any more but as a general rule preference is given to hand pumps. Some of the State Water Boards are less clear in their preference for hand pumps if only because piped water supply schemes are more interesting from an engineering point of view.

Foreign assistance in the field of drinking water and sanitation is relatively restricted in India. Firstly, this holds for the total foreign funds made available for this sector. In general, the major part of the investments in (rural) drinking water and sanitation come from the Indian government and the states. For specific states, however, foreign funds can mean an important contribution to these Indian funds. This, for instance, holds for Andhra Pradesh where 68% of the Plan funds for the year 1997-98 will come from Externally Aided Projects. Secondly, it holds for the number of foreign donors involved in (rural) water supply and sanitation. According to the Rajiv Gandhi National Drinking Water Mission, there were six donors (excluding UNICEF) active in the sector in 1995: Danida (Denmark), ODA (Great Britain), DGIS (the Netherlands), KfW (Germany), the European Union and the World Bank.

Whereas earlier projects were mainly construction projects, the 1980s show a shift towards more attention for so-called software aspects (health education, participation, organisation, etc.) also with the donor community. For them, this made the projects in the field of drinking water supply and sanitation more directly aimed at poverty reduction.

Selected projects

Three projects co-financed by the Netherlands (DGIS) and one project co-financed by Denmark (Danida) have been assessed as part of this study. For a full account of this assessment we refer to Manti (1997). Lack of co-operation from the implementing organisations in the Danish project in Karnataka made it extremely difficult to conduct the research. The following therefore draws heavily on the experiences in the Dutch funded projects in Uttar Pradesh and, to a lesser extent, in Karnataka.

1. SP-VI (Uttar Pradesh), implemented by Jal Nigam in co-operation with the PSU Foundation with support from DGIS. Started in 1987, this project ultimately intended to provide 13,559 hand pumps to 1,638 villages spread across six districts in the northeastern part of Uttar Pradesh. Two addendum phases have been sanctioned since then: one for the district of Lakhimpur Kheri and one for the district of Siddhartnagar. Although from the start already perceived as an integrated project in which next to the installation of hand pumps a community participation component was added, the implementation of the latter component only started after already more than 60% of the originally proposed hand pumps had been installed. Up to the end of 1995, a total of 17,260 hand pumps had been installed being 97% of the target. Nearly 25% of these hand pumps were specifically installed for the Socially Weaker Sections. From 1995 onwards, the community participation component includes training of 5,855 hand pump caretakers and 100 cluster level mechanics, each cluster comprising about 50 hand pumps.
2. SP-VIII (Uttar Pradesh), implemented by Jal Nigam in co-operation with the PSU Foundation with support from DGIS. Implementation of this project only started in 1995. The project is conceived as a water supply project with community participation and sanitation as integral parts from the inception. It is intended to construct 15,426 hand pumps in 3,348 villages spread across 6 districts (Aligarh, Moradabad, Badaun, Kanpur-

Dehat, Unnao and Ballia). Besides, the project aims at training of 15,943 care takers from the local communities.

3. Integrated Rural Sanitation and Water Supply Project (IRS&WS) (Karnataka), implemented by the Department of Rural Development and Panchayati Raj (RD&PR) in co-operation with the Project Advisory Group (PAG) with support from Danida. Implementation started in 1991 and the project was completed by August 1996 after three extensions. A second phase of the IRS&WSP was sanctioned in 1996. The project covered one Taluk in the districts of Bijapur, Chitradurga and Kolar and was preceded in the late 1980s by Danida support to the development and strengthening of a hand pump maintenance system in 4 districts including training of village-based hand pump caretakers and maintenance mechanics.
4. Integrated Rural Water Supply & Sanitation Project (IRWSS) (Karnataka), implemented by the Department of Rural Development and Panchayati Raj (RD&PR) in cooperation with the Project Support Unit with support from DGIS. The project, located in the districts of Dharwad and Bijapur, is conceived as an integrated project, aiming at better living conditions, and includes such activities as community participation, training of caretakers, decentralised O&M, environmental acre and sanitation facilities. Although intended to start implementation in June 1993 not much headway has been made with regard to the construction of piped water supply systems and hand pumps. This seems to be due, among other things, to the Dutch preference for groundwater sources and the extended hydrological surveys required because of this in combination with the Government of Karnataka preference for a faster implementation. In the field of environmental sanitation (e.g., building of Anganwadi buildings and household latrines) has already started as have the activities in the field of community participation.

The above projects have been selected in order to include (nearly) completed projects (SP-VI and IRS&WS) and recently started projects (IWSSP and SP-VIII). It will be clear that considering the relatively recent start of implementation in SP-VIII and the severely delayed implementation of the drinking water supply part of the IWSSP puts restrictions on this report, particularly in the field of impact assessment.

Conceptualisation of poverty

None of the projects formally specifies poverty reduction as their objective. The projects are principally aimed at the provision of improved drinking water and sanitation for the rural population. Looking down at the objectives of the different projects, it is clear that poverty is an issue that forms part of the projects without them becoming principally aimed at poverty reduction. Most projects do not get much further than the statement that special attention should be paid to, what are normally conceived, poorer sections: Scheduled Castes, Scheduled Tribes and women (see also under 'targeting'). This indicates that poverty reduction as such is not the prime objective of these projects. Although the Netherlands, for instance, formally take drinking water projects as falling under the general policy objective of poverty reduction, the Dutch embassy is less clear in this regard. This is mainly because these projects only touch upon specific issues that are elements in poverty reduction, such as participation and better health, but do not directly touch upon some other issues such as income. In effect, this means that the projects in general are restricted to specific issues captured mainly under resources and, to some extent, knowledge but leave out the larger part of livelihoods and rights.

When taking account of the different activities undertaken in these projects it is clear that specific criteria mentioned in Section 3 as important with regard to poverty (reduction) are part of the projects. This mainly refers to the so-called software elements that are taken up in all projects: community participation, health education and also institutional changes with regard to the government delivery structure. It should, however, be taken into account that these elements are not part of the projects because of their contribution to poverty reduction but because experiences have learned that without, for instance, a greater involvement of the target group in the projects, these projects are very likely to be unsustainable. However, software elements such as community participation, hygiene education, and institutional change are adopted by, for instance, the Dutch funded projects in Uttar Pradesh not as a means to contribute to rural poverty reduction, but to achieve the physical targets of the projects.

Concluding it can be stated that the projects do not show a clear conceptualisation of poverty and thus not of poverty reduction. The projects are mainly grouped under poverty reduction because they aim to provide one of the amenities to the rural population that is considered to be relevant for the physical well being of that rural population. The main aim is thus on increasing the health situation of the target group and it is in targeting we can see that these projects thereby pay (some) attention to the position of the poor and as such to the equity issue.

Targeting

As with basically all drinking water projects implemented by the Indian state water authorities (which up to now have been mainly focused on the problem village concept), the four projects under discussion here have entire villages as their immediate target, thus including the total population of these villages. In this regard it is thus important to pay specific attention to the equity question (i.e., are all sections of the population able to benefit from the facilities constructed under the project). All four projects state that specific attention has to be paid to women as well as poor (the latter being described, for instance, as low-income households, Scheduled Castes and/or Scheduled Tribes). This specific attention does not only hold with regard to installation of drinking water facilities (i.e., making sure that these poorer groups will be able to use the facilities constructed) but also to the non-physical components taken up in the project. Whether or not this also works out in practice remains to be seen in the case of the Dutch RWS/S project in Karnataka as the implementation of this project still has to gain momentum. In the other three projects, it can be observed that despite the specific attention mentioned in project documents, all have to a large extent failed to target a substantial part of their activities at the poor. This is mainly because the projects have adopted a traditional coverage approach in which participation of the target group, and particularly of the poor, overall has been inadequate.

Field observations in Uttar Pradesh and Karnataka (with the exception of the Dutch project in Karnataka where implementation of drinking water facilities is yet to gain momentum) show that the distribution of drinking water facilities is biased in favour of the better-off sections of the population. This may be due to the location advantage (e.g., better infrastructure facilities) and, more importantly, to proximity of power. The proximity of power of the better-off sections, generally, is due to their representation at the village meetings and the gram pradhans (= village head) generally being elected from among themselves or through their support. With regard to the non-physical or social field it can be stated that the projects were not clear about the special attention to be paid to the rural poor. It is noteworthy that the IRS&WSP, despite the efforts to integrate the community participation part right from the inception of the project, did not succeed to target the rural poor much better than the SP-VI project in Uttar Pradesh.

Major problems are encountered in the projects with regard to site-selection as well as with regard to the implementation of the social components. Partly this is due to the size of the projects covering hundreds of villages which leads to selection of villages by the implementing agency. Partly this is also due to the fact that Gram Panchayats (= village councils), which are supposed to play an important role in the execution of the SP-projects, in general leave the implementation to the established water users committees (called Jal Samitis) due to inadequate institutional structures and finances. These water users committees in turn are often dominated by those villagers who can raise the money to make the use of hand-pumps more hygienic and socially acceptable. There are clear signs that the implementation of social components is related to the financial contributions made, thereby limiting the influence of the poor.

Gender

In a recent evaluation report on the Indo-Swedish development co-operation programme it is remarked that 'the promises and deficiencies in water supply and sanitation policies and programmes affect women vitally. Women are at the centre of all water related household activities and it is they who bear the entire burden of drudgery and physical hardship involved in fetching water from distant and uncertain sources when their local hand pumps or pipe water supply systems break down'. In all projects this crucial role of women in drinking water is recognised. This leads to a call for specific attention to women, which is seen, among other things, in the training of women as caretakers and the involvement of women in water committees. Although some positive experiences have been gained from the projects (notably also SP-VI), these experiences at the same time have been piece-meal and relatively limited in size considering the sheer vastness of the projects.

In general, the projects (despite increasing stress on gender objectives) are yet to integrate a gender approach with regard to decision-making capacity and equality. The projects have instead concentrated on the accessibility of drinking water and sanitation facilities. Partly this seems to be due to a male urban bias with the implementing technical organisations that did not consider the need to relate the provision of rural drinking water and sanitation facilities with the effort of involving poor rural women in the process of decision-making. Also the fact that relatively small budgetary allocations within the projects for toilets and sanitation facilities point out that the projects are less oriented to the special needs of rural women. Finally, doubts have to be raised with regard to the involvement of women in the Jal Samitis and water users committees. Although women are involved it seems that their contribution to decision-making is limited, there is still a large dependence on the male members to seek, for instance, the intervention of block level mechanics, and the hand-pump care-taking by women might just as well be regarded as an additional responsibility upon the women.

Participation

As mentioned already above, participation of the target group, and particularly of the poor sections, has been inadequate as a result of the approach followed in which coverage determines the installation of the water supply facilities to a great extent. This is partly due to the fact that the water authorities in Uttar Pradesh and Karnataka, responsible for the construction part, are and principally remain technical oriented organisations. Involvement of the target group in the selection of sites, considered to be an important part in the process of creating a feeling of ownership and increasing usage, has been part of the SP-VI project but only for those hand-pumps that were left after the start of PSU's involvement. This makes SP-VIII the first Dutch project in the sector in Uttar Pradesh in which community participation and hygiene education have been introduced from the very start.

In the case of the Dutch project in Karnataka, participation of the local population particularly holds for the environmental sanitation component that is to be implemented by the village communities themselves with technical guidance, supply of locally not available material and payment for skilled labour by the Zila Panchayats. In the water supply component local people play a less clear role as the water works are executed by local contractors and supervised by local consultants under the overall control of the Zila Panchayats. Community organisation forms an important part of the project and is linked to hygiene promotion (e.g., through cultural groups). Village Committees have been formed in a large number of villages in the first batches. In general, local ownership is considered important in light of the need for proper operation and maintenance. Local, however, is not so much conceived as direct ownership by individual people but as ownership by the local elected bodies (i.e., Gram Panchayats) as they are regarded as being the proper entity to look after O&M. Considering the substantial lack of involvement of the poor in these Gram Panchayats it is not to be expected that this type of local ownership will automatically benefit the poor and thus contribute to poverty reduction.

It is clear from all projects that the target groups were not at all involved in need assessment, planning or the choice of technology. The technical approach adopted (making villagers mainly spectators), the urgency of providing drinking water and sanitation facilities, government rules with regard to the number of hand-pumps and standposts per specific number of people, the choice for deep hand-pumps and the consequent neglecting of existing shallow pumps, open wells, and private wells all have contributed their share to the lack of participation in the initial phases of the projects. Although the extent of participation is different with regard to implementation and operation and maintenance, the involvement of the target group here is at best partial. There is, however, a marked difference to better participation with newer projects such as the SP-VIII project in Uttar Pradesh.

With regard to operation and maintenance, it is important to point at the fact that the Jal Samitis (consisting of a maximum of five members) in SP-VI are sometimes treated more as fund collecting agencies than as a means for community participation. The generation of funds from the community, and particularly from the poor, remains poor, however. The same can basically be seen in the SP-VIII project despite the fact that the voluntary contribution to the installation, operation and maintenance of the hand-pumps is in fact a local tax and thus has to be paid every year. Within the IRS&WSP project it was observed that minor operation and maintenance depended on the contribution of individuals and that major operation and maintenance was left to the grants of the government.

Impact

The Dutch Karnataka project is, despite the official start in 1993, still in a much too early phase to say anything conclusive about the impact of the project. At the end of 1996, the water supply component of the project was basically still in a preparatory phase in the sense that designs and estimates for one of the four first packages of villages were under preparation while for the three others, tenders had been launched and were under evaluation. Slow progress in this field seems to be mainly due to the Government of Karnataka (GoK) which is unwilling to fulfil some of the central commitments made. These include the posting of staff and the delegation of authority to them and a further decentralisation and, eventually, privatisation such that power for implementation will be handed over to District Project Units. According to the erstwhile team leader of the PSU in Karnataka, the GoK has actually on several occasions complicated and delayed work unnecessarily by, among other things, insisting on bureaucratic procedures and for long insisting on the incorporation of existing facilities in the new schemes while knowing that these facilities do not even meet its own standards (PSU 1996: Annex 3).

Concerning the environmental sanitation component progress is more obvious although less than planned mainly due to such issues as delayed supply of materials and payments, and lack of skilled labour. At the end of 1996, a total of 10 aganwadi buildings and 225 household latrines (in 23 villages) were completed, while another 26 buildings and 350 latrines were under construction at that time. Besides, a few villages had started works on soakpits, drainage and lane paving. The latter already indicates that community participation and health and hygiene education were simultaneously undertaken. It should, however, be mentioned that the aganwadi buildings are mainly catering to the needs of the better-off sections of the population and that, considering the observed common practice of bathing and washing at the hand-pumps and water logging due to inadequate construction and cleaning of drainages, the integration of drinking water supply with environmental sanitation has not been achieved.

With regard to the other projects it is necessary to make a distinction between different elements when judging their impact. In the field of the *provision of physical components* it can be stated that SP-VIII is presently still under implementation and the two other projects (SP-VI and the Danish IRS&WS project) have made impressive progress although these projects are still to achieve full coverage. At the same time, the creation of sanitation facilities is less impressive in both projects. With regard to the *distribution of physical components* (showing the effectiveness of projects in meeting the needs of various segments of the hamlets/villages) it can be remarked that the SP-VI and IRS&WSP-projects are biased in favour of the better-off sections. In SP-VI, for instance, the disadvantaged make out some 57% of the total population, whereas the distribution of physical components remained at some 37% only.

The *utilisation of the physical components* reflects the demand and usefulness of drinking water and sanitation facilities provided by the projects. IRS&WSP has been more successful in influencing the use of traditional drinking water facilities, which are shown in all projects to meet the need for drinking water to a large extent. Often the new installations are used for exactly those activities (e.g. bathing, washing) for which they are not meant. This also shows that the projects have major difficulties in reaching the population through their awareness programmes. Certainly, the often low use of created facilities is also due to the functioning of the facilities. The *reliability of the physical components* can certainly be improved, although drinking water facilities are generally functioning better than sanitation facilities. In the field of training of caretakers, the SP-VI has made considerable achievements although less than anticipated. According to a government official (Interview) earlier involved in the Dutch financed drinking water projects in Uttar Pradesh, the PSU (funded by the Dutch for the implementation of software activities) could have done much more considering their staff and the funding available.

With regard to the software-components the following can be remarked. In the field of *health and hygiene* care (mainly through health and hygiene education of the target group) a lot still has to be done despite the fact that this component has been part and parcel of the projects (except for SP-VI) right from the start. Education in such fields as, for instance, handling and storage of water has been restricted to relatively small parts of the target area. The same can basically be observed with regard to *environment and sanitation care,* which is related to the changes in attitude of people towards better environment and sanitation conditions.

Sustainability

Sustainability in the case of drinking water and sanitation is mainly a question of whether the constructed facilities can be maintained. In all projects, (operation &) maintenance is supposed to be dealt with mainly by the users themselves. For this, some projects have set up local bodies, so-called water committees while others regard the Gram Panchayat as the local body. The water committees eventually are subject to the local elected Gram Panchayats. Sustainability then depends largely on the possibilities of these Gram Panchayats to raise sufficient funds for maintenance and on the availability of trained people to do the job. Training of caretakers is an explicit part of some of the projects and has to be regarded as essential. Field observations revealed that caretakers are not available among all villages.

Raising local funds is a more recent phenomenon. In parts of the SP-VIII project, specific activities have been initiated to raise local funds by introducing a user-fee that is collected by the Gram Panchayat and intended to be used for preventive and break-down maintenance of the hand-pump. Until such local systems are in place in all projects, dependence for maintenance rests largely by the state water authorities. Considering the general lack of funds for O&M at the state-level this means that the sustainability of the projects can be seriously questioned.

With regard to raising user-fees as a means of creating the possibilities for local maintenance of the water facilities it is important to look at the possibilities for involvement of the poor in this. Are they capable of providing such contributions and if they are not, what does that mean for the maintenance of the water supply facilities in their part of the village? In general, the projects under discussion pay insufficient attention to this issue. Specific activities geared at increasing the probability that the poor in the village can and will participate in the user-fees system (e.g., income generating activities) are not undertaken.

Important in sustainability is also the availability of alternative drinking water sources in the villages. As the Netherlands Embassy (RNE) noted, 'the Netherlands have reached at least that in many villages these alternative sources are not used anymore' (interview RNE). This is not regarded as an overall positive development as it leads to acute problems when the new facilities break down. In the choice of technology in the projects no attention has been paid to the existing drinking water situation in the villages (i.e., existing open wells, hand-pumps, etc.), except in the IRS&WSP project. Field observations, however, reveal that the traditional sources of drinking water and sanitation play a significant role. The inhabitants of the villages in SP-VI and SP-VIII, who have shallow hand-pumps or living close to such facilities, use these mainly for cooking and drinking while the water from the deep hand-pumps installed under the projects are used for bathing, washing and animals. In the Danish project in Karnataka, the villagers generally use the water from the hand-pumps and mini piped water schemes for all purposes including drinking and cooking. The general abundance of alternative sources in UP and the use made of these unsafe sources for drinking purposes indicate that inadequate demand has been generated through health education activities. This also seems to be the main reason for the fact that institutional latrines (i.e., at schools) are hardly used and in many cases damaged.

Replicability and scaling up

Probably the major drawback of the projects when looking at the possibilities for replicability and scaling up is funding. Those project activities that have to be considered essential in creating a better local environment for maintenance are basically financed by donor funds. The question seems justified whether the Indian and state governments would be willing to take over these activities. Without sufficient time and funds made available for community participation and health education activities it is to be expected that the possibilities for replication are severely limited.

Monitoring and evaluation

Monitoring and evaluation is in-built in all the projects. However, the focus is clearly on the physical and financial components and not on the impact on rural poverty reduction. Nor is there much stress on monitoring and evaluating the process of social components particularly with regard to the participation of the rural poor in decision-making. As such, the projects still have to develop an appropriate system of 'participatory impact assessment'.

Conclusions and suggestions

- The projects are all conceived as integrated projects in which next to the provision of safe drinking water facilities attention is paid to such issues as health education, environmental sanitation and community participation. In practice this integration is not achieved and certainly not on a scale large enough to cover the entire project areas.
- The projects are mainly grouped under poverty reduction because they aim to provide one of the amenities to the rural population which is considered to be relevant for the physical well being of that rural population. The main aim is thus on improving the health situation of the target group and it is in targeting we can see that these projects thereby pay (some) attention to the position of the poor and as such to the equity issue.
- In general, the projects do not get much further than the statement that special attention should be paid to, what are normally conceived, poorer sections: scheduled castes, scheduled tribes and women.
- As with basically all drinking water projects implemented by the Indian state water authorities (which up to now have been mainly focused on the problem village concept), the four

projects under discussion here have entire villages as their immediate target, thus including the total population of these villages. In this regard it is important to pay specific attention to the equity question (i,e. are all sections of the population able to benefit from the facilities constructed under the project).

— The traditional coverage approach adopted by all projects led to the failure to target a substantial part of the project's activities at the poor.

— Local ownership is considered important in light of the need for proper operation and maintenance. Local, however, is not so much conceived as direct ownership by individual people but as ownership by the local elected bodies (i.e. Gram Panchayats) as they are regarded as being the proper entity to look after O&M. Considering the substantial lack of involvement of the poor in these Gram Panchayats it is not to be expected that this type of local ownership will automatically benefit the poor and thus contribute to poverty reduction.

— Raising user-fees as a means of creating the possibilities for local maintenance of the water facilities is a relatively new issue in drinking water supply in India and is reflected in recent projects. In this regard, it is important to look at the possibilities for involvement of the poor in this. Are they capable of providing such contributions and if they are not, what does that mean for the maintenance of the water supply facilities in their part of the village? In general, the projects under discussion pay insufficient attention to this issue. Specific activities geared at increasing the probability that the poor in the village can and will participate in the user-fees system (e.g. income generating activities) are not undertaken.

— Probably the major drawback of the projects when looking at the possibilities for replicability and scaling up is funding. Those project activities that have to be considered essential in creating a better local environment for maintenance are basically financed by donor funds. The question seems justified whether the Indian and state governments would be willing to take over these activities. Without sufficient time and funds made available for community participation and health education activities it is to be expected that the possibilities for replication are severely limited.

13

HEALTH AND FAMILY WELFARE PROJECTS

Introduction

The health sector has often been seen as having only a marginal role in promoting poverty reduction. Indian government officials, and some donors, continue to see poverty in income terms and thus see employment generation as lying at the heart of poverty reduction. Nonetheless, in the past decade, as a multi-dimensional conceptualisation of poverty has taken root so the relevance for poverty reduction of efforts to improve access to and the quality of health services has become clearer. Many of India's poor lack access to decent health care, and this is one element of their powerlessness and social exclusion. Health, like education, is at the core of basic capabilities: without health, participation in the economic and social world is critically constrained. Improving access to health and providing basic health knowledge increases family security, another component of well-being. A single episode of illness requiring hospitalisation can cost 3-6 months earnings, and expenditure by the poor on health services is the largest source of indebtedness (Krishnan 1996; NSS Round Survey). At a macro level, improved health status has been shown to contribute to increased productivity, benefiting economic growth with potential longer-term 'knock-on' effects on poverty reduction.

Considerable achievements in expanding the public health system in India have been realised in the 50 years since Independence. Life expectancy has risen from 50 in 1960 to 61 in 1991, and under-five mortality has fallen from 106 to 79. However, there are serious problems with access, quality and efficiency, and key health indicators remain low compared to other Asian countries that started with a comparable resource base, such as Sri Lanka and China. In particular, women are poorly serviced, with for example very high levels of maternal mortality, which at about 450 per 100,000 account for almost a quarter of world maternal deaths. Total fertility remains very high at 3.7%, though declining, and at least 20% of fertility is unwanted. There are very large disparities in the level of human development between states, with the poor having least access to basic health services in Bihar, Rajasthan, Madhya Pradesh, Uttar Pradesh and Orissa.

The health sector has not traditionally been a major beneficiary of donor support, and donor assistance accounts for less than 1% of national health expenditure. The World Bank is the major source, with Denmark, Germany, Sweden, UK, USA, UNICEF, WFP, WHO, as well as a few international NGOs, also contributing significantly. The two major channels for donor funding have been the Area Development Project (ADP) and Integrated Child Development Scheme (ICDS), examples of which are examined in detail below. ADPs have, since the mid-1970s sought to strengthen health and family welfare services by promoting their integration, providing buildings, improving training, and strengthening Information, Education and Communication (IEC) strategies and monitoring mechanisms. The Integrated Child Development Scheme encompasses health, nutrition and education. It was put to trial in 1976, and since has received national priority with the aim of covering 60% of those rural villages and urban slums where the proportion of scheduled castes is higher than 30%.

The ADP model now appears badly outdated, since it lacks an emphasis on systems, resources and institutions. In the last couple of years many within government and the donor community have instead sought to promote a sector-based approach, recognising that the entire system, at centre and state level, has fundamental weaknesses, particularly a lack of capacity to plan strategically. These weaknesses have undermined the input-based approaches of the ADPs and, to some extent, the ICDS projects, as is apparent from the analysis below.

Selected projects

Three projects have been included in this study. For a full account see Banerjee (1997). The three projects are the following:

1. The Area Development Project (ADP) in Orissa funded by DFID/ODA since 1979. The main goal has been to expand the system of primary health care downwards to the village level

by constructing health sub-centres. Phase 1 (1979-87) covered five districts and concentrated on providing physical infrastructure (mainly sub-centres), as well as some training inputs. Phase 2 (1989-97), covering five new districts, had a greater stress on health and welfare education and on training. A third phase, if approved, will concentrate on policy and institutional reform at the state-level.

2. The Area Development Project (ADP) funded by Danida in two Districts of Tamil Nadu. Phase 1 (1991-89) concentrated on health infrastructure, but emphasized maternal and child health. Phase 2 (1989-95) continued these priorities, but also supported the development of a health information system and IEC. Phase 3 (1995-98) expands the project to three new districts and seeks to provide statewise support to human resource development, IEC and AIDS programmes.
3. The Sida-supported Integrated Child Development Services Scheme (ICDS) in Tamil Nadu. This emphasized innovative approaches to implementing the nutrition and pre-school components of ICDS in three districts. The project is far smaller than the two ADPs in financial terms. The regular ICDS elements are funded by the centre and state governments.

Statewise context

The ADP/ODA project in Orissa operated in a fundamentally less favourable environment than the ADP/Danida or ICDS/Sida projects in Tamil Nadu. Firstly, Orissa has markedly worse social indicators, with over 45% of its population estimated to be below the poverty line, compared with less than 40% for Tamil Nadu. Life expectancy at birth stood at 55 for Orissa in 1990-92, as against 62 for Tamil Nadu. All of Tamil Nadu's main health status indicators are better than the country average, while for Orissa it is the reverse. Orissa also has the largest tribal population in India, a group which is disproportionately poor and is perceived as traditionally being resistant to development. Over 80% of Orissa's population still lives in rural areas, where poverty tends to be more entrenched, compared to two-thirds for Tamil Nadu, and, finally, Tamil Nadu has enjoyed higher rates of growth in the agricultural and industrial sectors.

Political and institutional factors play a large part in explaining these differences, further underlining the contrast between the two states. Tamil Nadu has had a succession of governments with a strong political commitment to improving the state's socio-economic situation, which is reflected in its establishment of social welfare programmes dating back to 1962, and particularly since the early 1980s. These include a raft of pension provisions for landless labourers, destitute women, and the disabled, and reflect Tamil Nadu's success in attracting central government and donor assistance, and perhaps the fact that they were well-implemented, in contrast to many other states.

Tamil Nadu has, to some extent, forged policies according to local need within the Indian constitutional framework, and has been less dependent on the centre. Thus it drew up its own health policy in 1993, and was the first state to prepare in 1995 a comprehensive state plan of action for children and nutrition. Orissa, on the other hand, has no specific health or education policies of its own, instead adopting wholesale those of the centre. This dependency on central government for policy direction has resulted in the state's currently very limited capacity to tackle health sector issues strategically. The general perception is that the administration in Tamil Nadu has been more flexible and receptive to innovations, and donor-assisted experiments have sometimes later been adopted across the whole state, as in the ICDS-Sida project. It should be noted that steps have been taken by Orissa's current Health Secretary to strengthen policy capacity, backed by the ODA.

These differences should not be overstated, however. The weaknesses of the government structure in the health sector in each state are differentiated more by degree than by nature. Both may be characterised as rigidly hierarchical, mechanistic rather than strategic, target oriented, and in both opportunities for junior staff to take initiatives are stifled. If Tamil Nadu's health system has been effective in certain respects, such as achieving high immunisation rates, there remains enormous potential to increase the access and quality of service delivered to the weaker sections of society in particular. The Danida and Sida projects, like that of the ODA in Orissa, also struggled to institute the necessary moves towards more decentralised planning and improved relations with health users through more effective community participation.

Conceptualisation of poverty and targeting of the poor

The project documentation in all three cases does not spell out the potential linkages between project activities and poverty reduction. This is a shortcoming, since had a concerted effort been made to assess how activities might relate to the various dimensions of poverty, there might have been scope to alter project design or implementation in a way which strengthened those linkages. The projects concentrated on improving the access, quality and utilisation of health and family welfare (HFW) services. Neither the Sida nor the Danida project documents define target groups very explicitly, including the most recent ICDS/Sida project proposal. The ODA phase 2 document states that the main intended beneficiaries are the poor, especially in tribal areas. It demonstrates a good understanding of the demand-side as well as supply-side aspects which contribute to the low levels of utilisation of health services among the most disadvantaged groups. Thus, it lays stress on better communication of health information, including orally in tribal languages, and better training and mobility of health workers. At a more macro level, the ADP/ODA project is better targeted at the poor, given Orissa's status as one of India's poorest states, whereas Tamil Nadu stands as one of the five states with the best health and other socio-economic profiles. Some project staff feel that while three of the five states in which the ADP/ODA project operated in Phase 2 were particularly underdeveloped, much more could have been done to concentrate its efforts in the poorest parts of Orissa. The desire to have a project success may have conflicted with the objective of reaching the poorest.

Gender

Danida's interest in taking account of the gender dimensions of poverty is perhaps reflected in its decision to analyse 'Women in Development' in the ADP project in a separate report. This reveals, however, that gender analysis was not integrated into the design or implementation, and that little information is available on the extent to which the poorest women have benefited in terms of status, workload, and income earning capabilities. Nonetheless, the project has had an implicit rather than explicit emphasis on women's development since the principal beneficiaries have been women, as are the main service providers, whose status, income earning capacities and living conditions were improved by the project's activities. To some extent, the same goes for the ADP/ODA project, though in this case gender was specifically taken into account in the project documents, alongside caste, class and ethnicity. The ICDS/Sida project did not take specific account of the disadvantaged position of women, except in its inclusion of an 'adolescent girls scheme'. This sought to support and provide training to the more marginalised girls, often drop-outs from school. Field research and Sida's own documentation suggests that this had brought only marginal benefits, with the training not being sufficiently oriented towards improving income-earning potential.

Participation

The poor and marginalised, including women and scheduled castes and tribes, suffer a social, cultural and physical isolation which limits their access to health care. Barriers to access are reinforced by their lack of knowledge of available services, language differences, poor access to cash, restricted freedom of travel, and gender or caste intolerance. This analysis underscores the priority that one would expect to be accorded to knowledge dissemination and community participation activities in all three projects. In fact, with a few qualifications, measures designed to elicit the involvement of local people were either missing, ill-thought out or poorly implemented. Despite considerable rhetoric, participation was accorded a low priority at each phase of all three projects, though less so in the ICDS/Sida project. The consequences of this failure have been many and serious, including continuing low levels of utilisation, lack of ownership and absence of maintenance.

There was little or no participation of the poor in the identification and design phases of the project cycle, which instead were the preserve of the donor, and to some extent, the central and state government authorities. It is interesting to speculate whether the Danida- and ODA-assisted ADP projects would have accorded such a large share of resources to building health sub-centres had the views of the target beneficiaries been sought. Evaluations of both projects point out that the provision of buildings alone did not result in any significant increase in the quality of health services or the use made of them. They echo each other in concluding that since the health workers spent such a large proportion of their time outside of the centres in people's homes, then it was questionable whether concentrating on buildings was an effective use of funds. Evaluations of the two projects also indicate that the value of providing sub-centres was further undermined in very many cases by poor site selection. Often centres were constructed at some distance from the villages, in unhygienic surroundings or by burial grounds, all of which limited access or attractiveness of the service to potential users and to the health workers alike. The isolation of some centres increased the insecurity of the health workers, who are by and large young women and often not from the locality. In the case of the ADP/ODA project, rather than use often ill-suited government land, the project could have sought the participation of the community to see whether they would themselves offer land for the sub-centre. This appears to have been rejected due to government reluctance and because consultation would entail delays and affect building targets. Some observers suggested that the design of the ODA-funded sub-centre buildings was itself flawed, since the use of flat roofs in Phase 1 has resulted in most buildings leaking, and add that community consultation would have resulted in a smaller building design which could have been constructed and maintained at lower cost.

The top-down approach of the government/donor partnership resulted in very serious problems of maintenance, or indeed the almost total absence of maintenance in the ADP cases. Danida's dissatisfaction with levels of maintenance by the Public Works Department in Tamil Nadu led them in Phase 2 to make maintenance the responsibility of independent building agencies backed by the participation of the community. A decentralised approach to maintenance could profitably have been sought by the ODA in negotiations with the Government of Orissa. Instead of making maintenance the responsibility of the Rural Development Department, some money could have been allocated to block level officials or primary health centres, for example, who would themselves have been made responsible for petty maintenance. Phase 2 of the ADP/Danida project brought some success by creating Village Health Councils to involve the community in construction. Quality of construction was generally high, with a cost-saving of about one-third and higher levels of utilisation. However, community participation in construction was not capitalised upon, and did not become an entry point for wider community involvement. The result was that the Village Health Councils rapidly became defunct even before completion of construction. Community participation usually degenerated into a means of meeting construction targets, and thus a contribution in terms of cash and labour rather than active involvement in decision-making.

In terms of buildings site selection, construction and maintenance, the ICDS-Sida project would not appear to be very different from the ADP projects. The latest project proposal reveals no evidence that site selection and construction will involve the local community in any significant way. However, the Sida-assisted ICDS programme did include a range of activities intended to mobilise communities in support of the ICDS objectives, such as mass campaigns, motivation days, and ICDS centre days. The aim has been to popularise the activities of the ICDS centres in the villages in which they operate, and make them the focal point of various community activities. In this it has been reasonably successful in some areas. This explains why the Sida-assisted ICDS centres initially experienced low levels of take-up, when community involvement in identification and construction was very limited, but later utilisation increased significantly following awareness activities and as the realisation by poor households that their children were being well looked after, fed and taught in the centres. In 1994-95, an attempt was made in the Sida-assisted districts to develop a more participatory planning system. However, after initial training of district officers there was little further support and no follow-up training, and the impact has been correspondingly small, with all plans still formulated at the state level.

Both ADP projects stressed that participatory Information, Education and Communication (IEC) activities were a vital component of any strategy to increase utilisation levels. It is very curious, therefore, that it was not until 14 years into the ADP/ODA project that a social development officer was appointed, who remained in post only two years. At the time of her appointment, the project had already begun to support some women's groups, which had an IEC mandate, but without first instituting a system of training or monitoring. No system of reward or sanctions was developed to ensure that medical officials actively supported the women's groups. Senior officials played lip service to community participation, but provided little guidance, and more than half of key posts (e.g. District Mass Education Information Officers) remained vacant. The social development officer helped set up 220 women's groups in one district, but as there were no adequate arrangements to ensure that the government took over responsibility for these project-supported groups, they collapsed soon after she left the project.

A similar picture of neglect of IEC activities emerges in the ADP/Danida project. Despite criticism in Danida's 1986 evaluation, the 1996 evaluation again concluded that 'at all levels IEC activities were low on the priority list' and had not in practice been accorded the emphasis spelt out in the project documentation. There have been no attempts to involve local youth to form their own drama troupes or use traditional media. There was little evidence that IEC materials produced were used by the health workers, since they lacked the skill and confidence and time to carry out mass education activities. As in the ODA case, support from higher level health workers, such as the block extension educators, was lacking. This is partly, again echoing the situation in Orissa, because of lack of fuel for travel, but also because staff training has not focused on the communication and planning skills necessary for effective community participation.

Overall, staff training in the ADP/Danida case has been quite successful. The District Training Teams set up in Phase 1 were, in Phase

2, integrated into a higher level institutional framework, the Health Manpower Development Institutes. Creation of these institutes and the associated physical infrastructure was preceded by a specialist assessment of their future role in the context of health staff development for the whole state. The District Teams and the Institutes were a response to a situation where most health functionaries did not receive the management, programme implementation, monitoring and community mobilisation skills needed to delivery primary health care effectively. While there remains scope for improvements, including more effective training on community participation and greater focus on women's issues, an important strength of the ADP/Danida approach has been the development of an appropriate institutional framework for training delivery. Continued efforts are required to strengthen links between the Institutes and other training centres, but the prospects for their internalisation and sustainability are good.

This attention to providing training within a sustainable institutional context was sorely lacking in the ADP/ODA project. Phase 2 was intended to signal a move away from providing physical infrastructure towards training and IEC activities. In practice, it continued to be perceived as a 'buildings project', and training was implemented on a largely *ad hoc* basis through project staff. ODA's evaluation of its in-service training programme indicates that the state's delays in releasing funds resulted in overly intensive training sessions, and regular refresher training was not achieved. A state-level institution for training and communication activities was created with project support, but only in 1995, too late to feed into a strategic approach to training provision or to support the fledgling District Training Units. There is a widespread feeling that the cart came before the horse, that there were physical structures (District Training Unit offices) long before there was any strategy on how to operationalise them. Even before 1995, alternative institutions existed which could have provided an institutional framework, but instead District Training Units were established without a clear understanding of which part of the state bureaucracy would head the units, how they would be paid for, what the linkages would be with other institutions, and precisely what their role and function was. Some officials argued that, rather than bypass existing institutions, the ADP/ODA project would have done better to strengthen these institutions. Another commented, 'if you do training in a vacuum, it will vanish when the project ends'. The conclusion that institutional and strategic dimensions were lacking is hard to escape, for which the responsibility must be shared between the donor and government partners.

Sustainability and replicability

The prospects for sustaining benefits appear to be highest in the ICDS-Sida project and lowest in the ADP/ODA case. One factor underlying this is the relative success of the ICDS project in building links between different parts of the Tamil Nadu government machinery. The ICDS-Sida annual review team's finding that there were problems of collaboration between the health and social sector branches resulted in the appointment of a Joint Director (Health) within the ICDS Directorate (which is within the Social Sector branch). This opened the way for increased collaboration on all levels between health and social workers, including joint home visits by Health Visitors and Anganwadi Workers (ICDS). Regular meetings and activities now take place, which has helped to allay suspicions, increase effectiveness and improve the chances of sustaining project benefits.

Sida's focus on supporting innovative approaches also appears to have paid dividends, and there is evidence that a number of these innovations, such as low-cost teaching aids, cooking classes and kitchen gardens, are being replicated by non-Sida ICDS centres across the state. The prospects for sustainability are enhanced by the Government of Tamil Nadu's stated commitment to maintaining all aspects of ICDS which benefit the poor, despite budgetary pressures. Some aspects of the ICDS/Sida project are unlikely to be replicable, because its success partly lies in the double complement of staff at ICDS centres in Sida-assisted districts. Also, one Sida report questions whether a separate Sida-support wing should continue since its positive contribution may be outweighed by the tendency for it to undermine genuine participation by project staff in the planning process and reduce scope for replication.

The ADP/Danida project seeks to underpin the sustainability of the physical assets created in the very recent Phase 3 by vesting responsibility for construction and maintenance with the local panchayats, in partnership with the Government of Tamil Nadu and the local community. It remains to be seen how successful this will be, but the hope must be that by injecting greater decentralisation the current situation (where maintenance exists on paper only) will improve. The project document for the proposed ODA Phase 3 highlights the rapidly deteriorating state of the huge investments in health buildings made during Phases 1 and 2. Without the successful implementation of major heath sector reform measures, many of which are well-documented in the Phase 3 document, the prospects for sustaining benefits appear slight.

The sustainability and replicability of the Information, Education and Communication activities of the ADP projects appear highly questionable, partly due to the lack of priority which they received and, particularly in the ODA case, the inadequate institutional support for them. In both cases, the project-based approach resulted in a very high level of dependency on the personality of the Project Director, of which there were several over the life of the projects. This partly explains why specific and shorter-term activities, such as buildings construction, were more successful than those requiring long-term sustained effort, such as maintenance, IEC and community mobilisation. The prospects for continuing benefits from the training components are good in the ADP/ Danida project, and will depend on efforts to increase internalisation during Phase 3.

Impact on the poor

Any attempt to link donor-supported interventions with changes in health indicators is highly problematic due to the complex range of factors which affect health status, many of which are not directly linked to project activities. Impact is gradual and long-term. Various approaches might have been tried, and given the size and duration on the Danida and ODA investments, a baseline survey and use of control areas should have been considered. Some indication of impact on the may be surmised indirectly by assessing the quality and effectiveness of the delivery of project inputs.

ODA has made the most serious efforts to assess impact on the poor target groups, and has been rigorous in reviewing and evaluating Phase 2 in particular. Various studies were commissioned to examine the effectiveness of individual project components, such as women's groups and in-service training, as well as evaluations and an impact study. The latter concluded that at the end of Phase 2, 'it is difficult to discern any project impact at all in terms of improved health service efficiency or quality of care.' A separate ODA study compared districts where ODA had supported women's groups with non-benefiting areas. It concluded that the mobilisation activities resulted in some improvement in levels of utilisation, but was severely handicapped by its top-down implementation, the lack of training to group members in social mobilisation as a participatory process, and the absence of monitoring at either the district or project head office level. Buildings were the most significant output of the ADP/ODA project, but their impact on quality of service and utilisation levels appears small. Overall, the ability of the ADP/ODA project to benefit the poor must be judged to have been minimal.

Far less evidence is available to assess the impact of the Danida- or Sida-supported interventions. Danida's own evaluation (1994) indicates that the feedback and monitoring system has been very weak and has yielded little information on impact. However, its two major evaluations stand in contrast with Sida's rather slim desk study and annual reviews. In neither project was there well-developed concept of targeting the benefits to the poorest, and though the ICDS/Sida project did seek to reach the disabled and marginalised adolescent girls, it met with very limited success. In the health context, reaching the poor means making quality care accessible and taking steps to increase demand for such services. The ADP/Danida project achieved some positive results by increasing participation in construction, contributing to higher levels of awareness and utilisation, but overall its efforts to mobilise demand were unsuccessful.

There is some evidence that the health status of mothers and children has improved and malnutrition fallen where Sida-assisted ICDS centres have been established. Field evidence suggests that ICDS centres are positively viewed by beneficiaries, the vast majority of whom are poor, and this has been reflected in increased levels of attendance. Some of the beneficial impact of the Sida-assisted project has been compromised by recurrent delays in releasing funds by the state government.

Conclusions and suggestions

— Where the policy and institutional environment is very unfavourable, a sector reform approach may be more effective. The three projects studied sought to bring benefits to those marginalised by the health system without considering state-level reform, and thus project impact was moderated through the existing financial, managerial and institutional mechanisms. This proved to be a very serious handicap, particularly to the ADP/ODA project.

— The sector reform approach does also present risks, namely that working on upstream issues may lead to a loss of focus on the service users – the poor.

— Donors bring more than just money: involvement in Orissa was felt to have assisted in introducing new ideas. A more constructive partnership may be developing in the health sector: one senior official in the Ministry of Health explained that where once she had felt like a professional beggar, now she sees donor assistance as an enabling relationship.

— Many health sector officials at central and state-level welcomed strong conditionality by donors as a means for increasing the likelihood that extra (donor) resources are truly additional. However, rigid conditionality can create rather than solve problems. One major European donor's insistence on complete additionality in a major sector reform programme was seen as threatening the Ministry of Finance sanction for an already attractive package.

— The low utilisation rates in the ADP projects in particular suggest they are not providing what people want. A major component of this has been an insufficient emphasis on simple curative services as well as preventive care. The poor, like anyone else, want services which are appropriate and of sufficient quality. The ADP projects have given too much weight to improving physical accessibility of health services and not enough to quality and appropriateness.

— The gap between design and implementation is large. Community mobilisation received low priority in practice and was largely unsuccessful.

— Knowledge on effective Information, Education and Communication (IEC) strategies is not lacking – but donor and government prioritisation of IEC is. IEC requires monitoring and evaluation, should be given priority at the project planning stage and should involve beneficiaries.

— Failure to invest time in seeking the views of beneficiaries resulted in ill-sited health facilities, limiting access and attractiveness to users and health workers alike, and thus reducing impact on the poor and undermining sustainability.

— Greater community participation delivered higher levels of utilisation. These benefits would be greater if participation went beyond construction, and increased the poor's say in decision-making. This would also help remedy appalling maintenance problems.

— Genuine commitment and ownership by the state government is essential for effective sustainability and replicability. The government-donor partnership must seek to internalise project innovations as early as possible.

14

PRIMARY EDUCATION PROJECTS AND PROGRAMMES

Introduction

Literacy and education have both a direct role and an instrumental role in contributing to human development and poverty reduction. Illiteracy and lack of education are identified by the poor themselves as important dimensions of their lack of well-being.[1] Current thinking on poverty recognizes that improved educational provision is associated with greater access to services, knowledge, and influence, and thus makes a direct contribution to reducing poverty in its multi-dimensional sense. In addition, there is extensive empirical evidence to show that investments in education, particularly primary education, act as an engine of growth. The marginal rates of return to primary education are higher than to other levels of education, particularly when focused on poorer groups and females. Besides contributing to higher rates of growth of GDP, education expands human capabilities and enlarges people's choices. Improved education has been shown to increase farmers' productivity, lower fertility rates (delaying marriage, empowering women, improving knowledge and access to family planning methods, etc), and to have a positive impact on indicators of infant mortality, life expectancy at birth and disease (Ahmed 1995 and Suratwala 1992, in Varghese 1997: 5). In addition, investing in children brings benefits beyond the individual. To the extent that education improves the employment status and income levels of the individuals that are educated, it tends to have a positive impact on the well-being of elderly family members who are cared for by those children when they grow up.

At the time of independence the vast majority of India's population was illiterate. The 1951 census indicated an overall literacy rate of 16%, with female literacy of only 7%. Access to education for all between the ages of 6 and 14 was written into the constitution, and a major effort was made to expand provision in the deprived regions. Expenditure as a percentage of GNP on education as a whole increased from 1.2% in 1951 to 3.7% in 1991, and for primary education 0.5% and 1.7% respectively. Particularly significant is the shift towards primary education since 1970s, which is reflected in increases in new investment (plan) expenditure on primary education as a share of total investment expenditure on education. The increase from 28% at the end of the 1960s to 47% presently means that nearly half of all new investments in education are at the primary level.

The result has been that great strides have been made since Independence. School enrolment leapt from 19 million in 1951 to nearly 110 million in 1993-94, and census information for 1991 indicates a literacy rate of 52% compared with 16% 40 years earlier. Currently, over 94% of rural areas (above a certain size) are provided with a primary school within a walking distance of 1km. Yet huge numbers of children remain marginalised by the system, usually because they live in the most deprived or isolated areas. In addition, provision of school buildings does not necessarily mean provision of education. Particularly in rural areas, there are very serious problems of teacher absenteeism or of very low quality teaching. Also, where schools are provided without first seeking to engage the local community to raise awareness of the benefits of education, or to make it relevant and appropriate (culturally and linguistically), then levels of attendance are low. There is a tremendous need to improve quality and access for India's poorest, as it is they who are currently the least-well served.

Donor enthusiasm for primary education, at least in concrete spending terms, is in fact a fairly recent phenomenon. Their priorities, until the late 1980s, did not coincide with the stated priorities of the Indian government, since with a few exceptions donor investment in the education sector in India was concentrated in secondary and tertiary levels. This probably reflects prevailing beliefs as to what kind of education contributes most to economic development, with agencies such as UNICEF, ODA, USAID and others placing emphasis on science education, while others, including the World Bank and Sida, viewed technical and vocational education as the crucial aids to industrialisation and growth. Sometimes, donor interest in funding education appears to have had more to do with the requirements of their direct investments in the productive and economic sectors of the economy than with the development of education *per se.* UNESCO was one of the few international agencies which from the very beginning consistently argued for more spending on primary education.

Whereas the value of focusing of primary education for growth and poverty reduction was emerging strongly from the literature as early as the 1960s, it was not until the 1980s and 1990s that this consensus was confirmed among the donor community. This convergence that the lower levels of education should be promoted as a first priority was symbolised by their coming together under the banner of 'Education for All by the year 2000' at the World Conference on Education in Jomtien in 1990. This brought the GoI and donor stated priorities closely into line.

The donors' approaches to education have differed from those of the government in another important way. The Government has usually operated in a 'programme mode', where decisions are taken in the context of national needs, with a view to implementation on an all-India basis to deliver long-term benefits. Donors, in contrast, have tended to have a 'project perspective', unfettered by national considerations, at least in the short run, and with the brief of delivering the maximum benefits, often using innovative approaches, to project beneficiaries. This is changing, however, and the past few years has seen many donors sign up to the national DPEP programme, which is discussed below. Not only does this reflect greater ownership on the part of the Indian government, but this more coordinated approach, integrated within the national development strategy, is likely to be more sustainable.

Below we will seek to assess the ways in which European Union donors reached the poor through education in three individual projects. But first it is necessary to place these interventions into the context of the overall contribution made by donors to the education sector in India, and specifically with respect to poverty reduction.

The first major externally-funded primary education project was the UK-supported Andhra Pradesh Primary Education Project, started in 1983. The second phase, running from 1989 until 1996, took a slightly more holistic approach by taking account of the way in which social environment influences the demand for education. The project made two important contributions which were incorporated into many district level projects implemented in later periods, namely the establishment of teacher centres for mutual academic support and the provision of materials for teachers to experiment with to develop teaching aids. Yet, since the interventions were classroom or teacher training based, the project largely benefited those who were already enrolled and not the vast numbers entirely excluded from the educational system. In essence the project retained its rather narrow pedagogical focus, and its impact on poverty reduction was largely indirect and incidental.

The Swedish-funded Shiksha Karmi Project, starting in 1987 in Rajasthan, although without a poverty reduction mandate as such, contained two features with positive implications for poverty reduction. Notably, it was focused on rural areas in general, and remote rural areas in particular, in an attempt to reach those previously ill-served or excluded from the government system. Secondly, the project specifically targeted women, again particularly in the rural areas, through women's groups and by ensuring their representation in Village Education Committees (VECs). The Dutch-assisted Mahila Samakhya Project, starting in 1989, also promoted women's empowerment, and acknowledged the centrality of education in this.

Targeting of the poor and of women was subsequently built into the Indian government's District Primary Education Programme (DPEP), which is considered in detail below. However, it is undoubtedly the Bihar Education Project (BEP), funded by UNICEF, Government of India and the Government of Bihar, which was particularly influential in making poverty considerations central to the design of the DPEP. The BEP introduced the idea of focusing at the district rather than state-level, which allowed the project to target the most educationally backward districts of Bihar. It had a strong focus on community mobilisation, achieved through public meetings, including women on the village education committees, women's groups, involving the community in schools construction, and a participatory approach to school mapping. Uniquely it sought to encourage educational planning at a district rather than state-level, so that plans would better reflect local specificities.

DPEP represents a radical development, in terms of the government-donor relationship, its sheer scale, and its careful focus on excluded groups. Since DPEP is a national programme rather than a state-specific project, it accounts for a huge share of the extra resources for primary education provided through external financing, about 70% for the 1992-97 period. Though the bulk of DPEP funding comes from the World Bank, through its Social Safety Net account, European donors such as the EC and the ODA are contributors, and see themselves as supporting capacity building as well as providing financial resources.

Selected projects

Of the three major primary education projects we looked at, two form part of the District Primary Education Programme (DPEP) – Madhya

Pradesh funded by the European Union and Andhra Pradesh funded by ODA. The third, Lok Jumbish in Rajasthan, is funded by Sida. All three are still in the process of implementation, which makes it difficult to draw firm conclusions about their respective impact on poverty reduction. Lok Jumbish has been implemented since 1992, and has a more limited scope and budget than the DPEP projects, with an allocation of Rs. 960m for the 1992-98 period. Madhya Pradesh DPEP has been implemented since 1995, with a budget of Rs. 6850m for 1995-2001, covering 19 of 45 districts in Phase 1. The ODA is funding DPEP within 5 of 23 districts in Andhra Pradesh, with a budget of Rs. 2400m for the 1996-2002 period, though it is likely that World Bank funding will extend DPEP coverage to many other districts.

Conceptualisation of poverty and targeting of the poor

Both the Lok Jumbish project document and the DPEP framework reveal an approach centred on improving both the access to and quality of educational provision. But there is no explicit reference to the contribution that each can make to reducing poverty, either in terms of bolstering rights or, in the longer run, by strengthening capabilities and improving livelihoods. This lack of emphasis on poverty reduction was confirmed in discussions at the state and local levels, in which project administrators did not see themselves as playing a role in poverty reduction as such. What is more surprising is that education specialists in two of the three donor agencies also did not see any immediate link between their funding of primary education interventions and poverty reduction. This probably reflects the weak poverty focus, poor quality or total absence of education strategy papers within all three agencies.

The picture, however, is much less gloomy than it might first appear. A distinction should be drawn between poverty reduction and reaching the poor. Although one would expect that project functionaries, often with social science backgrounds, could better appreciate (or give greater weight to) the link between objectives and impact on poverty reduction, they *are* keenly aware of the importance of reaching the poor. This concern is apparent from the emphasis on *targeting* the poor within both DPEP and Lok Jumbish. Both projects seek to give priority to the educationally backward areas, defined in terms of female literacy rates for DPEP and average literacy rates for Lok Jumbish. Given that illiteracy is one dimension of poverty, in terms of lack of knowledge, access to services, and social exclusion, this targeting of areas of high illiteracy represents a direct attack on poverty. Secondly, there is a high positive correlation between educational backwardness and economic backwardness. Since educationally backward regions have higher concentrations of poor people, these interventions are likely to reach the income poor and contribute to strengthening their livelihoods over the longer run. DPEP's use of female literacy as the criterion is sensible, since it always lags behind male literacy rates, often by a substantial degree, and focusing on female illiteracy therefore contributes to reducing gender inequalities.

Whereas in the past the emphasis has been on targeting educational investments at states with low literacy rates, DPEP targets backward districts and Lok Jumbish targets backward blocks, making it more likely that each will actually reach the most needy. In principle this is especially true of the DPEP approach, since its use of school mapping is intended to further concentrate resources on those villages and hamlets with greatest need. In practice, in both projects the most educationally deprived are not always prioritised. Although Lok Jumbish starts by selecting backward blocks, village selection does not necessarily reflect a measured assessment of educational need, and non-educational factors may be involved. In the case of DPEP, it is not always the most needy districts which are selected as political factors may play a role, and within the districts it may not be the villages with the lowest literacy which are targeted first (though this did appear to be the case in the Andhra Pradesh district visited). Nonetheless, while this may not be ideal from the poverty reduction perspective, it remains the case that the national DPEP and Lok Jumbish guidelines specify minimum levels of illiteracy for the districts and blocks selected, meaning that all areas benefiting are needy albeit not necessary the very worst cases. Furthermore, the fact that in DPEP it is the state which decides district selection, within the national guidelines, reaffirms state-level ownership.

The whole thrust of both the DPEP and Lok Jumbish approaches is to increase access, particularly for scheduled castes/tribes (clearest in DPEP) and for girls. Concentrating on illiteracy inevitably results in a substantial focus on scheduled tribe/caste populations, as their literacy levels consistently lag behind those of the rest of the population. By implication, many of the children targeted are from families where there is no tradition of attending school, and thus both projects seek to address demand factors through mobilisation activities. In scheduled caste/tribe areas one difficulty is often the sparseness of the population, and thus DPEP contains provision for experimental approaches, including residential schools, mobile school and non-formal education. The Madhya Pradesh documents have exercised the DPEP option to lower for tribal areas the population threshold required before establishing a school from 250 to 200. In both Andhra Pradesh and Madhya Pradesh supplementary materials are either being used, or will be, to try and ensure a smooth transition between home and school by the initial use of tribal languages. There was, however, little evidence in the field of these measures having been implemented, though both projects are in the early stages of implementation. In Lok Jumbish tribal populations are targeted by ensuring that a number of 'tribal' blocks are selected.

One element within DPEP designed to increase access relates to school timings. The guidelines leave open the possibility of changing the school calendar so that school holidays rather than school terms correspond to the busy harvesting time, thus making it easier for poor households to allow their children to attend consistently. A final tool used to try and direct resources at the most needy is termed school mapping, an approach adopted in theory by all three projects. School mapping is intended to reveal which villages are the least well-served but have the largest school age populations, and prioritise resources there. This has been implemented in Andhra Pradesh, but in Madhya Pradesh less so, partly because of MP's Education Guarantee Scheme, which states that all habitations above a certain size have the right to schooling. In Lok Jumbish school mapping does not in practice contribute towards a strategy of concentrating resources on the most needy villages.

Gender

DPEP measures designed to increase the enrolment of girls include increasing the numbers of Early Childhood Education Centres, which may free the girl child from caring for a younger sibling and thus enable her to attend school. This is seen largely as a contribution to access rather than quality, but in practice the reality may be that girls were attending school *with* their younger sibling, and thus the Early Childhood Education Centres allow them to concentrate better on learning. In both cases, however, the centres are helping to reduce the gender bias. Plans for centres are reasonably advanced in Madhya Pradesh and are proposed for Andhra Pradesh where community demand is forthcoming. A further element is the stated commitment of both DPEP and Lok Jumbish to increasing the numbers of female teachers as a means of reducing barriers to girl enrolment.

Lok Jumbish has from the start sought to make women's development part of the programme strategy rather than a separate component. One aspect of this is the priority given to increase the numbers of women working at various levels within the organisation, not simply teachers, and with marked success. The project also has mobilised women's groups in some 700 villages in Rajasthan, and 'core teams' of three women in some 1500 villages. A recent monitoring mission found that these groups and teams had had some success in encouraging parents to permit girls to attend school, with girl enrolment rising by 4% in villages where groups are active. This is an important achievement, though small in the context of the Rajasthan. DPEP has promoted, at the central level, greater liaison between the MSS Women's Group programme and DPEP, with the former assisting in stimulating demand for education at the village level and with DPEP subsequently meeting it. In practice, coordination is often lacking, sometimes because of rivalry between MSS and DPEP officials, and the synergy which might potentially be realised is lost. Both DPEP and Lok Jumbish have sought to ensure that village education committees have a minimum representation of women. The extent to which the position of women is strengthened through such measures varies, and there is evidence from all projects that women may often remain marginalised and silent members.

Participation

Although both projects reveal a design which is targeted to reaching poor people, it is vital to ask whether the poor remain in focus as one moves from the document-based strategy to the reality of implementation. A fundamental strength of both projects which has the *potential* to safeguard the pro-poor objective is their stated commitment to decentralisation. Decentralisation may be seen to have happened in practice more readily in the DPEP projects, particularly the Andhra Pradesh DPEP. In the Karimnagar district of Andhra Pradesh (primary district for the field study), there was evidence of plans having being produced at the village level, and that the village education committee and other villagers had been consulted in their preparation, though this may be less true of the other four districts. The variations between these plans attests to a reasonable level of commitment and involvement of villagers. Village meetings have been held to discuss where new schools would be sited, which increases the likelihood that the site will be convenient to the poor majority, rather than the better off elite. (Investments, such as health centres, wells, or even post boxes may typically be sited close to the dominant groups rendering them less accessible to the more marginalised in the community.)

When planning reaches village level, the sheer of the enterprise makes it impossible for district or state-level authorities to control the process. This was not the case in Madhya Pradesh where only state and district plans in operation, and the planning process was more centralised. Below that, participation is moderated through the Panchayati Raj and through village education committees. This presents risks as well as opportunities since Panchayati Raj members may not view education at a top priority. The state context has a role to play in explaining differences between Madhya Pradesh and Andhra Pradesh. The latter's administrative systems have tended to be more committed to DPEP and sensitive to its objective of reaching the more needy. In Madhya Pradesh, it appears that a more political approach may be taken, and that officials may implement DPEP provisions less out of a sense of commitment to project objectives than because that is what they have been directed to do. Lok Jumbish does not have plans developed at the village level, only lists of activities, and in practice appears to operate in a less decentralised fashion.

It is a commonplace that participation is most effective when communities have a practical role to play and genuine involvement in decision-making. Two of DPEP's provisions which are in tune with this decentralise responsibility for petty funds to the Village Education Committees. Every school within the DPEP district is given an annual lumpsum of Rs. 2000 and each teacher is given Rs. 500 for locally-produced teacher aids. Although these sums are quite small, the decision to distribute sums directly to schools and teachers, in most cases via the Village Education Committees is a radical departure from normal practice and has been found to bolster the sense of local ownership. When DPEP was being designed, there was initially some reluctance to countenance the distribution of funds at the local level for fear that they may be misused, and perhaps because it removes an element of power and patronage from higher authorities. The decentralised approach was ultimately included within DPEP, however, partly because a desire to promote local ownership, and partly because it was recognised that misuse of funds is scarcely a problem which is limited to the local level. No such mechanism exists in the case of Lok Jumbish.

DPEP in Andhra Pradesh, and in Karimnagar in particular, has so far been highly successful in its social mobilisation. This is reflected in the unprecedentedly high levels of contributions made by villagers towards the construction of a village school or additional classrooms. The District Collector, the most senior district-level official, confirmed that government programmes had never before succeeded in eliciting anything but a token contribution from villagers. The district DPEP official decided to make a contribution of between Rs. 20,000 to Rs. 25,000 a pre-condition for the building a school in any village, representing roughly 10% of total cost. This is not a DPEP requirement, but field visits clearly demonstrate a very high level of satisfaction among villagers, and a sense that the new school is their school. This has practical benefits, including a new conviction that as it is their school and not a government school they have the right to insist that teachers attend regularly – teacher absenteeism being a very serious problem in rural areas. Involving the community from the start has, in Andhra Pradesh, kindled a willingness in many villages to contribute their labour free and to use locally available materials which are free or low cost, resulting in large savings and sometimes a better quality of construction.

The Rs. 3m that have been mobilised already within Andhra Pradesh's five districts represents a significant increase in resources available for DPEP. But is this affordable by the poor? The speed with which villages have collected their contributions suggests that it was. Villages decided themselves how much people should be expected to contribute, with some exempting the poorest from making any contribution at all, while others had a sliding scale where everyone made some contribution. In Madhya Pradesh contributions are voluntary and far lower. It is unclear what the reasons for this are, but it is possible that DPEP officials are approaching participation in a more mechanistic way, and thus not realising its full potential. In Lok Jumbish no contributions are expected.

One further aspect of the design of DPEP which underlines its recognition of the importance of participation is the fact that the only criterion for district selection other than female literacy is that a Total Literacy Campaign has been conducted there. These central government funded programmes met with mixed success, but even where they did not achieve large increases in literacy they have had a very important role in increasing awareness and demand for primary education, and encouraging a greater response to the participatory components of DPEP.

Sustainability and replicability

Both Lok Jumbish and DPEP take a holistic approach to education, seeking to improve quality and increase access through a wide range of measures. However, DPEP represents a shift away from the 'project mode' of thinking, of which Lok Jumbish is an example, towards a 'programme mode' which inherently has a greater capacity to respond to national concerns, both immediate priorities and long-term needs. It may also tend to be more sustainable than the project approach because it forms an integral part of the governments educational machinery, at central, state and district level. Lok Jumbish may not be seen as a 'donor' project, in the way that many externally aided projects are, but it nonetheless operates outside of the usual channels and is not subject to their control. This gives it considerable flexibility but may reduce its political constituency and sustainability in the long-term. It is interesting to note that the Rajasthan State Government has requested that DPEP be initiated.

DPEP's framework specifically identifies building institutional capacities at all levels as the *sine qua non* for ensuring sustainability of the system. It has sought to strengthen and augment the existing education sector institutions, such as the state and district level research and training institutes. It has also created a new organisational and professional support organisations, such as State Institutes of Educational Management and Training and Block and Cluster Resource Centres, all of which are designed to become an integral part of the state and district level administration. Finally, mobilisation activities have been supported through local level committees, such as the village education committees and parent-teacher associations, supported by the block, cluster and district level administration. This is functioning better in some districts than in others, but in general the care to ensure that DPEP has institutional roots bodes well for its sustainability. The prospects for success of this enterprise—building institutional capacities—are enhanced by the genuine strides towards decentralisation taken by DPEP. The normal practice of planning in India is to start with national plans, and then divide up the funds between states and then districts. This process has been reversed under DPEP. Under DPEP, first district plans are prepared, and only then are state and national plans drawn up. The process of preparing the district plan involves various departments, educational functionaries, teachers, parents and the public at large. This participatory process is widely seen as helping to build individual and institutional competencies.

Clearly, Lok Jumbish has also sought to ensure that the benefits it delivers are sustainable. It's approach is different to DPEP, as is illustrated by the description in its 1997 Report of the 'handing over' by the state of District Institutes of Education and Training (DIETs) to Lok Jumbish project. The objective is that Lok Jumbish develops the three DIETs, by improving the physical facilities, building capacity and links with other educational organisations, and introducing new staff selection procedures. The hope is that these will become pace-setter institutions which can serve as a model for the reform of the rest of the state's DIETs.

The DPEP concept is founded on replicability. A national bureau was established to make it easier for donor inputs to be harnessed efficiently, and to ensure that all donor's accept the nationally-defined framework thus reducing duplication. Potentially, the best of Indian and donor practices can be applied on an all-India basis, so that benefits are not confined to donor operations in 'pockets' of India. DPEP has already begun to deliver on its potential for 'mainstreaming' the lessons of experience, as many of its innovative features reflect lessons learnt from past donor-assisted projects. Lok Jumbish approaches replicability on a state-level. The intention is that the many innovations promoted within Lok Jumbish blocks can be generalised to the non-project blocks.

It is striking just how much a source of pride DPEP has been, both at the central, state and district government level. This high level of ownership is the surest guarantee of sustainability and replicability. In Andhra Pradesh, DPEP is seen as contrasting strongly with an earlier ODA-supported project. This was very much viewed as a UK-led initiative which, while it made important contributions, had a number of failings which might have been remedied had there been a greater sense of responsibility and ownership at a local level. It is striking that despite their rhetoric about ownership, the bilateral donors have had difficulty in adjusting to an Indian-led programmatic approach, though most are making efforts to do so. Donors, such as ODA, who are used to taking a 'hands-on' approach and providing regular technical and managerial inputs view DPEP as riskier. It is true to say that DPEP is 'riskier' in the sense that it affords donors fewer opportunities to influence quality directly, but it may be far *less* risky in the longer term as it prospects for sustainability outshine those associated with most donor projects.

An example of donor difficulty in adjusting is the reluctance of some donors to accept the DPEP guideline that donors would not have their own field offices in particular states to assist in DPEP implementation. This stipulation was in part the result of experience in the Bihar Educational Project, which, although successful, came to be perceived as a UNICEF project, whereby district functionaries and NGOs began to look to the UNICEF office rather than to the state Project Director for direction. One major European bilateral was adamant that it would not contribute to DPEP unless it could provide technical support to 'its' chosen state. (In theory donor inputs are not associated with particular states but contribute to the national 'pot'.) The government preferred to forgo the financial support rather than compromise its framework Another donor, which already has a field office, has been unenthusiastic about closing it down. This is more a difficulty for the bilateral agencies than the multilateral ones, since in the case of the World Bank the scale of its assistance alone renders such scrutiny impracticable.

Although many indications augur well for the long-term sustainability of DPEP especially, there are at least two causes for concern. The first applies to DPEP, particularly as implemented in Madhya Pradesh, and also to Lok Jumbish, namely that large numbers of new teachers appointed are at very low salaries (between 20% and 40% of the norm). This is largely because they are local recruits and have lower academic qualifications and less (or no) training. This reduces start up costs, but unless new recruits receive the intensive in-service training intended by the end of the project period, they risk not being absorbed as permanent teachers. Should their post fall vacant villagers would have fewer rights to demand that it be filled. The second cause for concern applies to DPEP, namely that it may be being scaled up and replicated too fast. The recent huge inflow of World Bank funding, although welcome at one level, goes against one of the important premises of DPEP – local capacity building and decentralisation. There is some evidence of creeping centralisation and a lowering of standards, in order that district plans, for example, are approved and disbursement authorised.

Impact

The various ways in which improved primary education provision attack the many dimensions of poverty have been described above. Assessing the impact of these projects on poverty will only be possible over the long-term, and then only if an adequate system of monitoring and evaluation is in place. Lok Jumbish does not appear to have a universally effective monitoring and evaluation capacity, though aspects of the programme, such as the Minimum Levels of Learning component, have been rigorously assessed in 15 blocks. This suggests a very significant increase in learner achievement of about a third or more after two years of implementation. There is some debate about the adequacy of the management information systems built into DPEP. So far the information available is quantitative rather than qualitative. The ODA has supported research to identify more clearly the priorities and means by which monitoring and evaluation of DPEP may be improved. This input is welcomed by the Indian government, though there are concerns that the approach being advocated may be overly complex and expensive.

There can be no doubt that both the DPEP and Lok Jumbish projects are making a very important contribution by making primary education accessible to many at society's margins. The analysis above of the targeting mechanisms, the degree of participation and the scope for sustainability and replication all suggest that future impact is likely to be positive and significant. It is clear that, although the project design and government and donor officials lacked an appreciation of the linkages between the projects and various dimensions of poverty, their emphasis and success at targeting resources at the least literate should result in a positive impact. The vast bulk of DPEP and Lok Jumbish resources are directed at those who have hitherto been denied any access to education. And there are indications, particularly in the case of the longer-established Lok Jumbish, that investments are resulting not only in increased attendance but, as mentioned above, increases in learner achievement of a third or more. This reflects the success of Lok Jumbish in improving the quality of training and developing more effective and appealing textbooks, for example.

Nonetheless, a number of reservations suggest themselves. It is important, for instance, to recognise that the mere inclusion of special targeting mechanisms within the project design may not necessarily bring benefits. Measures must be carefully assessed against the local context. Residential schools for tribal children may not, for example, always be welcomed, since they may result in children becoming culturally alienated from their families. Similarly, it can not automatically be assumed that using tribal language materials is the best approach. Sometimes several different languages are in use, and parents may prefer that their children be taught in the dominant non-tribal language for economic or social reasons.

Another component of both DPEP and Lok Jumbish which could have a limited or even negative impact relates to their common emphasis on the value of increasing numbers of female teachers as a means of encouraging girl child enrolment. In practice, though this measure has strong political support at higher levels, it sometimes raises practical difficulties. There tend to be few local women with sufficient education to become teachers, and therefore female teachers tend to be strangers in the local community. Evidence from the field suggests that they may feel isolated in the village setting, and lack sanitary and other facilities. Other difficulties are often not openly acknowledged. Women teachers tend to be young, and close to marrying age, but if posted in deprived areas they have few opportunities to find a suitable partner. If they are already married, there is little scope for their husband to join them due to lack of job opportunities. The commitment to increasing the numbers of female teachers, often by selecting a female as a school's second teacher, may mean in practice that the post becomes vacant after several years, if the teacher succeeds in arranging a transfer to a less isolated location. The underlying reason given for increasing the number of female teachers – as an incentive for girls to enroll–is also open to question. Measures to reduce gender inequalities must be carefully assessed in relation to the specific local context, and should be implemented in a way which does not threaten the quality of educational provision.

Finally, the DPEP framework includes provision for altering school timings as a means of facilitating access for girl children and the poorest. It is possible that this problem may loom larger in the eyes of well-educated urbanites than it does for the rural poor. What is certain, is that implementation has proven difficult, since teachers have been very resistant to changing holiday dates which may other coincide with those of their spouses', for example, and also because it has sometimes been used by teachers to justify absenteeism.

Conclusions and suggestions

— The creation of DPEP has transformed the nature of the donor contribution to primary education in India. Indian experts have developed a programme which is well-designed to meet the needs of the excluded, and which has integrated the lessons of Indian and donor experience. Donor-assisted projects have been very formative, but the current insistence that India coordinate and that donors accept the national framework represents a level of ownership far beyond the norm. The burden of accountability for the success of DPEP has shifted towards the Indian government, as individual donors have only limited scope to influence design and implementation. They are currently adapting to a new role as facilitators and capacity builders, a role which they claim to have desired all along. The preliminary evidence suggests that European donors are making this transition with some success. Their expertise, experience in the field and commitment to the social dimensions of development is welcomed by government officials. They are felt to serve, in some measure, as a counterweight to World Bank, which is sometimes perceived as placing output achievements before issues of quality and process.

— Lok Jumbish has had a positive impact on educational provision to the poorest in Rajasthan, both by training large numbers of teachers, providing and upgrading schools, and by paying special attention to gender disparities. Its minimum levels of learning programme has resulted in demonstrable and significant increases in learner achievement in 15 blocks. Lok Jumbish has also sought to promote greater decentralisation, though with mixed results, and has followed a highly participatory approach. It is to be hoped that, like earlier donor-supported state projects, that the lessons of Lok Jumbish will serve as a valuable input in the design and implementation of other projects or national programmes.

— It is still too early to come to any firm conclusions about DPEP's contribution to tackling the illiteracy of the poor. However, while DPEP will be more and less successful in different districts and states, it may prove itself to be the best donor-supported mechanism for bringing education to the poorest yet seen in India. In such a context, the role of donor financing of project-type interventions covering limited areas within states, such as Lok Jumbish, would need to be re-examined carefully. It may be that such projects may be felt to respond to specific local needs or have value as an alternative source of lessons based on different experiences.

Further specific conclusions include:

— DPEP's 'programme' approach offers brighter prospects for sustainability and replicability than the traditional project model. It promises to 'mainstream' the best lessons of Indian and donor experience.
— The Indian government should be encouraged to resist the temptation to scale up DPEP too rapidly, thereby undermining local capacity building, decentralisation and quality.
— Donors' intellectual commitment to ownership needs to be complemented by an increased determination to capitalise on the potential benefits as well as the risks of a more 'hands-off' approach.
— Decentralisation of planning down to village level increases the say of villagers vis-à-vis district level authorities, and is likely to bolster participation and sustainability.
— Effective decentralisation requires genuine commitment from state and district level officials.

— Making villagers responsible for the administration and use of even quite small sums, as in DPEP, helps sustain community participation and engender local ownership.
— Mobilising more than token community contributions to school construction increases local ownership with the positive 'knock-on' effect of reducing teacher absenteeism and improving prospects for maintenance.
— Greater efforts should be made to realise the potential synergy between women's mobilisation activities (e.g. MSS) and DPEP.

REFERENCE

1. The following analysis draws extensively on Varghese (1997).

15

TRAINING PROJECTS FOR WOMEN

Introduction

Two types of women training projects have been studied. The first is directed at farm women and seeks to impart knowledge and skills in agricultural technology through training and extension work. The origin of this type of project lies in dissatisfaction with the neglect of women's role in agriculture in most training and extension work in India and specifically criticism of the traditional Training & Visit approaches propagated by the World Bank. In 1982 the Ministry of Agriculture and Danida took an important initiative and launched the first such programme in India, the Women and Youth Training and Extension Project (in Karnataka). Prior to that there had been some training of farm women in Farmers Training Centres, but on a small scale and not followed up through extension work. So this was an innovative project. Since then similar projects have been established in Tamil Nadu, Orissa and Madhya Pradesh with support from Danida, and the Dutch have supported a comparable project in Andhra Pradesh. Today the Government of India has on its own established similar projects on a small scale in seven states, Himachal Pradesh, Punjab, Haryana, Rajasthan, Uttar Pradesh, Maharashtra and Kerala.

The other type of women's training is completely different in origin, scope and approach. This is organised under the so-called Mahila Samakhya (Education for Women's Equality) societies in a number of Indian states. Under the Mahila Samakhya programme women are trained in a variety of skills, including literacy, but the main objective in the programme is to contribute to collective empowerment of mostly poor women through organisation of groups. The origin of this lies in the National Policy on Education, adopted in 1986, which heralded a shift from a service delivery approach to an approach emphasizing the creation of a conducive environment for learning. Moreover, this policy emphasized the need to create learning opportunities for women who are disadvantaged owing to poverty and gender discrimination. The Mahila Samakhya programme started in 1988 in Karnataka, Gujarat and Uttar Pradesh and later in Andhra Pradesh. The Netherlands' Directorate General for International Cooperation (DGIS) has supported these programmes since the inception.

Although the two types of projects are very different in scope and approach, it is obvious that they both can be highly relevant for poverty reduction.

Selected projects

Three projects, two supported by Denmark and one by the Netherlands, have been selected for assessment as part of this study. For a full account of this we refer to Rajamma (1997). The three projects are the following:

1. Women and Youth Training and Extension Project (WYTEP), implemented by Government of Karnataka's Directorate of Agriculture with support from Danida. First phase of the project was carried out 1982-89, second phase 1989-97 (five year phases plus extensions). A third five year phase was under negotiation in 1997. First phase covered 11 districts in Karnataka, and second phase included the rest of the state (except Bidar district). Third phase is aimed at making results more sustainable and integrating the female cadre of Assistant Agricultural Officers (Farm Women) into the mainstream training and extension system. Under phase I 48.8 mill. DKK was spent, phase II had a budget of 59.7 mill. DKK, all financed by the donor.
2. Training and Extension for Women in Agriculture Project, (TEWA), implemented by Government of Orissa's Directorate of Agriculture with support from Danida. First phase of the project was carried out 1987-94 (incl. extension), second phase is scheduled for 1995-2000. First phase covered four districts, and second phase includes another four districts so that most of Orissa's districts are now included under the project. The districts covered under phase II are more marginal and poorer than the phase I districts. The budget for phase I was 13.8 mill. DKK, for phase II 24.7 mill. DKK, all financed by the donor.

3. Mahila Samakhya (MS) in Uttar Pradesh, implemented by the autonomous Mahila Samakhya Society with support from DGIS. First phase was 1988-93 and second phase runs 1993-97 (5 years). In Uttar Pradesh there has been Dutch funding of the programme in four districts, namely Saharanpur, Tehri Garhwal, Banda and Varanasi. The budget for phase II in all the states - Uttar Pradesh, Gujarat, Andhra Pradesh and Karnataka—is 30,0 mill. Dfl. However, there has been substantial underspending (compared to the budgets) and it is proposed to extend the programme for another five years.

The two Danida-supported projects have been selected because they demonstrate the range of these projects. WYTEP was the first and TEWA the third of the agricultural training and extension projects for women, and although they have similar objectives, they use different approaches to achieve their goals. The selection of the MS in Uttar Pradesh has more to do with the overall regional balance of all projects under assessment in this study. It could as well have been the MS project in Andhra Pradesh or Karnataka.

Geographical location

In WYTEP there has been emphasis on geographical coverage right from the beginning. In phase I it already covered more than half of Karnataka's districts and in phase II the entire state (minus one district). TEWA in phase I covered four districts, two relatively developed coastal districts and two less developed districts inland. The four districts included in phase II, however, are among the remotest and poorest in Orissa with a substantial tribal population (*'adivasis'*). Since Orissa as a whole is much poorer than Karnataka this in itself combined with district selection will tend to make TEWA more relevant to poverty reduction than WYTEP.

The four districts in Uttar Pradesh, where MS is supported by DGIS, are far from among the poorest in the state. Saharanpur actually belongs to the most developed third, and the other three, Tehri Garhwal, Banda and Varanasi, are somewhere in the middle. A slightly better distribution (from a PR perspective) is found among the districts that in 1996 were selected for inclusion in the extended programme. One of these, Sitapur, is among the poorest and most backward in the state, but Pauri Garhwal is in the upper third and Allahabad and Etawah in the middle. This should be viewed against criteria adopted in 1991 for selection of new districts, namely low female literacy, poor school enrolment of girls and low level of socio-economic development. But Uttar Pradesh like Orissa is among the poorest states in India and it ranks lowest in the human development index (notably because of discrimination of women). So even districts in the middle rank fairly low on an all-India scale.

Project components

The main aim of WYTEP is to increase agricultural production by providing agricultural training and extension services to selected women farmers so that they can disseminate skills to other women farmers. Small and marginal women in particular are targeted in their role as agricultural producers and the training mainly deals with agriculture. But it is also an important objective to strengthen the self confidence of women and improve their social status. The training is primarily conducted in Farmers Training Centres (FTCs) some of which have been constructed under the project. The selected women are brought to the centres for ten days training courses. The training is followed by extension work in the villages over a period of three years, carried out by female Assistant Agricultural Officers - Farm Women (AAO-FW), trained under and financed by the project. Their training includes (although not for all) half a year at a Danish agricultural school, an important but also very costly motivational factor. In the villages the AAO-FW support the formation of women's groups.

Under phase II of the project some of the trained women farmers have been given five days additional training at the FTCs in order to function as link workers who can play a key role in continuing the extension work and keep the groups together after the AAO-FW have left the village. There is also a component of the project targeting farm youth, employing more or less the same approach.

The overall objective, increased agricultural production (with added emphasis on food security), and the main philosophy, training small and marginal women farmers, are the same in TEWA as in WYTEP. But the approach is different. Under TEWA the training of women farmers takes place in the villages. It is carried out by Lady Village Agricultural Workers (LVAWs), trained under the project for 14 months—and some of whom also get half a year's training in Denmark. The LVAWs work closely affiliated to the ordinary Training & Visit extension system, but they focus exclusively on women. The LVAWs stay in the villages and work with groups of women farmers for a period of four years. Under phase II, however, it is planned that the LVAWs after working for two years with the farm women only shall shift to a family-based approach, but utilising the TEWA methodology.

The development objective of MS is to provide basic educational opportunities for women - particularly poor women - in rural areas in a way which contributes to their development and empowerment. MS conducts two types of training programmes, skill based training and training aimed at imparting a new set of values and attitudes. At the core of the programme is the formation of women's groups, Mahila Sanghas, which discuss the problems faced by the women and how to overcome them. These are supported by motivators at two levels, Sakhis, who are often illiterate women trained to mobilise women and facilitate meetings at the village level, and Sahayoginis, who are more educated women with responsibility for ten village sanghas. The content of the training activities varies according to the felt needs; literacy and health are recurring themes, but the range of topics addressed includes forests, veterinary care, anti-alcohol, violence, wages, legal rights, accessing government schemes and panchayati raj. Many groups concurrently function as savings groups. Special components under MS are child literacy centres and Mahila Shiksha Kendras (6 months residential schools for teenage girls).

Targeting

None of the projects studied has PR as direct objective. But all projects try to target economically weak and disadvantaged groups in such a way that PR nevertheless becomes an important outcome. Both WYTEP and TEWA primarily target small and marginal women farmers, whereas landless labourers are largely bypassed. However, under TEWA there is a small component which includes landless people in such activities as mushroom growing. MS takes special care to reach the most disadvantaged women both in terms of caste, class and ethnic group. Among the most vulnerable groups identified are landless, illiterates, destitutes, widows, woman headed households and SCs/STs.

Participation

WYTEP was initially implemented in top down fashion, but has moved towards more participatory approaches from the second phase. However, the target group has not been involved in project identification and design, and even during implementation the extent of participatory involvement is limited. There is a tendency for the AAO-FWs to work according to a fairly rigid methodology and to convey more or less predetermined messages. Under TEWA the approach has been more participatory since the beginning, although it has also here been largely confined to the implementation phase of the project cycle. In the initial stages of implementation the LVAWs have conducted benchmark surveys and used Participatory Rural Appraisal techniques to identify the needs and wishes of the women farmers and to promote their involvement in the project activities. On the whole TEWA is more flexible and more conducive to learning and feed-back.

The approach taken under MS is more genuinely participatory. Here the point of departure is a set of principles that are quite strictly adhered to. But the entire programme is oriented towards process rather than output and there is a lot of variation and flexibility in implementation. MS "has tried to offer rural women the opportunity to reflect critically on their lives—to understand socio-economic processes which impinge upon it—to maximise individual and collective self-expression, and promote personal and political growth". Through group discussions the women's felt needs are identified, and with the assistance of the female motivators the groups decide how they can best address the problems raised. The learning process is thus in focus.

There is little doubt that the somewhat more participatory approach adopted by TEWA in comparison with WYTEP contributes to better fulfilling project objectives. It is not possible, though, to compare these two projects with MS which is so different in scope and approach. In principle it is very positive to apply a genuinely participatory approach and to focus on the processes that are supposed to bring about empowerment and development. No doubt, this can strengthen the women on a personal level and as a group and that is in itself an important objective. The risk is that the felt needs of the women do not necessarily coincide with the most important issues of development (e.g. in terms of PR).

Gender

One way of conceptualising gender in a development context is to distinguish between strategic and practical gender needs (Moser, 1993). The strategic needs of women are those which challenge their subordinate position in society. They relate to gender division of labour, power and control, to discrimination in terms of ownership rights and wages and to sexual oppression and physical violence. The practical needs of women in contrast are those they identify in their socially accepted roles in society, i.e. needs that improve the lives of women without challenging the societal order. These needs encompass improved livelihoods, higher income, better access to education, health, drinking water, reduction of drudgery etc.

The three projects studied here all deal with both strategic and practical needs of women. In WYTEP and TEWA the approach addresses mainly the practical needs by providing training in agricultural methods which can bring about improvements in their livelihoods. However, there is also a secondary emphasis on strengthening the women's self-confidence, dignity and social status. In MS the focus is on strategic needs in so far as discrimination of women and attempts to overcome it through an empowerment process lie at the heart of the programme. But practical needs are also addressed through literacy courses, child care centres and discussions of a range of topics. Evidently, both strategic and practical needs of (poor) women are relevant in a PR context.

Sustainability and replicability

Both TEWA and WYTEP are implemented by the Directorates of Agriculture under the respective state governments. Although Danida has financed the female staff—AAO-FWs in WYTEP and LVAWs in TEWA—the prospects of integrating them in the established governmental training and extension system are quite good. In TEWA all the LVAWs are posted in existing vacancies of the extension service, and the project agreement stipulates that their salaries will be paid by the Government of Orissa after seven years of appointment.

In WYTEP the situation is a little more complicated because there is a running battle over the issue of integrating the AAO-FWs in the general seniority list in the Department of Agriculture. WYTEP and Danida have been pushing hard for this for a number of years, and Danida has made the solution of this issue a conditionality for supporting a third phase of WYTEP. But this has met opposition in the government and particularly among the male AAOs. Their resistance no doubt contains an element of male prejudice towards women in the role as agricultural advisers. But there is also a more substantial argument, namely that most of the AAO-FWs do not hold a degree in agriculture, but in home science (with some supplementary training). This complicates the solution of a vexed issue.

The role of the (Indian) Danida advisers in both WYTEP and

TEWA also has implications for sustainability. The WYTEP adviser was one of the persons who initiated the project and she has served as adviser for 15 years. She deserves a lot of credit for this innovative project, but her total commitment to the cause of the project also has a flip side: She has become 'project owner'. Her dominating role has contributed to some of the problems in the integration of the project in the administrative government set-up. In TEWA there is less of a problem, but it is obvious that the use of Danida advisers in general both strengthens project implementation and at the same time risks to create problems in the transfer of projects to complete government responsibility.

MS is different in that its direction is entrusted to an autonomous MS Society at state level with a non-bureaucratic director. The autonomy no doubt is an advantage during implementation, but puts a question mark on sustainability. At the moment it is uncertain what will happen when the foreign donor funding is terminated.

At the village level the sustainability of all three projects depends primarily on the viability of the women groups created. One of the objectives of a possible third phase of WYTEP is to strengthen these groups with an added emphasis on their empowerment potential. There are also plans for training male extension workers in dealing with women farmers. When the AAO-FWs withdraw from a village, the extension work is handed over to men. It remains to be seen how this works out and also whether the link workers are sufficiently trained and motivated to continue to work as such. In TEWA the situation and problems are roughly the same as in WYTEP, but in both these projects there is at least a continued regular extension service that can take over after the project. This adds to sustainability of the results. MS in contrast is not integrated in the government system and hence faces a more uncertain future. Time will show if the women's groups formed have enough viability to survive.

Regarding replicability it can be argued that WYTEP has been replicated on an extensive scale both in the other Danida-supported projects, in the similar DGIS-supported project and in those established independently by the Government of India. However, it is a modified 'WYTEP model' that has been found to be most replicable. The training in Farmers Training Centres (under WYTEP) is relatively costly compared to training in the villages as practiced in TEWA and the other Danida-supported projects. The village training model has other advantages as well so there are good arguments for building on this in the future.

MS is a relatively low cost venture in comparison with the agricultural training projects with their large professional staff etc. Since it exists in a number of states it has already been shown to be replicable. If the necessary financial means can be found it can both be replicated and sustained.

Monitoring and evaluation systems

In both WYTEP and TEWA monitoring largely deals with quantitative outputs (number of women trained etc.) and the financial side. The two projects—together with TANWA, the similar project in Tamil Nadu—were evaluated in 1991, at a time when TEWA had hardly taken-off. More interestingly, a participatory impact assessment of WYTEP was carried out (by 'Outreach') in 1994 in connection with a major evaluation of Danida-supported agricultural projects in several countries.

Also in MS the monitoring is primarily in terms of quantitative output (number of groups formed etc.). Since the focus is on social processes, which are difficult to monitor, it is important that participatory impact assessments become a regular feature of the programme. An evaluation of MS was carried out at the same time as this study and we have not been able to draw on it.

Impact in terms of poverty reduction

It must be remembered that none of the projects has PR as its main objective. However, all the projects want to benefit the economically weaker sections, in the cases of WYTEP and TEWA mainly in the shape of small and marginal women farmers, in the case of MS more broadly economically and socially disadvantaged women. There is no doubt that all the projects in different ways contribute to PR, but it is equally clear that this objective can be strengthened.

WYTEP has been a pioneering project which for the first time has provided agricultural training and extension to a large number of women farmers in a systematic way. They have learned seed selection, plant protection, dryland technologies, animal husbandry, vegetable cultivation, post harvest technologies, organic farming, sericulture, vermiculture etc. There is no doubt that generally the training and extension is relevant and that some of what they have learnt is also put into practice. But of course it is a problem that less than 10% of the women were found to be decision makers (in the period 1991-94); in most cases it was either their husband or their father. This obviously is a consequence of the traditional gender roles. The implication of this is that it is easier for the women to translate their knowledge into practice in such areas as post harvest technologies, sericulture, animal husbandry and vegetable cultivation where the role of women traditionally is strong.

Many women refer to increased crop yields as a positive result of their training, but in the absence of any detailed studies (and benchmark surveys) it is impossible to separate the impact of WYTEP from other factors that have contributed to improved yields. In a number of cases new activities taken up by the women have increased their already heavy workload, but by and large the women find it worthwhile. There are also a few examples of the introduction of labour saving devices and technologies, e.g. for peeling groundnut shells. Many women express the view that they have gained self confidence and self esteem from the project, an important dimension of the impact. In this context the ten days training courses in the Farmers Training Centres, that bring the women away from their families and usual surroundings and together with other women, should not be underestimated. But it is extremely difficult for most women to get away for such a long period, so there is also a negative side to this. Specifically the training centre training prevents most poor women from getting trained because they have even greater difficulty in being away from the village for ten days.

The biggest problem in WYTEP has been the tendency for slightly better-off women to be the main beneficiaries. The 1991 evaluation strongly criticised the youth component of the project for primarily involving youths from larger farms and farms with irrigation. But also in the women component it has proved difficult to direct the benefits mainly to small and marginal farm women, although things have improved over the years. In 1992-93 more than 20% of the trained farm women came from families owning more than 4 ha and another 20% from families owning 2-4 ha. Later the proportion of women with less than 2 ha has increased. Especially in the early years many of the trainees were young unmarried girls, many of them already well educated. There is also a caste factor in this, a tendency for the dominant caste women to be overrepresented. In contrast Scheduled Castes and Tribes have been underrepresented, and landless agricultural labourers have been entirely bypassed by the project.

In terms of overall impact TEWA in many ways is similar to WYTEP. The training and extension activities are comparable—seed selection, plant protection, organic manure, vegetable cultivation, grain storage—but in TEWA there is more emphasis on food security. This is a priority of the women, whereas men often have a preference for cash crops. In TEWA like in WYTEP the women testify about increased crop yields, but also here it is uncertain how much is owing to the project in comparison with other factors. In some areas, where the women are heavily involved in field operations, the project has increased their workload, but they find it worthwhile. Apart from improving the agricultural skills and knowledge of the women the project has brought about increased self confidence and recognition from others.

The most important difference between WYTEP and TEWA is that in the latter the training takes place in the villages. This makes it much easier for the women to take part in the training. It also means that poorer women can participate. Hence TEWA has been more successful in actually reaching the target group of small and marginal women farmers. The general level of poverty in Orissa is also much higher than in Karnataka, so on the whole TEWA is more poverty oriented. But even in TEWA the landless agricultural labourers are largely bypassed, although some landless women are involved in groups that have taken up mushroom cultivation.

Mahila Samakhya, finally, has assisted the women's groups in getting better access to the various government programmes (hand pumps, health facilities, school enrolment, scholarships for SCs/STs etc.). In some cases savings groups have taken up income generation activities, but in this respect the programme still has a lot to do. There is a need for more skill training. However, there exists a particularly successful example in Banda district where a group of women were trained as hand-pump mechanics and later have taken up maintenance and repair work in different places. Through campaigns the MS women have influenced the wage rate in several places so as to increase it and make it less unequal. The workload of women has been reduced through the establishment of daycare centres for children. The women have increased their knowledge about health, legal issues and a host of other topics and many have become literate. On the whole there is no doubt that the programme has contributed to empowering the women involved. Although the extent of course varies from group to group and from woman to woman, generally they have become more mobile and have acquired critical awareness and bargaining power.

It is clear that the achievements under MS have been more in its contribution to empowerment than in concrete economic benefits. There is a need to move beyond awareness raising towards supporting the women's groups in roles that will more directly improve their livelihoods.

It is a problem that we have not had access to any material that could provide more solid documentation of the impact of MS. Such material may be available in the 1997 evaluation. It is understood that most of the women benefiting from the programme are poor, but even this is undocumented.

Conclusions and suggestions

— Women training projects can be highly relevant in a poverty reduction context—both when they impart technical skills and when they aim at promoting an empowerment process, or, to put it differently, both when they address women's practical and strategic needs.
— The projects studied here have been innovative in the way they have targeted women in development. Credit for this should go to the donors as well as to the Indian institutions that have plaid an important role in the design and implementation of the interventions. Specifically the projects for farm women have paved the way for similar government programmes in other Indian states.
— The projects under study have all contributed to poverty reduction in the wide sense. The agricultural training projects have enabled the women to introduce new methods in agriculture, horticulture, animal husbandry, sericulture etc. and thus increase productivity and improve livelihoods. The programme dealing with education for women's equality has also brought some material benefits, but the emphasis here has been on awareness creation, mobilisation and organisation of the women in order to enable them to improve their social and economic situation.
— WYTEP has been a pioneering project, for the first time systematically addressing the training and extension needs of women in their role as agricultural producers. The training centre model, however, has made it difficult for many women to participate and has especially prevented many poor women from benefiting from training. So although the target group of small and marginal women farmers is well represented among the trainees, many better—off women and young, unmarried girls have constituted a sizable part of the trainees. The poor, landless agricultural labourers have been bypassed by the project.
— TEWA has built on the experience from WYTEP. By focusing on training in the villages the barrier to women's involvement has been removed. Thus TEWA has been able to reach the target group of small and marginal women farmers more effectively.

But even here the landless women have been largely bypassed by the project.

- Under both WYTEP and TEWA and in similar projects it should be considered how landless agricultural labourers could be included in the target group offered training. Since they actually carry out a lot of the field work, although not in a decision-making role, this could be relevant to everybody (otherwise they may resist the introduction of new methods). However, their training clearly has adequate economic compensation as a necessary prerequisite, and moreover the training should be adapted to their needs and given with a view of building up their skills and capacities in such a way that they may use their increased qualifications to improve their remuneration.
- Mahila Samakhya has succeeded in mobilising, training and organising—largely poor—rural women in such a way that they are in a better position to fight for their rights, have their dignity respected and improve their livelihoods. Although something has already been done there is a need to strengthen the support to the women's groups in activities that bring direct material benefits.
- The relevance of all the projects to PR could be increased if this objective was clearly stated to be one of the primary objectives.
- In selection of districts the prevalence of poverty should be used as an important criterion. This will almost always be strongly correlated with substantial gender inequality and discrimination of women.
- All the projects use participatory methods to some extent least in WYTEP and most in Mahila Samakhya with TEWA somewhere in the middle. There is scope for a more participatory approach in WYTEP (and to some extent TEWA), perhaps combined with greater flexibility in design and implementation.
- Regarding sustainability, the prospects of integrating WYTEP and TEWA in the regular governmental agricultural training and extension system are quite good, although in WYTEP it requires a solution of the contested position of the AAO-FWs. While the strong role of the Danida adviser has primarily been an advantage during implementation it also contributes to making integration somewhat more difficult. The sustainability of Mahila Samakhya depends on the availability of the financial means

(when the donor pulls out). In all three projects—and particularly Mahila Samakhya—sustainability moreover depends on the viability of the women's groups that have been formed.

— Monitoring in all the projects is largely in terms of quantitative outputs plus the financial side. There should be more monitoring of process and poverty reach. There is a lack of benchmark surveys and indicators. Under one of the projects a participatory impact evaluation has been carried out. This should be taken up by others..

16

URBAN SLUM DEVELOPMENT PROJECTS

Introduction

According to official census figures, the number of Indians living in urban areas has doubled over the period 1971 to 1991 from 109 to 218 million. At present, India counts some of the largest cities in the world and there are more than 20 cities with more than one million people within their boundaries. Earlier the rural-urban migration was the main reason for the rapid urbanisation in India but at present this migration only contributes some 20-25% to the growth. The main reason at present is the natural population growth. The rapid urbanisation has led to severe problems in the field of housing, employment, public facilities, transport, sanitation and health to name some of the most obvious ones. It will be clear that these 'deficiencies' are extremely prevalent in the urban slums. In these slums, particularly women, children and elders form the most vulnerable groups.

Over the years, the Indian government (central and state) has set up a large number of projects to tackle some of the major problems in urban areas. These run from self-employment schemes for urban poor and basic services schemes to housing programmes. Particularly the latter type of projects seems to form the basis for many of the urban poverty reduction programmes initiated.

Selected projects

Also foreign donors have supported specific projects and programmes aimed at urban slums. Five of these projects, assisted financially by the

UK, the Netherlands and Germany have been assessed as part of this study. For a full account of this assessment we refer to Benjamin (1997). The five projects are the following:

1. The Dutch funded Bangalore Urban Poverty Programme (BUPP) in Bangalore (Karnataka). The BUPP started as a pilot project for two years from November 1993 to October 1995, with a further extension for three more years. The programme is executed under the responsibility of the Ministry of Urban Affairs and Employment in New Delhi, the Housing and Urban Development Corporation, and the Karnataka Government's Housing and Urban Development Department. The aim of the project is to develop and test a model of sustainable comprehensive urban poverty alleviation based on the concept of enduring and effective community participation. The project is implemented by a Steering Committee consisting of a specifically established Project Support Unit (acting as coordinating body), the Government of Karnataka (e.g., Karnataka Slum Clearance Board) and local NGOs. One of the explicit aims of the project is to link programmes of both government and NGOs as the concept of 'convergence'. The project initially selected 10 slums and later added another 5 to the list. Although it was considered important that an NGO is already working in a slum, also slums where no NGO worked were included. Development tasks here were taken over by the PSU. At slum level, residents were to be organised into groups of 20-40 families [so-called Slum Development Teams (SDTs)]. The SDTs are supposed to develop plans for Habitat improvements and related interventions with the support and help of the field level NGO and under overall guidance of the PSU.
2. The ODA funded Visakhapatnam Slum Improvement Project (Andhra Pradesh). This project follows the Urban Community Development (UCD) approach which was first started in Hyderabad. The emphasis in this approach is on city wide upgrading including the provision of basic amenities and related health, education and community development inputs, and housing. Covering 170 slums with an estimated target population of 200,000, the project started in 1988 and was officially concluded in 1996. The main emphasis is on organising the community into local groups which can manage the facilities

created and be responsible for cost recovery. Institutionally, a UCD wing is created in the municipality to coordinate their functions with other planning interventions. At the level of each slum settlement, the community is formed into smaller groups, called Neighbourhood Committee (incorporating a women's group and a youth wing). This NC is supposed to have half its members as women addressing gender issues. In addition, there is a Project Steering Committee (PSC) which is to include elected representatives.

3. The ODA funded Chinagadili Habitat Improvement Scheme Phase II (Andhra Pradesh). The Chinagadili project is perceived as an integrated project covering such activities as environmental improvements, health and education activities, economic support programmes and the creation of community based organisations. With an estimated target population of 30,000, the project started in 1996 and is supposed to end in 1998. Management is in the hands of the same UCD wing mentioned above for the Visakhapatnam project. The main objective is to create conditions for sustainable poverty reduction and improvements in the quality of life of families in the Chinagadili relocation area, Visakhapatnam.
4. The German (KfW) funding through HUDCO, focused through existing programmes. The building centre operations are part of HUDCO operation. Building centres are promoted by HUDCO and the GoI as a 'lab to land technological intervention'. The centres are managed by autonomous societies (e.g., NGOs) under GoI and HUDCO guidelines. The objective is to provide cost effective, innovative and affordable technology transfer and training at the grass-roots besides decentralised production of materials and components, sales outlets, and housing guidance, counselling and information.
5. The German (KfW) funding through HDFC, which is also focused through existing programmes. The housing in Kerala follows established HDFC norms. HDFC has identified two lines of credit: via NGOs and via state government housing authorities with the aim of developing mass housing. In this study two NGOs have been included: (1) the Alleppey Diocesan Society (ADS) with organisation, training for income generation, credit unions, insurance schemes, infrastructural works and marketing programmes as main activities, and (2) the Changanacharerry

Social Service Society (CSSS) which implements such activities as training and awareness building, community health, low cost sanitation, rehabilitation, family and child welfare, women's empowerment, savings and credit, sericulture and other economic programmes.

Institutional arrangements

Donor relationships with field offices vary with the three donors. In the BUPP case, Dutch NGO funds routed via the Government of the Netherlands and India through HUDCO arrive at the PSU via a indirect circuit. This implies that donor interests are themselves not singular but represent heterogeneous interests. The ODA relationship is more direct; being established with the Visakhapatnam Municipality and in particular its UCD wing. In a sense, the UCD wing and the ODA form a close working alliance for implementation issues. In contrast to the BUPP where a completely new structure is created, the UCD is centred on reorganising the municipal government in a way to co-ordinate different departments. KfW's relationship with the operational and policy mechanics is marginal. With regard to the building centres funded through HUDCO it should be remarked that the centres are managed by autonomous societies (i.e., NGOs) under HUDCO guidelines. The NGOs have the autonomy to define the objectives in the local context. Some lay more stress on training, while others stress on the development of new technology. Thus, in summary, the donor influence in the Dutch case is complicated, heterogeneous and shifting. In the British case, its direct and interventionist. In the German case, it is in-direct and almost marginal.

Institutional arrangements have also been influenced by project formulation. In the BUPP case, it started as smaller scale programmes being implemented by Habitat NGOs supported by Dutch NGOs. The BUPP was seen as a scaling up of these efforts via NGO networking. In recent years, the BUPP has strengthened its links with government agencies. These are especially with those of the State Government, since they decide on land issues. In a sense, this has helped to improve the legitimacy of the BUPP to both governmental and slum community, although this link may not be to the liking of some of the NGO group. In the British case, the ODA selected an ongoing and reasonable successful programme, which had already achieved some credibility. There is little information on German funding. It seems though, that as per a broad policy, institutions at the central level were selected for funding on the basis of their operations in the Habitat sector.

Project activities

The projects in general were regarded not only as participatory in nature but also as integrated or comprehensive projects. In the BUPP case, this, among other things, means attention to employment generation via promoting micro credit through a savings and credit society. Besides, the project tries to converge existing governmental and non-governmental activities in the field of income generation. Attention to education is included through *balwadies* and implemented by NGOs. Health issues are left to mainstream governmental interventions. Being a project in which NGOs play a central role, the capacities of the NGOs to implement different activities aimed at poverty reduction determines the extent to which the project can be regarded as a comprehensive project. In effect, the main activity relates to housing. The BUPP focuses mainly on habitat improvement and infrastructure improvement related to this and, as a consequence, the project suffers from a pre-occupation with land-title issues. The confusion on land issues has plagued the project right from its inception. One of consequences of these complications is that the project has suffered from extensive delays. These delays were also due to unrealistic expectations from NGO networking and the time consuming routing of funds (which has to go through the GoN, GoI and HUDCO). These delays have meant a lack of funds for actual implementation and stressing on 'soft' aspects such as community mobilisation to buy time.

In the ODA Visakhapatnam project, housing is far less important. In this UCD approach, the main aim was to find ways and means to get basic services and civic improvements: upgrading/lining of the canal system to reduce flooding, roads, sewerage and drainage improvement, basic health, education and efforts at income generation. The housing component, which is included in the UCD project, suffers from some of the complexities of implementation issues mentioned above for BUPP. It is, however, important to note that the UCD approach, stressing on several types of intervention, can bypass the housing component if it seems to go against local interests. The Chinagadili project, in contrast to the official description, is a site and services project for poor groups resettled from central city areas in Visakhapatnam. There are some modifications in the way the community is organised in local groups to manage services and for cost recovery. Essentially, this makes that this project focuses, like the BUPP, on housing. The same is true for the KfW funding of HUDCO's building centres. The funding for building centres is, by definition, selective and not comprehensive. KfW's funding for housing through HDFC is comparable to the BUPP and Chinagadili cases

Poverty concept and targeting of the poor

Various studies have shown that housing by itself falls very low on the priorities of poor groups and, particularly, of the poorest. In contrast, access to multiple economic and survival opportunities are critically important as are such issues as access to clean water and avoiding flood prone conditions. In addition, promoting conventional housing usually results in many ways in which the poor are affected negatively. As such, housing can have a regressive impact on poverty reduction and hides more critical (livelihood) issues requiring attention. Basically, this is the case with all projects except the ODA funded Visakhapatnam project following the UCD approach. That is to say that these projects have a narrow conceptualisation of poverty and one that can have the opposite impact on poverty than intended.

The BUPP, as mentioned, has been selective in focusing mainly on habitat improvement. Moreover, the project was also selective with regard to slums to be taken up. Problems with land titles, which require state intervention, forced the project to select only notified slums with minimal conflict over land issues. It is likely that the poorest of the city have not been targeted by this selection. Moreover, the groups with the least legal claims are not able to participate. In the ODA funded Chinagadili project another issue strengthens the case that the project has not targeted the poorest. Being 7 km away from the main city and 12 km from the city centre and the port where the most jobs are, many of the originally resettled people at Chinagadili have returned to the city. As one of those who returned to the city remarked: 'If I have a job and food here, I can sleep on the footpath. What do I do with golden house 16 km away'. Remaining (and settling) at Chinagadili were mostly economically more stable groups.

In the case of KfW/HDFC projects in Kerala, it can be mentioned that the implementing NGOs in their own programmes focused on some of the issues faced by the poorest such as drinking water. Instead of reinforcing these interventions, HDFC focused on housing. The loans provided for housing, although subsidised, is tied to a strict repayment schedule suggesting that loans are mainly offered to the better-off and more stable households. As such, the project does not target the poor. The KfW funding for building centres, being a technocratic approach to PR of those related to the building industry, does not directly address the specific and more immediate needs of the poorest of this industry. That leaves the Visakhapatnam project supported by ODA. Being basically an upgrading project with only little attention to housing it is directed at PR through its focus on those issues that are regarded as important by the poor themselves. As such, it has a comprehensive and multi-dimensional conceptualisation of poverty. The project, moreover, emphasises improving civic amenities and getting infrastructure while keeping the settlers where they are, thereby avoiding already the issue of the legitimacy of land claims.

In sum: The conception of poverty in the BUPP is habitat related (i.e., inadequate housing and deficient infrastructure), while it is more comprehensive in the ODA project following the UCD approach which focuses specifically on issues of absolute poverty, access to basic civic and social services and inclusion of slum areas into mainstream urban management. Within the Chinagadili project, the conception of poverty here is different from the UCD approach adopted in Visakhapatnam. Here, the mass resettlement of poor families is taken as a given and the main issue is adequate shelter as a way to alleviate poverty. Finally, the donor's conception of poverty in the KfW projects, similarly to the BUPP and the ODA in Chinagadili, is very much in the housing approach. The difference here is the emphasis on centralised institutions.

Ownership and participation

The approach within the BUPP is aimed at improving the habitat of poor people in a participatory way. It visualises the NGO community playing a key role. Their networking would help in project formulation, have an overall advisory role, and direct the implementation process. The project agency The Project Support Unit (PSU), is an independent agent acting as an interface between NGOs and government departments, and also field level NGOs involved in implementation. The 'ownership' of the project relates closely to the role played by PSU. Initially, its functioning was closely aligned with key local NGOs in a directive and supervisory position. These in turn, were linked to their Dutch counterparts via the Habitat Coalition. As the implementation proceeded it soon became evident that land issues were most critical, especially when housing had to be attempted. Here, a good working relationship with the State Government was fundamental. In recent times, the PSU is more closely aligned with State Government agencies. Thus, ownership has shifted from the grouping of NGOs to the State government. This is also because legislation relating to development work in slum areas is at the State level, along with most legislation relating to land issues. This is especially when attempting to undertake housing programme drawing from central government financing. One result is selecting only notified slums with minimal conflict over land issues.

The ODA funded Visakhapatnam project attempts to build on the existing UCD approach, emphasising the role of the local government. The urban community development wing, within the municipality, helps to converge slum development inputs in a coordinated way with mainstream municipal functions. The ODA, however, has played a strong interventionist and directive role, with the local government playing the role of an implementation agency. Ownership is very much with the ODA. Indirectly, the programme is also influenced by the State and Central government since the administrative wings of the local government (rather than its representative face) play a key role. The local government, community groups have a consultative role.

In the Chinagadili project, housing and infrastructure is expensive and promoting civil engineering forms of solution. Not surprisingly, donor funding is critically reinforcing ODA's ownership of the project. KfW funding is routed via national level agencies, the latter playing a critical directive and policy role. Local bodies (NGOs, or State housing boards) are implementers of their policy. There seems little choice for beneficiaries or the local government to decide on policy issues. This is even more entrenched in the case of the NGOs implementing HDFC programmes. Here, although their other activities are more contextualised having a more important bearing on local poverty (in its absolute and perhaps relative sense) the implementing institutions have little autonomy to make foreign funding more effective. 'Ownership' rests mainly with the routing agency. Local groups are 'beneficiaries', with little more than a consultative role.

The local population is in none of the projects directly involved. In the BUPP, the NGOs are supposed to be the intermediary between the people and the project. From the Chinagadili project, a small but innovative approach can be learned: the incorporation of existing organisations of poor groups (rather than promoting new ones) in the management and, to a certain extent, decision-making process. The general neglect of existing local organisations and politicians, thereby responding to the 74th Constitutional amendments, has to be regarded as a lost opportunity. The heavy donor involvement in, for instance, the ODA project in Visakhapatnam and the BUPP, has meant the strengthening of administrative wings of local and state governments, and central level political and bureaucratic interests. Not surprisingly, local elected representatives are even more marginalised. KfW funding for building centres does not directly recognise the issues raised by workers of the construction industry via their representative or developmental organisations. Again, KfW funding for housing construction routed via the HDFC and according to its norms completely misses out potential opportunities provided by the 74th amendments.

The role of NGOs

NGO involvement in the three funding agencies has been quite different. In the ODA programme, NGOs play a service oriented service role to the UCD wing. This is seen to be part of the 'convergence' strategy. In the Chinagadili case, a micro-credit programme carried out by a church based group has been very successful and forms an important part of the project implementation. NGOs in KfW funding fit in a role prescribed by the fund routing agencies (HUDCO and HDFC). Here, the HDFC has a more restricted and strictly operational role for NGOs. HUDCO, in the case of the building centres, promotes some degree of autonomy within general guidelines in defining the kind of training and product development. Thus, in the German case, the intermediately routing organisation plays a critical role in defining the institutional space for NGOs.

The most dominant role, both formative and directive/supervisory role has been in the BUPP programme. This also may have been related to the serious implementation issues plaguing the BUPP programme. Initially, the implementation process visualised a networking role for NGOs, and a relationship between them and the community groups where they operated benign. Both of these assumptions turned out to be seriously faulty and affected the implementation process. Discussions with field staff and residents highlight the protection of 'turf' by one NGO against another wanting to operate in the same neighbourhood. This is even if the two work on quite different issues for instance health and education. This conflict over 'turf' may also be reflected in the fact that the rotation of NGOs in the Steering Committee (SC) has not happened. In effect, this may have also created a rift between field NGOs and those in the SC.

Internally, the project office (BUPP office) supposed to co-ordinate local actions by NGOs at the field level, and the formation of various community based organisations (CBOs) responsible for both formulating and implementing development activities (especially habitat related). The CBOs were to have equal women representation in decision-making. All this, including the project office, was supposed to be supervised by a body of select NGOs (represented by rotation) and key government officials who would provide advise and also help to 'network' activities. Moreover, whereas the NGO coalition was supposed to play a key managerial and advisory role, it has little institutional space or capability to deal effectively on the land issue. It is not surprising, that at present, with more experience, the PSU has taken a lead role in sorting out land issues, and strengthening their links with state government institutions rather than the NGO community. This shift of alliances too has not been without tension.

Another issue relates to the capability of NGOs at the field level. Most are specialised in a particular area and the responsibility of organising a range of slum upgrading components went beyond them. In interviews with NGOs in Bangalore, some mentioned that it was in fact better to limit a programme to the particular skills available, rather than propose a comprehensive one requiring NGOs to take on additional responsibilities.

Legitimacy is a major issue in a NGO driven programme like the BUPP. Residents do not necessarily view NGOs attempting development work without some form of self-interest, an element of cynicism and suspicion. Some go to the extent of placing them at the same level as politicians and bureaucrats. This has several points to it. Slum communities are very heterogeneous, with complex fractures. In this situation, for an NGO to set up a representative organisation to take decision on the group's behalf, is not easy—especially to local residents. For instance, this can seriously affect the efficiency of infrastructure improvements.

The community must also be convinced that the NGO has official credibility to solve substantial issues in their favour. These invariable relate to land, and not the strongest point of NGOs. The community organisations that they set up are also not necessarily the ones that take a lead role in land issues. In most of the slums we visited, it turned out that most of the community organisations set up by the NGOs were perceived locally as being women's organisations (due to the mandatory 50% representation) and responsible only for women's issues (children's crèches, birth control, and health issues). 'Real' issues like that of land or negotiating with the government were largely in the domain of the Sanga or existing organisation operating via administrative or political channels.

Sustainability and replicability

The BUPP in Bangalore is by definition not comprehensive. The institutional structure, in which a Steering Committee consisting of the

PSU, the GoK (e.g., Karnataka Slum Clearance Board) and NGOs is supposed to lead the way, has little hopes of being replicable at a larger scale and becoming more comprehensive unless substantial institutional changes are made. The KfW programme may be sustainable but its efficacy in poverty alleviation is limited. The sustainability of the ODA programme though is dependent upon its relationship with local political agents. Till now, they have had little role, and thus while the situation is much more promising than the BUPP programme, this too faces uncertainty.

One of the main differences between the BUPP and the ODA projects at Visakapatnam and Chinagadili is the minimal involvement of the local government in the former. In the BUPP, involvement with the government happens over land issues as related to habitat related infrastructure issues—and thus, these are mostly state level agencies or under direct state control. Few issues are related to lower level of governments. This contrasts with the ODA case, which is build around local government organisations. As in the BUPP, KfW funding too bypasses local government, being routed through NGOs or central or state government institutions. All the projects leave little institutional space for elected representatives. In fact, it is quite the reverse. This is significant because while project staff and formulators view local politicians as a 'threat', discussions with residents in Visakhapatnam, Chinagadili, Bangalore and Alleppey suggest that residents of poor areas do not share the same perspective.

The issue of sustenance after donor funding, as illustrated in the above issue, relates closely to the political space given to elected representatives. In the ODA project, this important group was given little space, thus building a serious threat to programme and project staff of the entire UCD department after donor withdrawal. Thus, while the advantages, coverage, and infrastructure of a municipalised programme was sought, it was equally important to ensure political commitment. At present, people in the slums in Visakhapatnam, see it as a ODA programme rather than a UCD-municipality run programme. While this may be good publicity for the ODA, it affects sustenance in a very serious way. In a sense, the political face of community organisation is very deeply rooted.

In sum: Except for the KfW funding of HUDCO's building centres none of the projects is sustainable after donor funds dry up. The only other possible exception has to be made for the ODA project in Visakhapatnam. Sustainability here depends largely on the possibilities to incorporate the local politicians in the project.

Impact in terms of poverty reduction

Considering the selective conceptualisation of poverty (i.e., with regard to housing) within most of the projects, the impact of these projects on PR is negligible at best and regressive at worst. Promoting conventional housing—being the main intervention within the HDFC, BUPP and Chinagadili projects—has a negative effect on the poorest of the poor by displacing them from central city locations, which provide a multitude of employment opportunities. This is due to programmes requiring clear titles and needing beneficiaries to build according to pre-determined housing plans. Access to low interest subsidised loans means that better placed poor and middle-income groups try to move at the poorest. Thus, doing conventional housing including sites and services, can seriously affect the economic security, health and environmental conditions of the poorest.

The Urban Community Development Programme (ODA) in Visakhapatnam is most effective in addressing the immediate needs of poor groups. This is particularly when its housing component is bypassed, with the focus then on health, education and provision of basic infrastructure and civic amenities irrespective of tenure conditions. This was also successful because it was a citywide programme pushing policy to include slums in all categories of tenure. This is unlike the BUPP and, to an extent, the KfW, where the selection of declared slums and those households who had clear titles, meant that the poorest were neglected.

The impact of employment and economic support programmes is less clear. Discussions with beneficiaries point to few successes (particularly in the ODA and DGIS cases). KfW funding does not directly deal with this issue. However, in almost all cases, indirect support in terms of micro-credit organisation seems to be working well. The UCD approach is implicitly the least disruptive of employment providing local economies. This is due to the programme stressing upgrading poor groups in their existing locations that provide access to multiple economic opportunities in an urban context. In contrast, resettlement projects in the form of site and services have the most regressive impact on economic opportunities of poor groups. Attempting to replicate economic opportunities is extremely difficult.

Conclusions and suggestions

— The local population is in none of the projects directly involved. Project agencies define participation in terms of consultation or along non-critical issues. This erodes their credibility. Contextualising interventions in light of the 74th amendment (on local government) will not only result in self-sufficient programmes, but target funds better and help to build positive political support. Moreover, the heavy donor involvement in, for instance, the ODA project in Visakhapatnam and the BUPP, has meant the strengthening of administrative wings of local and state governments, and central level political and bureaucratic interests.

— The most serious shortcoming in all projects is on the economic front. None have taken direct note of the urban economy and how these projects fit into this. The UCD approach is implicitly the least disruptive of employment providing local economies. This is due to the programme stressing upgrading of poor groups in their existing locations which provides access to multiple economic opportunities in an urban context. In contrast, resettlement projects in the form of site and services have the most regressive impact on economic opportunities of poor groups. Attempting to replicate economic opportunities is extremely difficult.

— Considering the selective conceptualisation of poverty (i.e. with regard to housing) within most of the projects, the impact of these projects on PR is negligible at best and regressive at worst. Promoting conventional housing — being the main intervention within the HDFC, BUPP and Chinagadili projects — has a negative effect on the poorest of the poor by displacing them from central city locations which provide a multitude of employment opportunities. This is due to programmes requiring clear titles and directing beneficiaries to build according to pre-determined housing plans. Access to low interest subsidised loans means that more well placed poor and middle-income groups try to move out the poorest. Thus, doing conventional housing including sites and services, can seriously affect the economic security, health and environmental conditions of the poorest.

— NGO involvement in the three funding agencies has been quite different, running from a service-oriented role in the Visakhapatnam project to a successful micro-credit programme carried out by a church-based group in the Chinagadili case. In the German case, the intermediately routing organisation plays a critical role in defining the institutional space for NGOs (e.g.

Table 16.1: Ranking table for the EU-projects in urban slum projects

	DGIS	ODA	ODA	KfW	KfW
	BUPP	Visakhapatnam	Chinagadili	HDFC housing	HUDCO building centres
Conception of poverty	Narrow focus: focus on 'shelter' concerns	Comprehensive	Very narrow: concerns with shelter issues	Very narrow: concerns with shelter issues	Not explicit Indirect impact via skill upgrading
Impact on absolute poverty (including the lowest 10%)	No	Yes	No	No	No
Impact on relative poverty	No	Maybe	No	No	No
Scale: city wide or select settlements	Selective	Citywide	Selective by default	Selective	Selective
Identification process: beneficiary/ local groups participation	By 'select NGO group	By local government	By local government/ project design	By implementing NGO	By implementing NGO
Design process	Select donor NGO and select local NGOs	Existing programme, modifications by donor	Donor	Routing organisation HDFC	Routing organisation: HUDCO
Conditionality by donors	Yes, on NGO involvement	Yes, creation of UCD cell, cost recovery	Not known	According to HDFC norms, cost recovery by NGO	According to HUDCO norms
Ownership	Select NGO State goverment	Donor	Donor	HDFC	Local building centre
Livelihood issues					
Responsive to local economy: recognition of existing resources	No	Indirect, but accommodative	No	No	To some extent
Inputs: organisational awareness building	Yes	Yes	Yes	No	No

	DGIS	ODA	ODA	KfW	KfW
Inputs: skill oriented	Yes	Yes	Yes	No	Yes
Participation					
Form of participation: consultative/ substantive	Consultative	Mostly consultative	Some substantive, some consultative	No participation	Some consultative
Participation on land, tenure	Minimal	Some	Not applicable	Not applicable	Not applicable
Participation on maintenance of community facilities	Yes	Yes	Yes	Not applicable	Not applicable
Inclusive of new groups/exclusive	Minimal	Some	Yes	No	No
Substantial space for elected representatives, representative process	Minimal, being presently attempted	Minimal	Some, being presently attempted	No	No
Feed-back possibilities for beneficiaries	Some	Some	Reasonable	None	None
Role of NGOs	Formative, supervisory and implementation	Consultative, and some implementation	Consultative, and some implementation	Implementation	Implementation and formative
Institutional space for indigenous/ existing community organisations	No	No	Yes	No	No
Sustainability without donor funding	No	Maybe	No	No	Yes

restricted in HDFC and aimed at more autonomy in HUDCO). The most dominant role, both formative and directive/supervisory, has been in the BUPP programme. Here, however, the networking between NGOs did not work out. Moreover, the rotation of NGOs in the Steering Committee (SC) has not happened. In effect, this may have also created a rift between field NGOs and those in the SC.

— In some projects, the NGOs are supposed to provide for the 'civic representation'. This assumption is misplaced, however. In none of the projects, except for the Chinagadili project, do exist representative organisations like Sangas incorporated in the implementation process. Instead, the programmes aim to create parallel organisations that in reality end up being concerned with non-critical issues.

— Except for the KfW funding of HUDCO's building centres none of the projects is sustainable after donor funds dry up. The only other possible exception has to be made for the ODA/DFID project in Visakhapatnam. Sustainability here depends largely on the possibilities to incorporate the local politicians in the project. All approaches are de-politicised: They do not provide a space for civic representation.

— The Urban Community Development (UCD) Programme in Visakhapatnam is most effective in addressing the immediate needs of poor groups. This is particularly when its housing component is bypassed, with the focus then on health, education and provision of basic infrastructure and civic amenities irrespective of tenure conditions. This was also successful because it was a citywide programme pushing policy to include slums in all categories of tenure. This is unlike the BUPP and, to an extent, the KfW, where the selection of declared slums and those households who had clear titles, meant that the poorest were neglected. The impact of employment and economic support programmes is less clear, although, in almost all cases, indirect support in terms of micro-credit organisation seems to be working well.

— The UCD-based approaches are the most comprehensive in dealing with poverty. They hold the potential to be sustainable after donor funding is withdrawn, especially if they manage to create room for elected representatives to play a more substantive role.

17

NGO PROJECTS

Introduction

The NGO sector is not comparable to the other sectors as its defining characteristics are the institutional mode of intervention rather than nature of the project intervention. NGOs are involved in many of the projects that have been covered in the other sectors studied: watershed management, forestry, irrigation, and so on. Their increased involvement is a sign of the growing awareness amongst donors and others that local NGOs possess certain attributes and potentials that can greatly enhance a project, particularly when sustainable poverty reduction is concerned. However, when delineating this sector, we wished to go beyond projects that simply involve NGOs in particular components of a project in order to achieve participatory planning, build sustainable local institutions, or generate local ownership for example. Rather, we have chosen to focus upon bilateral aid that first and foremost focuses upon the institutional and organisational nature of NGOs as the reason for support and only thereafter considers the type and form of the intervention undertaken by the local NGOs.

The sector's relevance for poverty reduction has been acknowledged for a long time amongst those who have sought to find alternative means by which to approach poverty reduction. NGOs have long been associated with development strategies that seek to utilise and build upon the poor's own knowledge, approaches towards development that emphasise the process of achieving development and not just the end objectives to be achieved, and in general terms seek to counter the more traditional top down, centrally managed with external expertise, approach towards achieving development with poverty reduction. Yet, it is only relatively recently that such thinking has begun to influence to approaches of the bilateral and multi-lateral donors. Factors behind this change in thinking include the growing rejection of the central role of the state in the development process and the emergence of poverty reduction as a priority objective for many donors which together with other contemporary priorities such as democracy, good governance, and gender, have placed far greater importance upon the role of participation in development.

Local NGOs are perceived as being potentially more participatory, more flexible, less hierarchic, more capable of building upon groups own organising practices and thereby of supporting a self-help approach towards development. It is also important to note that the self-help approach towards development is more in tune with the philosophy behind economic liberalisation, albeit with a pro-poor orientation and a more collectivist political philosophy at the local level.

The Government of India's approach towards the use of NGOs in its own development programmes has changed quite radically over the past ten years or so. It is now accepted that NGOs have an important role to play as part of the voluntary sector and they increasingly figure in both central and state-level programmes.

Currently there are over 20,000 NGOs registered under the Foreign Contributions Regulation Act (FCRA) in India and at least as many who are not. There is no doubt that a majority of these are present due to the availability of funds from both the government and international donors and that a considerable part of the development work undertaken by NGOs is project-oriented with little attempt to bring about a greater political involvement of the beneficiaries or for that matter to bring the interests of the beneficiaries into the broader political arena of development and development policy. They are primarily implementing agencies for programmes conceived elsewhere.

However there is a substantial minority for whom development is no longer merely based upon a charitable concern. These NGOs have instead pursued empowerment and self-help promotion through their activities. Much of their work is aimed at achieving a greater presence for their beneficiaries in the process of development at both local and macro levels. For these the aim is to achieve sustainable development by securing rights through organisational and institutional development. In sectors such as forestry, irrigation, wasteland improvement, watershed management and prioritising specific social groups such as women, scheduled castes and scheduled tribes, much of their work both directly and indirectly, is concerned with changing the relations that give rise to marginalisation, vulnerability and poverty at the local level.

To some extent, what is being witnessed amongst NGOs in India today is a desire to re-engage the local with the state. If NGOs' work in the sixties was primarily rooted in charitable development projects, the seventies and eighties witnessed an increasing tendency for many NGOs to view themselves as an alternative to the state, a development supported by the more general critique of the developmental role of the state in the international development discourse and by a more positive international aid policy towards NGOs. But what we are now witnessing in the nineties is local NGOs working in a more collaborative relationship with the state.

One form this collaboration is taking is that of NGOs taking on local responsibilities on behalf of the state. Today there are over 200 schemes for which NGOs can receive funds from central government or central agencies such as the Council for the Advancement of People's Action and Rural Technology (CAPART) and many more funding possibilities at state level and below.[1]

The second form is a more critical collaboration whereby NGOs are increasingly seeking to affect development policy through advocacy and lobbying, not only around particular issues as in the recent case of the Namarda Dam Project, but more generally in working for the recognition and attainment of the rights of those previously passed over in the formulation of the country's development strategy. NGO networks based upon a particular sector such as watershed management or minor irrigation, or based upon an administrative area, are one means by which this strategy is being pursued by Indian NGOs today.

Overview of donor involvement in the sector

Bilateral aid is by definition government to government aid and this has placed an obstacle in the way of donors who wish to support directly the work of local NGOs. Consequently most donor aid to NGOs passes via northern NGOs to southern NGOs and is therefore not part of bilateral aid and therefore not covered by this study.

As stated above, most donors are increasingly bringing local NGOs into their bilateral aid programmes through involving them in specific project components, but the NGOs are not the partner in this context, the partner remains the implementing department or ministry under which the project is found.

Several of the donors have utilised semi-autonomous organisations as a means by which to provide funding to local level NGOs and to programmes based upon the principle of local self-help group generation. For example CAPART, HUDCO and NABARD are all organisations working in this area with the government's full support as well as funding.

Danida is the EU Donor that currently works through CAPART, with 40 million DKK being channelled to NGOs in this way since 1980. DGIS has previously supported NGO projects through CAPART, but ceased to do so for some 10 years ago.

In 1996 Danida was supporting 14 such NGO projects. At the same time it is clear that support to local NGO projects are only a minor element within Danida's aid portfolio to India; that support to these is seen as being the responsibility of Danish NGOs. It is also the case that there is no explicit focus upon self-help as a development priority in Danida's conceptual framework for development in India or elsewhere. The situation with the other EU donors studied appears to be the same. The more orthodox sector approach being preferred with the aid being channelled through government institutions with the perceived advantages being that there is capacity building of government institutions, that the reach of government is greater, that the opportunities and possibilities for innovation, replication and scaling up are greater; and that administratively it is less demanding on the part of the donor.

Somewhat in contrast to this general attitude of the EU donors, BMZ has sought to take NGO support one step further by reaching an agreement in the 1993 Indo-German Aid Negotiations for GTZ to establish the Self-Help Fund project (GTZ-SHF) with a funding of 6 million DM and the Small Project Fund (GTZ-SPF), also of 6 million DM. Both of these began operating in 1994 and with both projects BMZ via GTZ can enter into direct partnership with local NGOs. This is quite unusual in that the fund has been established prior to partner institutions being identified. With the other EU donors, such funding of local NGOs tends to be on a one-off basis through small funds available for allocation under the Ambassadors' own authority.

The difference between the GTZ-SHF and the GTZ-SPF is that in the latter project local Indian organisations can approach the fund with a specific request for support for an activity that lies outside the scope of the normal bilateral domain. These requests can come from the private/NGO sector or the public sector, but the basic principle is that the fund operates as a demand driven activity.

In the case of the GTZ-SHF, the fund is designed to be used as a means for enabling capacity building of NGOs and involves far more technical assistance.

In the case of all of the EU donors investigated there is no sector paper as such that focuses specifically upon NGOs, not least because it is not seen to be a sector in its own right. However several of the donors have produced reports that explore the potential of working with local

NGOs. More often than not these are prepared from another sector perspective, for example from within the social sectors or forestry. The *Report on Alternative Mechanisms for the Funding and Management of Health and Population Projects in India* prepared by Tata Consultancy Services, November 1996, for The Health and Population Office of the Overseas Development Administration is one such example.

For its part, the GTZ-SHF has a background concept paper entitled *Money isn't Everything,* but again no sector paper as such. What it has established is a Core Group of local Experts whose responsibilities include the formulation of a strategy for facilitating the capacity building of local partner NGOs. Intrinsic to its work is the development of a conceptual approach to the work of GTZ-SHF and its partners and the translation of this into policy and practice.

Finally, should be noted here that the donors, bilateral and multi-lateral, appear to coordinate very little if at all in their work with and approach towards local NGOs and NGO funding vis á vis the Indian government.

The NGO projects selected for assessment

For the purpose of the study Danida's support to two NGOs via CAPART and the GTZ-SHF was studied through three local NGO partners, see Rajasekhar (1997). A third Danida/CAPART project has been studied for the Forestry Sector paper (Kripa,1997). This is the largest single NGO project funded by Danida through CAPART. It is an Agro-Forestry project being implemented by one of the largest Indian NGOs, BAIF, with a total project fund of 19.5 million DKK. Basic details of these projects are presented in the following table:

Conceptualisation of poverty

Danida's work with NGOs via CAPART does not have its own specific logic vis a vis poverty and poverty reduction, but falls into its more general approach towards poverty reduction in which NGOs are seen to have certain specific advantages over other institutional intervention mechanisms when projects involve local participation, local institutional capacity building and building upon the coping strategies of the poor. This has increasingly been the case in sectors and areas such as forestry, irrigation, watershed management, and urban slum improvement.

In the case of the GTZ-SHF, the partnership concept present in the project is based quite explicitly upon a multi-dimensional

Table 17.1: Basic Details on the Selected NGOs

Name of the NGO	Location	Area	No. of Villages	No. of groups	Total Staff	Donor agency
NIRPHAD	Mathura District, U.P.	Naujil and Mathura Blocks	123	N.A.	N.A.	Danida/ CAPART
PHCC	Dindigal District, T.N.	Palani Hills, near Kodai canal	N.A.	N.A.	N.A.	Danida/ CAPART
RDO	Nilgiris District, T.N.	Four blocks	56	56	17 (excl. village workers)	GTZ-SHF
SHARE	North Arcot Ambedkar District, T.N.	One block	28	*	6	GTZ-SHF
Homo Sapiens	Nalgonda District in A.P.	One mandal	13	10	5	GTZ-SHF
BAIF	Karnataka State	1 block in each of 10 districts	46-106 families in each block	N.A.	N.A.	Danida/ CAPART

conceptualisation of poverty with the argument that local NGOs are the most best institutional means with which to generate a sustainable strategy partly based upon the poor's own organising practices, but with considerable institutional capacity building being developed through the partnership relationship with the SHF.

> 'The non-governmental organisations play an important role in poverty reduction. They strengthen the self-help potential and the mobilisation and social integration of disadvantaged and marginalised population groups. We must remember that non-governmental agencies are independent and autonomous actors and should not be regarded as mere implementing agencies of official cooperation. Over and above their role of empowerment of the poor, they play an important role as partners of governments.'
>
> — Carl-Dieter Springer, Federal Minister, BMZ

The poor's own perception of poverty, the multi-dimensional nature of poverty ranging from assets to rights, the linkage of the poor's own coping strategies with other institutional actors such as local government, are all built into the thinking behind the GTZ-SHF.

Table 17.2: Objectives and activities of the selected NGOs

NGO	Stated Principal Objectives	Main Activities	Target Groups
NIRPHAD	Providing economic infrastructure to the poor so that human development occurs.	1. Providing economic infrastructure such as agricultural extension, irrigation, livestock development 2. Providing infrastructure of human development	Small and Marginal farmers belonging to depressed castes
PHCC	Protecting the deteriorating natural resources	1. Alternative practices in agriculture and forest lands. 2. Suitable technologies for natural resource management. 3. Plantation of trees and perennial crops in dry lands. 4. Creating local expertise.	Small farmers owning 2 to 5 hectares of land.
RDO	Facilitating self-help promotion	1. Enabling the people to possess the land. 2. Planting perennial crops on the lands controlled by the poor for the stable income flow. 3. Education of children	Deprived sections of the community.
SHARE	Total empowerment of the poor through income generating programmes.	1. Enabling the poor to undertake income generating activities through skill upgrading, marketing and raw material support. 2. Providing education and support services for the poor and their children	The poor and marginalised women.
Homo Sapiens	Not applicable as project under forumlation	Not applicable as project under formulation.	Tribals with a focus on women
BAIF	Initially to support agro-forestry amongst landless allotted waste land. Subsequently changed to poor landowners.	1. Increase the income of beneficiaries 2. Reduce beneficiaries dependency on forest resources. 3. Reduce beneficiaries dependency on casual labour and out-migration. 4. Demonstrate the feasibility of intensive afforestation and agro-forestry models.	Initially landless households subsequently Scheduled Caste, Scheduled Tribe and other weaker sections having marginal landholdings.

Table 17.2 provides an overview of the objectives and activities of the NGOs studied.

With the GTZ-SHF partners, the emphasis is upon working towards a better situational analysis and needs assessment of the poverty situation in the locality where the NGO functions. In the case of one partner, Homo Sapiens, this resulted in a period of more than one year between the establishment of a partner relationship and the submission of a project proposal for funding. In most instances, a project will arrive on a donor's table within one or two weeks of contact being established. This has undoubtedly led to a better conceptualisation of poverty, a point acknowledged by the NGO itself and reflected in the consequent project's nature and design. It also contrasts quite strongly with the Danida/CAPART projects in which the conceptualisation of poverty, in so far as it is present, is rooted in the philosophy of the individual NGO's approach towards development together with what the NGO perceives to be necessary for a proposal to be accepted by CAPART/Danida. In the case of BAIF, for example, it is present in terms of the delineation of the target group, initially as landless households, subsequently as Scheduled Caste and Scheduled Tribe households. In the case of BAIF, the lack of a multi-dimensional approach to poverty is reflected in the activities proposed and even further in the comments that came from local villagers, for example women from the targeted families.

Even when the donor seeks to work towards a better conceptual approach as in the case of GTZ-SHF, much depends upon the establishment of a positive partner relationship between the donor and the NGO. NGOs can be notoriously resistant to change if they have operated for a number of years and if they are also receiving funds from other donors. Strong personalities amongst NGO leaders can also lead to conflicts in the relationship. Ultimately, a donor remains a donor even while seeking to act as a partner in the development process and the different needs and interests of the donor and the partner will always be a potential source of tension no matter how good the relationship is.

Targeting

Targeting in the Danida/CAPART project is sectoral (irrigation, resource management, basic health, social forestry) and institutional. The latter is in fact as much determined by the level of intervention, i.e. local, as by the type of institution, i.e. NGO.

Beyond this, the targeting remains the task of the NGO and in the case of the three Danida/CAPART NGOs investigated, it has to be said that it was not always the poor, let alone the poorest of the poor, that were being targeted. There is an argument from some donor quarters that more than 90 per cent of those in the rural sector are relatively poor and that any rural project will directly reduce poverty for some of the rural poor. BMZ-KfW for one has expressed such a view. Having accepted this argument, targeting is considered thereafter in terms of who are most likely to utilise the resources, technologies, and other inputs from the project and thereby make it successful and sustainable. If donors are prepared to present such a view, then NGOs are also ready to accept it, not least as targeting that improves the chances of a project being successful in terms of resource utilisation, increased income, technological adoption, etc., will better secure a second phase or a second project and thereby the continued funding of the NGO.

The consequence at the local level for such a policy on targeting is that the poorest are passed over and it is the stronger rather than weaker sections of the local community that tend to benefit. In the cases of NIRPHAD and BAIF, possession of land was one of the most important criteria for targeting. Landless and women in the landed families were only targeted through secondary components that were poorly conceived and experienced high failure rates.

Good targeting of the poor and the poorest is not the focus of the SHF as such, but it should be the outcome of an effective partnership if the parties can work in a dynamic and mutually supportive manner. As mentioned above the partner relationship can be affected by many different factors on both sides. RDO has targeted on the basis of village, selecting communities in which the community as a whole can be described as poor. Working in the Nilgiri Hills, RDO selected villages populated by migrants who came from Andhra Pradesh over the past 30 years or so in search of employment and land. The households, for the most part landless, have been encouraged to illegally occupy forest lands, to clear and terrace the land and to plant tea bushes. They then seek B Memo status with the Land Revenue Department by paying an annual fine for illegal cultivation of forest lands. These in turn provide evidence of occupancy that can lead to a claim for occupancy rights after ten years. Targeting was therefore on a community basis and given the fact that the majority of the community differed only in extremes of poverty, this has been quite effective. The relationship with SHF has supported the ongoing activities, but has also resulted in the communities being mobilised in smaller groups to increase participation and participation of the poorest and women in particular. It has also introduced savings and credit programmes for the groups in order to diversify and strengthen the coping strategies of the poor involved. In so doing, the poor have been better targeted in general as well as in more specific terms of gender, lack of alternative employment/income generating activities, etc.

The role of SHF in strengthening the poverty components of other NGO activities is apparent in the case of the other partner NGOs investigated as well. Again it is a combination of the capacity building activities incorporated into the partnership relationship that seek to improve the conceptualisation of poverty and targeting of the poor on the one hand, and the project component support provided which enables a greater diversity of component activities as well as greater support for generating sustainable self-help groups.

SHARE requested support for their ongoing programme on manufacturing palm leaf products with a sub-component involving women specifically. GTZ-SHF agreed on the condition that the programme was broadened to include those not traditionally involved in this production in order to broaden the poverty reducing impact. GTZ-SHF also proposed expansion of the programme to include a savings and credit component in order to diversify the possible coping strategies of the poor.

Gender

Gender awareness is intrinsic to the needs awareness approach with the GTZ-SHF. This is reflected in the women-oriented components implemented in most of the partner NGOs. The example of SHARE has already been mentioned, here they sought to enhance both the income generating potential of women and to support their ability to press for their rights with respect to employment etc. Gender awareness within the self-help groups is given a relative high priority in all the self-help groups on the part of GTZ-SHF and appears to be implemented by the four partner NGOs although with varying degrees of success.

In the all of the NGOs studied the gender dimension existed in the documents as part of the overall objectives, but in practice, the role of women was subordinated both in terms of the design of the project components and in terms of gender sensitisation generally. This merely reflects the wider problem of gender awareness being a part of the general discourse amongst donors and NGOs, but the reality being far from positive. Again in SHARE's work, the income generating activity based around palm leaf products has the aim of enabling the target group to pay for education and health care. However, many of the women involved consider girl children to be a burden because of the need to pay a dowry. Many female children work in the craft centres in order to acquire money for their dowries and little emphasis is placed on their education. The inability to transcend this somewhat token approach to gender in development interventions has yet to be addressed by NGOs and their donors.

Participation

All of the NGOs investigated place emphasis upon the participatory side of their development activities. The problem appears to be that while stressing this, the NGOs tend to generate their project proposals on the basis of their own identification of the problems faced by the proposed beneficiaries and participation follows afterwards in terms of involving the beneficiaries in the subsequent implementation. Consequently the identification and design phases of the project involve little or no participation. It has to be said that the Government of India and donors tend to reinforce this failure by bringing NGOs in at a late stage of the project development as 'organisations to get the people involved in a project'.

As has already been mentioned, the Danida/CAPART process of identifying partners and projects tends to be reactive in that NGOs submit proposals to CAPART who then forward those they think fit Danida's interests. There may be a degree of appraisal and modification of the proposals prior to the acceptance and disbursement of funds, but these tend not to be major changes in practice. Due to this process, it is difficult for donors to press for participation to be a central element in the original identification and design of a project. The problems that can arise from this reactive role of the donors and of working through intermediaries are illustrated by the example of BAIF.

In the early 1980's, during the Janata Government's administration, there was a proposal to give C & D class waste lands to the landless for the purpose of afforestation. This led to BAIF proposing an Agro-Forestry project in Karnataka and via CAPART, BAIF approached Danida. Danida sent a pre-appraisal team which recommended the project. 8 years after conception, the BAIF Agro-Forestry project began to be implemented in Karnataka. Poverty reduction was implicit in the project as the land was to be given to the weakest sections of society as identified by BAIF. However, the government went back on its commitment for 'technical reasons'. The landless thereby dropped out of the project, but the project went ahead with the same proposal, but a modified target group. Would this have been possible if the poor had played a central role in the identification and design of the project?

In the case of GTZ-SHF the situation varies from NGO to NGO. In some cases, as with Homo Sapiens, considerable time is given to needs assessment and context analysis prior to project formulation. This introduces a high degree of participation into the identification and design of the project. In other instances, the project is already formulated, but the partner relationship, if established, requires that modifications be made and additional component development be undertaken by the NGO with a stress on participation. This is held to be central to the self-help philosophy behind the GTZ-SHF.

Local ownership in the NGO projects

Local ownership is intrinsic to the NGO sector as funding is to local NGOs who have primary responsible for identifying, designing and implementing the projects. In many evaluations, the NGO can nominate external experts to evaluation team and NGO self-evaluation is also widely accepted by donors as part of the assessment.

At the same time, with both Danida/CAPART and GTZ-SHF, the fact that the NGO and the local organisation/self-help group are not the same organisations makes it difficult to assess the location of project ownership. Often the beneficiaries themselves find it difficult to separate between their own organisations and that of the NGO. For their part, the NGOs are often guilty of merging the two in practice despite their presentation of the two as being separate in their own project documents and presentations of their work. Local ownership and ownership by the poor targeted by the intervention are clearly not the same thing.

Sustainability

The sustainability of the projects undertaken through the NGOs is quite difficult to ascertain, particularly in the GTZ-SHF as this is a relatively new project. Given the nature of the sector and its stress upon the institutional capacity of the NGOs in generating participatory, group-based, components, it should be that sustainability should rank high in any assessment of the sector. However there are clearly a number of problems with this assumption.

First, the lack of clarity in the relationship between the local NGO and the project groups and in their respective roles and status is a major weakness. Often the failure to clearly conceptualise the self-help group as an independent institution has lead to a high level of dependency of the group upon the NGO. While this might be unavoidable in the short run, in the longer-term the NGO should be able to withdraw from the day to day management and organisation of the group and its activities—savings and credit, production centres, forestry management, etc. As yet this appears not to be the case in any of the NGOs investigated.

Secondly, the NGOs can begin relatively quickly with the implementation of projects at the local level, but the linkage with other institutions, both NGOs and government institutions in support of securing and /or improving the rights of the beneficiaries and their organisations to better political services, improved economic and physical security, land rights, etc. takes considerable time. This is not helped by the short duration of funding for most NGO projects. It also requires that the NGOs are willing to broaden their conceptual approach to local development to embrace these other actors. NGOs generally have not been particularly open to such thinking tending to be both individualistic and not particularly willing to collaborate with the state. GTZ-SHF has stressed the need to move towards networking and a critical engagement. Again this is part of the partnership relationship. In the Danida/CAPART cases investigated, this is left more to the individual NGOs.

Thirdly, sustainability of such local interventions is beset with many of the problems of other sector projects, not least with respect to economic and technological sustainability. With respect to the former, credit and savings programmes are increasingly becoming a mainstay activity within the NGO sector, but as yet there is little evidence that such groups can become economically sustainable. Economic sustainability in other areas is now being approached by some NGOs through seeking government funding to carry out particular activities. This is not the case amongst the NGOs investigated with respect to the projects funded by the donors. However, other activities undertaken might involve government funding and it is the aim of the GTZ-SHF that NGOs should look to this possibility as part of a longer term strategy.

Finally, there is the question of technological sustainability. In the case of NIRPHAD, the sinking of wells as part of the project to improve cultivation of more commercial crops has only added to the increasingly deteriorating situation with respect to the water table level. With wells now beginning to fail and little in the way of watershed management being practised or encouraged, the beneficiaries are facing greater vulnerability. Diversification of strategies is being encouraged in the GTZ-SHF partner NGOs, but similar problems of sustainability are present with projects too much dependent upon one specific activity approached in a particular way.

Replicability

Replicability in the NGO sector can take several forms. On the donors side replicability is principally a question of willingness to extend the practice of working with NGOs as partner institutions. Where there is such a willingness then the principal problem faced is at the level of aid negotiations with the Indian government. Can funds be provided directly to local NGOs? To whom are such NGOs accountable with respect to development activities, fund utilisation, etc.? The Danish experience with CAPART as an intermediary in the donor-NGO relationship has not been a particularly positive one and Danida is now withdrawing from any further financing of new NGO projects in this way.

The examples of NGOs funded by Danida via CAPART demonstrate the quite fundamental flaw embodied in a donor-NGO relationship where the project is already identified and designed prior to the relationship being established. The possibility of replicability does not really exist while this situation remains as the donor faces a take it, modify it, or leave it choice.

This is perhaps one of the main reasons as to why for most donors, apart from the funds allocated from the limited funds for which Embassies have local granting authority, NGOs remain local actors to be utilised within broader projects, for example the Gomti Urban Development Project funded by ODA in which two NGOs, SPARC and SEWA, were brought in at a late stage in the project's design for local institution building and participatory planning.

For the NGOs, replicability possesses three possible dimensions: expanding the scale and area of existing activities based upon the existing NGO organisation, setting up the same activities on a similar (small) scale in new locations with new NGO organisations, or entering into advocacy, not least via NGO networking, to consolidate and extend their work. The dangers of the first approach is that NGOs become large, bureaucratic, and are no longer truly local organisations. The second offers the possibility of replicating the strengths of being small and local, but in relations to other development actors such as the government, they represent a weak lobby. The third dimension in many ways avoids the problems of the first two, but at the same time runs counter to contemporary NGO culture although there are signs of change here.

The GTZ-SHF is the only example we have found so far of an EU donor actively working towards greater inter-NGO collaboration in the form of sharing experiences via workshops, Core Group support, and similar activities on the one hand, and on the other hand by working towards NGOs critically engaging with the state as part of their process oriented project development. This extends down to the self-help groups through the aim of both strengthening their own management and organisational capacities as well as through cluster formation, establishing federations, and facilitating linkages with local government and local financial institutions.

On the basis of these actions, the replicability of the SHF is probably quite high, but of course for the donor it remains a relatively low budget, but administratively demanding project with substantial results only likely to emerge after a number of years.

Monitoring and evaluation systems

The four GTZ-SHF NGOs are all required to provide regular accounts of their activities and regular evaluations by local consultants are also carried out as part of the partnership relationship. These are coordinated from the main GTZ-SHF office in New Delhi and its local southern office in Bangalore. As the project has only been functioning for three years and the current complement of 36 partners has been built up over these years, the possibility for measuring the poverty reducing impact has been limited. Nevertheless information is being collected within and from the NGOs, not merely as a part of their assessment, but as a means through which to build upon the overall objective of local organisation capacity building by the GTZ-SHF. Currently, as part of the work of the Core Group, a research project is to be funded covering a number of the south Indian partners in which the poverty reducing impact of their work will be assessed.

For all of the NGOs investigated, Danida and GTZ funded, project appraisals and evaluations are carried out on behalf of the donors along the same lines as with most other development projects. In the cases of the Danida/CAPART NGOs, the degree to which these feedback into the work of either the donor, Danida, or the NGOs is difficult to assess, but would appear to be negligible. Danida's decision to discontinue such funding is believed to be partly based upon the findings from these, but dissatisfaction with CAPART as an intermediary has also been a factor here.

Impact in terms of poverty reduction

The scale of the impact is limited by the scale of the interventions. NGO projects tend to cover relatively small numbers of beneficiaries in quite small localities. Even the BAIF project although having a Karnataka dimension, in reality covered a small number of households scattered across the State.

The impact upon the poor within those localities would appear to vary considerably. The problems concerning the adequacy of the targeting of the poor has been discussed above. The objectives of the different projects investigated vary considerably as do the development philosophies of the NGOs themselves and these carry important consequences for the type of intervention and the target group identified, but in so far as it is possible to assess, those projects that have been examined were not disasters either from a project perspective or from a poverty reduction perspective.

In the cases of BAIF, NIRPHAD and PHCC, the target groups are small and marginal landowners, not the poorest, but nevertheless relatively poor. The farmers, 906, 350 and 500 respectively, mainly male, believe that their condition has improved due to the projects. In the cases of SHARE the beneficiaries are around 700 many of which are female with the project's focus on palm leaf production. Again these beneficiaries spoke of an improvement in their condition. With RDO, the situation is not so easy to assess due to the fact that only 17 acres have been planted with tea bushes so far, the legal status of the land is not yet settled, and the return to tea leaf production has not yet begun to take place. Support for the project is high amongst the villages targeted however. Finally, Homo Sapiens has yet to proceed with its project so the impact cannot be assessed.

Conclusions and suggestions

— It is clear that NGOs do possess a particular institutional advantage that can enhance a broader development strategy, but this requires that the donors, the NGOs and the Indian government can recognise and agree as to what that role can be. Conceptual thinking on State-NGO-poor relations from a development perspective is largely absent amongst the donor agencies. Amongst the six donors studied, only BMZ appears to have anything that might be loosely described as a sector approach towards NGOs and a firm commitment to provide bilateral funds to NGOs. This has been developed within the overall framework of German aid policy and has then be communicated from BMZ down to the country level and to GTZ. Only subsequently has there been an attempt at inter-donor discussion/dialogue on the matter. Outside the other EU donors, it is believed that the Ford Foundation has a policy that is somewhat similar, and possibly NORAD.

— Success in supporting local NGOs for poverty reduction would appear to be linked to a good partnership relationship between the bilateral donor and the partner NGO institutions. Given the history of NGOs, their ideological positions vis-a-vis government and donors and foreign funding, their natures (strong personalities as leaders, small fiefdoms etc.), such a partnership is both very difficult to establish and is extremely time consuming for the donor. At the same time, inter-donor coordination is central to the sector not least because NGOs are getting adept at playing funding agencies off against each other. It also appears to be absent.

— Intermediaries such as CAPART create one too many institutional intermediaries between the donor and the self-help group that the NGO sector is supposedly aimed at. On the other hand they do provide a solution to the delivery of bilateral funds to NGOs and the help with the problem of accountability, not least in the guaranteeing of funds.

REFERENCE

1. See Reddy, S. & Rajasekhar, D., (1996) Development Programmes and NGOs, BCO, Bangalore.

18

ASSESSMENT OF SPECIFIC INTERVENTIONS

Each of the preceding sections of this chapter has ended with a number of project- and sector-specific conclusions. The next and final chapter in turn will bring the overall conclusions from the entire study. In between we provide a big assessment table which in a way summarises the content of the analysis of the 33 projects and programmes that were subjected to detailed study. The assessments in the table deal with a total of 16 dimensions (or indicators) of each the projects ranging from conceptualisation of poverty over targeting, gender, participation, sustainability, replicability and monitoring to overall impact (based on 4 dimensions of poverty reduction). In each case these are judged to be either substantially positive, moderately positive or negligible (in only one case was the assessment negative). The assessments are built on the researchers' study of documents, visits to projects and interviews with staff and beneficiaries.

This table should be interpreted with some caution. Needless to say, it is difficult to summarise important and complex dimensions in projects in a single ++, + or 0. We may not in all cases have done justice to each and every dimension of every project. The result should be seen as more broadly indicative, and taken as a whole we do believe that the table at a glance provides some clues to where some of the strengths lie and some of the weaknesses. This will be dealt with at a more general level in the following chapter.

Table 18.1: Assessment of projects taken up in this study

	1	2	3	4	5	6	7
Sector	Water-shed	Water-shed	Water-shed	Water-shed	Irriga-tion	Irriga-tion	Irriga-tion
Project	KWDP	DVP	KIWMP	KAWAD	TIPP-II	OLIP	TRP
Donor	Danida	EU	KfW	DFID	DGIS	KfW	EU
State	Karn.	UP	Karn.	Karn.	Karn.	Orissa	TN
Project Dates	1990-97	93-2001	94-2000	1997-?	1996-?	n.av	1984
Conceptualisation of poverty	0	0	0	++	+	0	+
Poverty orientation (design)	Indirect	Indirect	Indirect	Direct	Indirect	Indirect	Indirect
Targeting: design	+	0	+	++	++	+	0
Targeting: implementation	+	+	+	n.ap.	n.ap.	+	n.av.
Gender: design	+	+	+	+	+	0.	0
Gender: implementation	+	+	0	n.ap.	+	n.ap.	n.av.
Participation: design	0	0	0	+	0	0	0
Participation: Implementation	+	+	+	++	+	+	+
Sustainability	+	+	+	++	n.ap.	n.av.	n.av.
Replicability	+	0	+	+	n.ap.	n.av.	n.av.
Monitoring and evaluation	0	0	0	n.ap.	n.ap.	n.av.	n.av.
Impact							
Livelihoods	+	+	n.ap.	n.ap.	n.ap.	++	+
Resources	+	+	n.ap.	n.ap.	+	n.av.	n.av.
Knowledge	+	+	n.ap.	n.ap.	n.ap.	n.av.	n.av.
Rights/entitlements	+	+	n.ap.	n.ap.	+	n.av.	n.av.
Overall	+	+	n.ap.	n.ap.	n.ap.	n.av.	n.av.

Table 18.1: Assessment of projects taken up in this study

	8	9	10	11	12	13	14
Sector	Forestry	Forestry	Forestry	Water	Water	Water	Water
Project	JFMP	BAIF	SFP	SP-VI	SP-VIII	IRS&WS	IRWSS
Donor	DFID	Danida	Sida	DGIS	DGIS	Danida	DGIS
State	Karn.	Karn.	Orissa	UP	UP	Karn.	Karn.
Project Dates	1992-98	1990-97	1983-96	1987-	1995-	89-2000	1993-
Conceptualisation of poverty	0	0	0	0	+	0	+
Poverty orientation (design)	Other	Direct	Indirect	Indirect	Indirect	Indirect	Indirect
Targeting: design	0	+	+	+	+	+	+
Targeting: implementation	0	0	0	0	0	0	n.ap.
Gender: design	0	+	0	+	++	++	++
Gender: implementation	+	+	0	0	+	+	n.ap.
Participation: design	0	0	0	+	++	++	++
Participation: implementation	++	++	+	0	0	0	n.ap.
Sustainability	++	0	0	0	n.ap.	0	n.ap.
Replicability	++	+	0	0	n.ap.	0	n.ap.
Monitoring and evaluation	++	+	+	0	n.ap.	0	n.ap.
Impact							
Livelihoods	+	++	+	0	n.ap.	0	n.ap.
Resources	+	++	+	+	n.ap.	+	n.ap.
Knowledge	+	+	+	0	n.ap.	0	n.ap.
Rights/entitlements	+	+	+	0	n.ap.	0	n.ap.
Overall	+	+	+	0	n.ap.	0	n.ap.

Table 18.1: Assessment of projects taken up in this study

	15	16	17	18	19	20	21
Sector	Health	Health	Health	Education	Education	Education	Women
Project	ADP	ADP	ICDS	DPEP	DPEP	LJ	WYTEP
Donor	DFID	Danida	Sida	EU	DFID	Sida	Danida
State	Orissa	TN	TN	MP	AP	Raj.	Karn.
Project Dates	1979-97	81-2000	1989-98	1995-	1996-	1992-	1982-
Conceptualisation of poverty	+	0	0	0	0	0	0
Poverty orientation (design)	Indirect	Indirect	Direct	Direct	Direct	Direct	Indirect
Targeting: design	++	0	0	++	++	++	+
Targeting: implementation	0	+	0	+	++	++	+
Gender: design	+	0	+	++	++	++	++
Gender: implementation	0	0	0	++	++	++	++
Participation: design	0	0	0	++	++	+	0
Participation: implementation	0	+	+	+	++	+	+
Sustainability	0	+	++	++	++	++	+
Replicability	0	+	++	++	++	+	++
Monitoring and evaluation	++	+	0	++	++	+	+
Impact							
Livelihoods	0	0	0	0	0	0	+
Resources	+	+	+	++	++	++	++
Knowledge	0	+	+	++	++	++	++
Rights/entitlements	0	+	+	+	+	+	+
Overall	0	+	+	++	++	++	++

Table 18.1: Assessment of projects taken up in this study

	22	23	24	25	26	27	28
Sector	Women	Women	Slums	Slums	Slums	Slums	Slums
Project	TEWA	MS	BUPP	HDFC	VSIP	CHIS-II	HUD-CO
Donor	Danida	DGIS	DGIS	KfW	DFID	DFID	KfW
State	Orissa	UP	Karn.	Kerala	AP	AP	Kerala
Project Dates	87-2000	1988-97	1993-	n.av.	1988-96	1996-98	n.av.
Conceptualisation of poverty	0	+	+	+	++	+	0
Poverty orientation (design)	Indirect	Direct	Direct	Direct	Direct	Direct	Indirect
Targeting: design	+	++	+	+	++	+	0
Targeting: implementation	+	++	+	-	+	0	n.av.
Gender: design	++	++	++	++	++	++	n.av.
Gender: implementation	++	++	n.av.	n.av.	n.av.	n.ap.	n.av
Participation: design	0	0	++	++	++	++	0
Participation: implementation	+	++	+	0	+	0	–
Sustainability	+	+	0	0	+	0	++
Replicability	++	++	0	+	+	+	+
Monitoring and evaluation	+	+	n.av.	n.av.	++	++	n.av.
Impact							
Livelihoods	+	+	+	0	++	+	0
Resources	+	++	+	+	++	+	0
Knowledge	+	++	n.av.	n.av.	n.av.	n.ap.	n.av.
Rights/entitlements	+	++	0	n.av.	++	0	+
Overall	+	++	+	+	++	+	n.av.

Table 18.1: Assessment of projects taken up in this study

	29	30	31	32	33
Sector	NGOs	NGOs	NGOs	NGOs	NGOs
Project	NIRPH-AD	PHCC	RDO	SHARE	Homo Sap.
Donor	Danida	Danida	GTZ	GTZ	GTZ
State	UP	TN	TN	TN	AP
Project Dates	n.av.	n.av.	n.av.	n.av.	n.av.
Conceptualisation of poverty	++	++	++	++	++
Poverty orientation (design)	Indirect	Indirect	Direct	Direct	Indirect
Targeting: design	+	+	++	++	+
Targeting: implementation	0	+	++	++	+
Gender: design	+	+	+	++	+
Gender: implementation	+	+	+	++	+
Participation: design	0	0	0	++	0
Participation: implementation	++	+	+	++	+
Sustainability	++	+	+	n.av.	+
Replicability	++	++	++	++	++
Monitoring and evaluation	n.av.	n.av.	n.av.	n.av.	n.av.
Impact					
Livelihoods	++	+	+	++	n.av.
Resources	++	+	++	++	n.av.
Knowledge	++	+	+	+	n.av.
Rights/entitlements	+	+	+	+	n.av.
Overall	++	+	+	++	n.av.

Key:

++	substantially positive
+	moderately positive
0	negligible
–	negative or adverse
n.av	not available
n.ap.	not applicable

19

CONCLUSIONS

In undertaking the study of poverty reduction in EU donors' aid to India, we have entered into a quite detailed analysis of the organisations involved and the programmes and projects that they are responsible for. To attempt to synthesize the detail in a conclusion is always prone to the problems of generalisation. The importance of such an exercise is that it can focus attention on the core findings and the recommendations that they give rise to; the danger is that one focuses on the condition of the forest and overlooks the state of the trees.

All of the EU donors studied wished to strengthen the poverty reduction objective in their aid to India, in line with the overall objectives of the European Union's aid. However, beyond this stated desire on the part of the six EU donors, the degree of commonality quickly begins to disappear. In asserting the priority of poverty reduction over other objectives, in communicating the objective through to the lower levels of their management systems, and in general operationalisation of the objective, the six EU donors reveal considerable variations in their commitments to poverty reduction and the poor.

It can well be argued that to focus upon poverty reduction in isolation when examining donor agencies' aid to India is to ignore the role that other objectives have to play in determining the nature of that aid. While we do not dispute the one-sidedness involved in the foregoing study, we would at the same time argue that if poverty reduction is the over-arching objective of EU donors' aid then such an approach is legitimate. Secondly that a focused examination of the status of that objective can have the positive outcome of serving to enhance poverty reduction in the future. At least we would hope that this would be the case.

Generally it can be concluded that while the rhetoric of poverty reduction is quite considerable and the overall impact of projects on poverty reduction is quite positive, the operationalisation of the poverty reduction objective remains a problem. Closer examination of the aid practice of EU donors studied indicates a lack of commitment and direction to the poverty reduction objective. While there are indications of changes underway and improvements in many areas with respect to poverty reduction, there remains an uncertainty and a certain lack of clarity on the part of the donors that affects the overall picture and must give rise to serious concern for the future. Problems in a number of areas support this concern on our part.

Donor strategies

On the basis of the research undertaken in 1997, the promotion of poverty reduction is not the overarching priority in any of the six EU donors' strategies in India. At best it can be seen as being a leading priority alongside a number of others. In particular the interests of trade, investment and the private sector of the donor country also figure as leading factors in the formulation and implementation of India aid strategies. One should not exclude the fact that business considerations can support the poverty reduction objective, yet with aid it would appear to be more accidental than planned. There is a strong case that such interests run counter to the poverty reduction objective and seriously erode its status and the fulfilment of its goals.

In addition to conflicting interests weakening the poverty reduction objective, the shift towards a sector structuring of aid on the part of the six EU donors would not appear to be linked to the PR objective or to facilitate the pursuit of that objective. Ideally a good country strategy should be able to demonstrate the linkages between the donor's operational priorities and its priority objective of poverty reduction. A sector strategy should then provide a more detailed discussion as to how interventions within a sector contribute to the overall poverty reduction objective in the country strategy. For all six EU donors, there is little evidence of sector papers, where they exist, fulfilling this need as poverty reduction is weakly represented or absent from these papers. Furthermore, for all of the donors studied the portfolios of projects and programmes are products of long engagements in delivering aid to India. Consequently the selection of sectors by countries within which to concentrate their aid programmes reflects decisions made on grounds that are not necessarily so relevant today. Poverty reduction has not been a priority consideration. Sectors chosen for aid appear to reflect a country's supposed comparative advantage: Denmark linked to agriculture, Sweden to forestry, Netherlands to water etc.

On dialogue and coordination

The complexity of India for aid donors lies not only in size of the country and the extent and diversity of poverty, but also in the political and administrative complexities present. The nature and scale of the development problems, not least some 400 million people below the poverty line, would suggest the need for close dialogue and coordination amongst the donors and between the donors and the government. This would also support the need for greater ownership of aid-supported development strategies by the recipient government, as espoused in the sector approach towards aid.

There is, however, very little coordination between the donors and at both the union level and at the state-level there is little policy dialogue. In particular there has been remarkably little attempt to discuss respective conceptions of poverty and strategies for poverty reduction on the part of the donors and the Indian government. Not only does this undermine the principle of the local ownership in policy and strategy development, it threatens the entire basis for pursuing poverty reduction successfully in a sustainable and replicable manner.

The marginal status of aid in the Indian context, around 1% of GNP, of which the contribution of the six EU donors is relatively small compared to that of the World Bank and Japan, is part of the problem. The donors feel that they possess little leverage, the Indian government can justifiably argue that aid makes little overall contribution to development, and inter-donor coordination does not seem so important given the sheer size of the country and number of aid opportunities existing. But if the relative size of the aid contribution to development is small, the amount of aid from the perspective of the donors is large. Secondly, the relative size is the basis for arguing that it is the quality and not the quantity of the aid that is important. Both dialogue with the Indian government and coordination with the other donors are central to enhancing the quality of aid and not least its capacity to achieve poverty reduction.

Those EU donors committed to poverty reduction should therefore play a greater role in furthering the objective beyond the circle of EU donors. During and around the 1996 India Development Forum's meeting in Tokyo a number of the EU donors together with the UNDP were involved in efforts to put social development more firmly on the agenda of this and future IDF meetings. Previously such meetings had been dominated by macro-economic issues in which the World Bank had been central. This is an example of how greater EU coordination and pressure could increase the status of poverty reduction on the part of donors' aid strategies for India.

But donor coordination together with greater dialogue with the Indian government on poverty and poverty reduction could enhance the quality and effectiveness of that aid as well. The low risk of duplication in aid interventions due to the size of the country and the relative size of the aid contribution to the development budget is a poor argument. The limited degree of sector coordination amongst donors is not enough. The isolated instances of donors sponsoring or organising multi-donor-government talks on a particular sector at state or union level is also not enough. Neither is the occasional donor-government conference on poverty and approaches to poverty reduction. At the very least, the UNDP's attempts at organising working groups of donors on particular themes or sectors need to be taken seriously and actively supported by the donors.

Management

The six EU donors have widely different management systems ranging from a 'hands-off' approach characterised by the EC and Sida, to the 'hands-on' approaches of the ODA/DFID and Danida. At the field level there is little doubt that donor technical and advisory inputs can improve the quality of project design and implementation. If poverty reduction is communicated through the donors' organisation to the field level, then there is a possibility of engaging the poor in identification and design and not just implementation and evaluation. It is also possible that the institutional and economic sustainability of projects might be improved. On the other hand, such engagement on the part of the donors could erode local ownership, undermine movement towards devolution and decentralisation, and reduce the replicability of the interventions. Much depends upon the sensitivity of the engagement by the donors.

This in turn depends upon the quality of the country expertise on the part of the donors. While the creation of a strong country base in the donor agency might create problems amongst others with respect to increasing costs, efficiency in donor staff utilisation, and complex decision-making structures, it can considerably improve the formulation and operationalisation of country strategies and aid policy objectives. It can also facilitate better dialogue with the Indian government enhancing both the innovation and the local ownership embodied in sector programming. It also provides the basis for better inter-donor coordination.

As stated, the commitment to innovation is strong amongst the donors. Yet a substantial number of the aid interventions continue to be quite standard interventions. On the part of the Indian government there was considerable support for the introduction of new ideas and practices by the donors, but there was also a strong argument that donors should disburse allocated funds more rapidly. In the context of a bureaucracy that is quite averse to taking risks and where initiatives tend to be stifled, the donors can play a critical role in promoting innovation. The officials in the Ministry of Finance and some line ministries were ready to point to developments in participatory methods and gender specific approaches introduced by donors. It has to be accepted that promotion of such innovations might delay disbursements.

At the same time, innovations with respect to poverty reduction are more difficult as these often require a less acceptable form of change. They tend to go beyond institutional capacity building and the enhancement or improvement of existing practices. To secure the introduction and implementation of such changes often requires a greater commitment and (political) will on the part of the government partner. This requires in turn, a strong commitment from the state and the higher echelons to press such changes through. Close cooperation, the establishment of greater ownership on the part of the government for such changes, continuity in dialogue and support, require a country capacity that most of the EU donors are reluctant to commit at the present point in time. ODA/DFID perhaps is the exception to this with its decentralised BDCOD in New Delhi.

Monitoring and evaluation of aid interventions is also central to an effective system of aid management. While this has improved in recent years in India, it continues to remain very much a donor-driven affair. It is questionable as to how much benefit such monitoring and evaluation brings to more general development effectiveness. Weaknesses in monitoring and evaluation are considerable with respect to poverty reduction. The majority of reports yield very little information on the impact of donor interventions and even less on their impact upon the poor. Projects lack any attempt at baseline studies in order that change and improvement be assessed; frequently little attempt is made to assess the condition of the poor before designing and implementation starts; appraisals tend to take a standard form within narrow time limits and to be preoccupied with the technical aspects of the project. Such weaknesses have been acknowledged by some of the EU donors who are making a conscious effort to address the problem.

Joint evaluations with the Indian government have also begun to take place in recent years. A positive step, not least in terms of securing greater Indian ownership, in practice it also entails a number of problems. Such evaluations have tended to be somewhat cumbersome and there are differences of opinion concerning such matters as to how critical one might be and as to whether criticism should be made public.

Poverty objective and targeting

In approaching poverty in this study, we have sought to emphasize its multi-dimensional nature. In this way we believe the complexity and diversity of poverty can better be approached. This in turn paves the way for better interventions for poverty reduction, not least in terms of targeting, sustainability, and replicability. While economic criteria such as low income or inadequate consumption may provide a point of entry for identifying and locating poverty, dimensions such as lack of productive assets, social exclusion, vulnerability, political marginalisation must be included in the design of projects and the more general formulation of programme strategies.

Four dimensions have been utilised in this study: livelihoods (from improvement to impoverishment), resources (from access to exclusion), knowledge (from expansion to reduction) and rights (from possession to alienation). With these four dimensions, the aim is not only to capture the diversity and complexity of poverty to be found in different situations and localities, but also to introduce the relational nature of the poverty. While indicators such as income or life expectancy permit a comparative analysis of peoples' conditions, the poverty concept used here also incorporates the relations that secure or deny peoples' access to, or possession of resources and the entitlements that these secure. Tenancy rights for example are central to securing poor cultivators access to formal credit, women's rights in areas of land ownership or inheritance are central to securing an improvement in the condition of poor rural women.

Effective targeting of the poor is one of the most obvious requirements in poverty reduction and essential in many interventions if benefits are to reach the poor. From the evidence collected for this study, it is clear that most of the interventions supported by the six EU donors do not specifically target the poor. More often than not the target group is a community or a population located within a specific geographic locality. While this might avoid causing political and social frictions within a locality it also means that the interests of the poor become subsumed within those of the community or population as a whole. The rich and the powerful are likely to benefit disproportionately where this is the case.

The degree and effectiveness of targeting is also dependent upon a number of other factors. The type of intervention, the resources that might be involved, the sector in which the intervention is located are all significant here. However, it is important that donors are aware of the limitations present in reaching the poor and that the poverty reduction objective is not pursued by simply broadening the definition of the poor to include a whole community or even the rural population. Not only will this undermine the potential that does exist in many interventions to target the aid better, it devalues the whole poverty reduction objective in aid.

Improved targeting is particularly called for in the productive sectors in which a focus on resources often leads to the wealthier sections benefiting most. For example, irrigation water is provided to land and thereby to cultivators. The beneficiaries are the cultivators in a particular locality, not merely the poor cultivators. To describe irrigation projects as targeted at the poor in a region is often a distortion of the reality unless an extremely loose definition of the poor is being utilised. Targeting can be pursued through specific criteria (income, consumption, assets etc.) or by proxy. The latter approach is administratively easier and often politically more acceptable. It can take the form of social or geographic targeting. In social targeting a group is selected on the basis of a composition primarily of poor people, for example landless agricultural labourers, scheduled castes and tribes, or women. In geographic targeting, an area is selected on the basis of the majority of its inhabitants being poor; the size can range from hamlet up to a district or state in the case of India. While social and geographic targeting are quite common, all six of the donors could nevertheless do a great deal more to strengthen their poverty focus by enhancing these approaches.

At the same time it must be recognised that the poorest of the poor are not being adequately reached by the majority of the interventions supported by the six EU donors on the basis of the evidence collected for this study. In addition to being very poor in absolute terms, the poorest groups are often socially and culturally excluded and geographically marginalised. As such they are the least able and thereby the last to access any benefits from a particular intervention. In addition to being difficult to target with the majority of interventions due to their lack of resources, assets and productive means, their exclusion leaves them disconnected from the channels and means through which development aid is delivered. This makes reaching them costly in terms of administrative and financial resources. One conclusion that donors should perhaps draw is that it is the government that is best placed to engage with the poorest of the poor and that donors should seek to encourage and to enhance this capacity.

The state context in India

The distribution of aid to the individual states in India is not equitable. In the first half of the 1990s the five States of Gujarat, Maharashtra, Andhra Pradesh, Karnataka and Tamil Nadu in the west and south of India received well over half of the total amount of aid allocated to individual states. The state allocation of aid by the EU donors reflected this bias. Yet in terms of both per capita income and other development indicators these states are not amongst the poorest and in a number of cases they are well above the average.

Conversely the five northern states of Rajasthan, Uttar Pradesh, Madhya Pradesh, Bihar and Orissa in which 40% of the total Indian population reside, receive only 20% of the state-allocated aid. Here are some of the poorest states in India. The argument that the institutions do not exist through which to reach the poor in these states, that there are problems of bureaucratic malfunctioning, corruption etc., may be correct, but it leaves the poor effectively abandoned by the donors concerned. While the EU donors do support some projects in some of these states (Uttar Pradesh, Orissa) there is a clear need to address the general reluctance on the part of the donors to go further and to find ways and means by which to support poverty reduction there. It might be that by having donors concentrate on different states one could improve effectiveness in terms of the number of India's poor being potentially in reach of an aid intervention.

States in India are also important when considering the issue of local ownership. While aid to India as a whole might be relatively very small, for some of the states, aid is of central significance in certain sectors. The study suggests that there is a good deal of genuine ownership on the part of the state governments. This perhaps reflects the capacity and strength of the Indian government system in contrast to the majority of countries in Africa for example. At the same time, this strength is also a weakness when one considers the lack of ownership at the local level. Too many of the interventions are implemented through partnership government institutions in a top-down manner. The EU donors need to increase their efforts to strengthen the local ownership of projects and particularly to ensure that the intended poor beneficiaries are included in the decision making processes.

Sectors

An important emphasis is placed in several of the six EU donors' aid policies on aid to the social sectors in the study's categorisation (education, health, drinking water, women and slums). Both with the older generation of drinking water projects and with the pedagogically oriented education projects such as ODA/DFID's APEP, there is a general lack of special mechanisms by which to target the poor and thereby to maximise poverty reduction. Social sectors tend not to need to be so sophisticated in their targeting mechanism in order to reach the poor as compared to the productive sectors (watershed, irrigation and forestry). Nevertheless social sector interventions need to address the demands for services expressed by the poor and not merely to supply services along 'traditional' lines. Greater attention to the multi-dimensional nature of poverty and the inter-connectedness of different factors in both generating and reducing poverty is essential.

More recent projects have been better to move in this direction and evidence from the study suggests that the poor have been better served. Yet the gap between rhetoric and reality remains not least with respect to the participation of the poor in the identification, design, implementation and monitoring of projects. It could well be that given the nature of the social sectors, and the relative success achieved in more recent interventions by the EU donors, a greater allocation of their resources to well-designed social sector projects would strengthen the poverty reduction of their aid programmes.

The problem with achieving poverty reduction in the productive sectors is that control over assets and resources is highly biased away from the poor. Possession of assets or control over them is the basis for systems of social and political inclusion and exclusion. Poverty is the economic consequence of this. Aid to these sectors with a focus upon specific resources is inherently problematical if poverty reduction is an objective of that aid. All too often it is those who are already productively active who benefit most from the aid and these do not often include the poorest. In that the degree of benefit is proportional to the share of resources one already possesses greater polarisation if not impoverishment of the poor can be a consequence. Land ownership in agriculture is a good example. Irrigation and agricultural services, which effectively go to land and thereby to people, will benefit the larger cultivators more than the landless sharecroppers. While greater productivity in agriculture is a *sine qua non* for both successful development and poverty reduction, the latter can only be achieved if instruments are used to ensure the poor receive a reasonable share of the benefits. In that the power basis influencing the distribution of benefits is rooted in local factors of political leadership, land ownership etc., the involvement of external actors and the state can be central.

Productive sector support therefore needs to embrace both the existing distribution of resources as well as any increase in resource stocks. Issues such as the nature of land and tenancy rights, the terms of agricultural employment, the state of literacy and knowledge in a society, need to be taken up in order to secure poverty reduction. Again, this is a call for a wider conceptualisation of poverty along the lines proposed in this study when formulating aid interventions and in the linking of measures and instruments to pursue poverty reduction in these sectors.

Approaches to poverty reduction

Donors express a clear sensitivity to the problems of specific disadvantaged groups in their policy rhetoric. In practice, there appear to be significant problems in implementing their expressed commitment.

In India as elsewhere it has long been recognised that certain general categories of the population find themselves in a particularly disadvantaged position in comparison to that of the general population. Already under colonial rule a number of caste and tribal groups were identified as being the target of consistent and systematic discrimination. Not least they experienced very low incomes, patterns of minimal consumption and possessed no influence. Defining them as scheduled castes and tribes was the basis for positive discrimination policies aimed at countering some of the economic consequences of their low social status. Fifty years after Independence, while there have been some absolute improvement in the position of the scheduled castes and tribes, they remain seriously and systematically disadvantaged. Successive Indian governments have largely failed to approach the problem of caste and ethnic discrimination in any new and innovative way. For their part, the EU donors appear to accept the status quo. Programmes continue to be designed and supported with the standard systems for implementing identification and targeting of beneficiaries. Innovation at best lies in the pressure for greater participation by beneficiaries in implementation and monitoring and evaluation.

In the post-Independence period another group, women, has been recognised as facing similar problems. While not all women are poor, the clear tendency is for women to be poorer and more oppressed than the men within the same social groups. Women are often amongst the poorest of the poor. However, women have a crucial role in production (agriculture, animal husbandry, crafts, minor forest products) as well as in reproduction (childcare, cooking, procuring water and firewood). So there are strong arguments for targeting women in donor-supported interventions. Many of the projects assessed in this study do stress the need to have such a gender focus within the project. In the social sector projects in particular, women tend to be amongst the main beneficiaries. However, in the productive sector projects the benefits accruing have mainly gone to men. This would appear to be a tacit acceptance of the fact that it is men that control productive assets and to run counter to relatively strong gender profiles presented by most of the donors studied. At the same time the donors in their engagement with the government system have been quite successful in promoting greater gender sensitivity in the field of development programmes and projects.

Clearly, as in the case of groups discriminated on the basis of caste and ethnicity, more needs to be undertaken with respect to gender on the part of donors, both EU and others. While it might well be the case that the elevation of gender as an issue in development policy is partly a consequence of donor pressure and initiatives over the years, the lack of innovation in approach and the regular failure to translate rhetoric into practice remain.

Participatory approaches, as mentioned, are recent and significant phenomena within the field of development practice in India. Whereas a decade ago most of the donor-supported interventions were implemented in accordance with the somewhat bureaucratic traditions entrenched in the line ministries of the Indian government system, today all of the EU donors studied are moving away from this top-down approach. For their part, the different government institutions involved in development programmes and projects are gradually accepting the need for this quite fundamental change in practice. It is taking time however, and some institutional partners are moving more on this issue than others.

In practice, the implementation of participatory approaches by the donors is not all that it is presented to be. There is considerable variation between the donors and between the different sectors and projects within individual donors' portfolios. In most instances participatory approaches are confined to the implementation stage of the project, typically through the formation of beneficiary committees as the principal way to secure some form of involvement on their part. There is little participation in project identification or design, nor is there very much in monitoring and evaluation. It must be recognised consequently that the influence of the beneficiaries on the different aspects and phases of a particular development intervention is often quite minimal. Within this somewhat depressing picture is the interesting finding from the cases researched for this study, that projects in the productive sectors show a more positive assessment with respect to the participation of the poor than those in the social sectors.

Delays and difficulties on the part of the donors in introducing innovative practices cannot be blamed upon partnership problems with government institutions alone. Problems are also to be found rooted in the organisation and management systems of the donors, in failures to communicate policies to field level, or simply in failures to implement policies along the lines called for in policy documents.

As for the importance of participatory approaches themselves, they are no panacea for development problems. While they can capture the immediate needs and interests of the beneficiaries, these might reflect short-term interests that can undermine development improvements in the longer-term. In addition concerns of environmental sustainability or the interests of marginalised groups not targeted might not be represented. Participatory approaches tend to both ignore the interests of those not targeted and to assume a considerable degree of homogeneity amongst those who are targeted. It has to be recognised that this does not reflect the reality of socio-economic life at the local level in India; that all too often the voice of the 'community' or group is not that of the poorest. It tends to be male, higher caste and stronger than the average in terms of resources, assets, knowledge etc. Generally participatory approaches need to be both refined and applied with greater sensitivity and understanding. They also need to be linked with other methodological approaches if the poor are to be better served by development interventions.

The regeneration and promotion of Panchayati Raj Institutions (PRIs) has been at the forefront of recent government policies for greater participation in the processes of governance and development. For their part, donors have indicated through their choice of institutional instruments in more recent interventions that they envisage a significant role for PRIs in development. It would certainly appear to be the case that there are advantages in giving elected PRIs a role in project implementation, design and monitoring. There is a strong argument that support to PRIs can strengthen local democracy through increasing the capacity of local government and by promoting greater participation in processes of planning, programme implementation, budget allocation etc. The strengthening of local democracy can enhance the work of the state at national level, it can also bring the needs and interests of the locality into the considerations of policy and development generally at the national level. There is also a strong case for arguing that greater local democracy combined with devolution of responsibilities and resources to decentralised government can promote poverty reduction through introducing the interests of the poor into policy, programme interventions, and the general distribution of resources and services.

At the same time, there are equally obvious risks involved in supporting decentralisation and the increased reliance upon the PRIs. Local elected government institutions can easily reflect the inequalities of the local society to the benefit of local elites. The consequence can be the further political exclusion of the poor and their increased marginalisation in service delivery, resource distribution etc. Successful decentralisation from a pro-poor perspective requires not only the enhancement of local institutional capacity, but also a strengthening of the PRIs' relationship to the state in order to secure the necessary accountability, transparency and affectivity.

The majority of the EU donors studied preferred as a matter of principle that bilateral aid should go through the government system and that it should not be channeled to Indian NGOs. There are four main reasons for this. First, working through government in itself can contribute to a strengthening and improvement in the capacity of government institutions. Secondly, working through government also gives better opportunities for replication and scaling up successful interventions and approaches. Thirdly, there is a reluctance to begin generating parallel organisational and management structures as the problems these can give rise to often outweigh the advantages of bypassing government bureaucracies. Fourthly, it is administratively demanding to work through local NGOs because of their size, the limited nature of their involvement, and the need to generate and sustain monitoring systems and accountability mechanisms acceptable to both donor and recipient.

However, as with the Indian government, the EU donors' attitude towards Indian NGOs is changing. Increasingly Indian NGOs are being brought into projects in which the principal partner is a government institution. In specific tasks such as institution building at the local level, training activities and social mobilisation, NGOs are often seen to possess a comparative advantage over government institutions. For their part, Indian NGOs have become adept in developing and applying participatory approaches and for many of them, poverty reduction is a central objective for their activities. As with the PRIs, experience with Indian NGOs varies by donor, by state, and by sector. On the whole, the contribution of NGOs has been to involve the poor in the development intervention and thereby to strengthen the poverty focus in those areas and sectors in which the EU donors have used them.

Impact and sustainability of European funded interventions

All of the projects examined in this study have been assessed for their impact in terms of poverty reduction. The assessment has been based upon the general criteria discussed in chapter 3: livelihoods, resources, knowledge and rights. Once more we would point out that assessments were carried out with a focus on poverty reduction only and that they are made by the researchers on the basis of project documents, visits to projects, and interviews with concerned staff and beneficiaries. What is lacking from these assessments is the type of data that comes from long-term monitoring involving longitudinal benchmark surveys and similar methods. Aggregating the more detailed assessments of the individual projects provided in chapters 9-17 has the advantage of providing an overview of the findings. However, in doing this, there is the danger of too little information being presented and a somewhat distorted picture emerging in comparison to that presented in chapter 6 and analysed in chapters 4-8. In this case, taking the overall assessments of the projects' approaches and consequences for poverty reduction reveals a considerable variation between sectors and donors on the one hand, but at the same time degree of success overall that is far from depressing. As Table 19.1 shows, of the 33 projects assessed 8 were found to have had a substantially positive impact on poverty reduction while 13 were assessed as having had a moderately positive impact and 3 had a negligible impact. Most of the remaining 9 projects examined are too recent in origin to have produced a measurable impact. In a few cases there was a problem of lack of information.

Table 19.1: Summary of overall assessments of 24 projects.

Overall Impact	Negative	Negligible	Moderately positive	Substantially positive
Poverty orientation				
Other	0	0	1	0
Indirect	0	3	6	2
Direct	0	0	6	6

Projects with a direct poverty orientation are achieving their overall objectives quite successfully it would appear and those with an indirect poverty orientation are having a positive impact in more than 70% of cases.

It is also evident from the study, although not shown in Table 19.1, that projects conceived and planned in the 1990s are having a greater impact upon poverty than the older projects assessed. While the more recent projects are usually at a far earlier stage of the project cycle, it would nevertheless suggest that the changes that have occurred in donors' policies and practices during the past decade or so are having consequences. In particular the increased emphasis on poverty reduction, the adoption of new methods of implementation, the greater gender sensitivity, and the utilisation of a broader range of institutions and organisations in the different phases of projects.

The sustainability of the improvements in the 1990s and of the process of change underway cannot be assessed with any certainty as yet. A number of factors do appear to be present that bode well for the future however. Here we would name the ongoing review process whereby donors appear to be actively examining their development management, organisational structures and development approach; the indications that similar processes of introspective analysis are underway within the Indian government at central and state-levels; and last but not least, the evidence that European donors' aid programmes are having an impact on poverty reduction presented in this study.

To return therefore to the question posed in the title of this book: as to whether the poor matter in European aid to India. It would appear that they do and that the donors' strategies are having an increasing impact on poverty reduction. However the more detailed discussion of EU donors' aid in the study does reveal that the overall positive picture in Table 19.1 is potentially misleading in a number of aspects. Today, there in fact remain many problems and the changes and improvements achieved to date are far from being secure for the future. It remains the case that while the poor do matter, they do not matter enough. To secure better poverty reduction the EU donors must continue with the changes introduced in the 1990s and pursue further improvements in management and organisation, further innovation in approaches and methodologies, and make far greater attempts at inter-donor and bilateral cooperation and coordination. Poverty rarely goes away. One can achieve changes for the better in both absolute and relative terms, but the processes that give rise to poverty have a habit of surviving and the poor being reconstituted in new forms, with new problems. If we look at India as a whole, the percentage of poor below the poverty line has been reduced from the time of Independence to today by some 50%. At the same time, the absolute number of poor has risen from some 250 million to 400 million so that today 25% of the world's poor live in India. That demands attention. They have a right to be attended to.

BIBLIOGRAPHY

Baden, Sally & Kirsty Milward (1996). *Gender and Poverty.* Sida Task Force on Poverty Reduction, Working Paper 2. Stockholm.

Baker, Judy L. & Margaret E. Grosh (1994). Povertry Reduction Through Geographic Targeting: How Well Does It Work? World Development, 22,7:983-995.

Bamberger, Michael & Abdul Aziz (1993). Poverty Alleviation Strategies and the Role of Targeted Programs for the Poor. In Michael Bamberger & Abdul Aziz, eds. The Design and Management of Sustainable Projects to Alleviate Poverty in South Asia. The World Bank, Washington D.C., pp. 3-17.

Banerjee, S. (1997), Health Sector Report. Mimeo.

Baulch, B. (1996), The New Poverty Agenda: A disputed consensus, in: *IDS Bulletin,* Vol. 27, No. 1, Brighton, Sussex.

Beck, T. (1994) Common Property Resource Access by the Poor and Class Conflict in West Bengal, in: *Economic and Political Weekly,* Vol. 29, No. 4: 187-197.

Benjamin, S.J (1997), A comparative study of aid to India from EU and selected EU donors and its relevance for poverty reduction: funding urban poverty reduction by the ODA, KfW and Dutch funding. Unpublished report.

Besley, Timothy & Ravi Kanbur (1993). The Principles of Targeting. In Michael Lipton & Jacques van der Gaag, eds. Including the Poor. The World Bank, Washington D.C., pp. 67-90.

Bose, S., Harriss-White, B. & Rogaly, B. (eds.) (1999), Sonar Bangla? Agricultural Growth and Agrarian Change in West Bengal and Bangladesh. Sage. London.

Boserup, Ester (1970). *Women's Role in Economic Development.* St. Martin's Press, New York.

Bourdieu, P. (1991), *Outline of a Theory of Practice,* Cambridge University .

Cassels, Andrew (1997), A Guide to Sector-wide Approaches for Health Development: concepts, issues and working arrangements', WHO, Danida, DFID, European Commission.

Chambers, R. (1995), Paradigm shifts and the practice of participatory research and development, in: N. Nelson and S. Wright (eds.), *Power and Participatory Development—theory and practice*, London, Intermediate Technology Publications.

CIDA (1991), Sustainable development—discussion paper, CIDA.

Cox, A., S. Folke, L. Schulpen & N. Webster (2000), 'Do the Poor Matter? A Comparative Study of European Aid for Poverty Reduction in India'. ODI Working Paper, London.

Cox, A. & J. Healey (2000), 'European Development Cooperation and the Poor'. Macmillan Press Ltd., London.

Datt, Gaurav & Martin Ravallion (1993), Regional Disparities, Targeting, and Poverty in India. In Michael Lipton & Jacques van der Gaag, eds. Including the Poor. The World Bank, Washington D.C., pp. 91-114.

Datt, Gaurav & Martin Ravallion (1996a), Macroeconomic Crisis and Poverty Monitoring: A Case Study of India. World Bank Policy Research Department, Washington D.C.

Datt, Gaurav & Martin Ravallion (1996b), Why Have Some Indian States Done Better Than Others at Reducing Rural Poverty? World Bank Policy Research Working Paper 1594. Washington D.C.

Dev, M. (1995c), Government interventions and social security for rural labour, in: The Indian Journal of Labour Economics, Vol. 38, No. 3, July-September: 419-441.

Development Assistance Committee (1999), Making Aid Work for the Poor: Poverty Reduction—Donor Policy and Practice (Draft), Paris, DAC.

Drèze, Jean & Amartya K. Sen (1989), Hunger and Public Action. Clarendon Press, Oxford.

Drèze, Jean & Amartya K. Sen (1995), India: Economic Development and Social Opportunity. Oxford University Press, Oxford.

Eade, Deborah (1997), Capacity-building, an approach to people-centred development. Oxford: Oxfam Publications.

Edwards, M. & Hulme, D. (eds.) (1996), Non-Governmental Organisations—performance and accountability—beyond the magic bullet, London, Earthscan/Save the Children.

Engberg-Pedersen, L. (1998), Studying Poverty: Concepts and Approach in Webster, N. (ed.) In Search of Alternatives: Poverty, the Poor and Local Organisations CDR Working Paper 98.10. Centre for

Development Research. Copenhagen: 11-30.

Farrington, J., Bebbington, A., Wellard, K. and Lewis, D.J. (1993), Reluctant partners—non-governmental organizations, the state and sustainable agricultural development, London/New York, Routledge.

Folke, S. (1998a), Swedish development cooperation with India - in a poverty reduction perspective. CDR Working Paper 98.1. Copenhagen.

Folke, S. (1998b), Danish development cooperation with India - in a poverty reduction perspective. CDR Working paper 98.2. Copenhagen.

Frontline, October 31, 1997, pp. 4-20 (various articles and authors).

Gaika, R. (1991), Poverty alleviation programmes in rural India: an assessment, in: Development and Change, Vol. 22.

Ghosh, A. (1992), Planning in India - the challenges for the nineties, New Delhi, Sage Publications.

Government of India (1961), Third Five Year Plan 1961-66, New Delhi, Planning Commission.

Government of India (1985), Seventh Five Year Plan 1985-90, New Delhi, Planning Commission.

Government of Uttar Pradesh (1991), Draft Eighth Five Year Plan 1992-97 and Annual Plan 1992-93 Vol. 1, Lucknow, Government of Uttar Pradesh, December.

Government of India (1992), Eighth Five Year Plan (Volume II), New Delhi, Government of India.

Government of India (1994), Indian Public Finance Statistics 1993, New Delhi, Ministry of Finance/Department of Economic Affairs.

Guhan, S. (1995), Social expenditures in the Union budget, in: *Economic and Political Weekly*, May 6-13.

Gulati, A. & Bhide, S. (1995), What do the Reformers have for agriculture?, in: *Economic and Political Weekly*, May 6-13.

Gulati, A. (1996), Harvesting the crop, Interim Budget 1996-97, in: *Economic and Political Weekly*, April 13.

Gupta, M. (1984), in: Indian Journal of Agricultural Economics, Vol. XXXIX, No. 3: 451-456.

Gupta, S.P. (1996), Recent economic reforms in India and their impact on the poor and vulnerable sections in society, in: Rao, C.H. & Linneman, H. (eds.), Economic reforms and poverty alleviation in India, New Delhi, Sage Publications.

Hansen, S. (1987), India, development and aid—Norway's contribution and future options, Bekkestua (Norway), Economic Research, Policy and Planning.

Haq, Mahbub ul. (1997), Human Development in South Asia 1997. Oxford University Press, Karachi.

Indira Gandhi National Open University (198?), School of continuing education, Rural Development: Indian context (Block 3 - Asset based programmes and performances) and Rural Development: programmes and performance (Block 4 - Target group-oriented programmes and performance, New Delhi, IGNOU.

Jackson, Cecile (1996), "Rescuing Gender from the Poverty Trap". *World Development* 24, 3: 489-504.

Kabeer, Naila (1994a), Not all women are poor, not all poor are women: conceptual, methodological and empirical issues in the analysis of gender and poverty. Mimeo.

Kabeer, Naila (1994b), Reversed Realities. Gender Hierarchies in Development Thought. Verso, London.

Kabeer, Naila (1996), "Agency, Well-being & Inequality. Reflections on the Gender Dimensions of Poverty". *IDS Bulletin* 27, 1: 11-21.

Kabeer, Naila, ed. (1997), "Tactics & Trade-offs: Revisiting the Links Between Gender and Poverty". *IDS Bulletin* 28, 3.

Karl, M. (1995), Women and empowerment—participation and decision-making, London, Zed Books Ltd.

Khanna, I. (1989), The plan of action on Integrated Rural Development—India, in: UN/Interagency Committee on Integrated Rural Development for Asia and the Pacific, *Integrated Rural Development in Asia and the Pacific—a framework for action for the 1990s,* Bangkok, United Nations.

Khanna, B.S. (1994), Panchayati Raj in India—rural local self government (national perspective and state studies), New Delhi, Deep & Deep Publications.

Kripa, A.P. (1997), Comparative Study of European Aid for Poverty Reduction in India - The Forestry Sector. Unpublished report.

Kumar, A.K. Shiva (1996), UNDP's gender-related development index: a computation for Indian states, in: *Economic and Political Weekly,* April 6: 887-895.

Lane, J. (1995), Non-governmental organizations and participatory development: the concept in theory versus the concept in practice, in: N. Nelson and S. Wright, *Power and participatory development—theory and practice,* London, Intermediate Technology Publications.

Lineberry, W.P. (1989), Assessing participatory development—rhetoric versus reality, Boulder, Westview Press.

Lipton, M. & Maxwell, S. (1992), *The New Poverty Agenda: An Overview,* IDS Discussion Paper No. 306, Brighton, Sussex.

Lipton, M. and Toye, J. (1990). Does Aid Work? A country study of the impact of official development assistance. Routledge: London.

Manti, D. (1997), Rural drinking water and sanitation: a comparative study of European aid for poverty reduction in India, Guntur, mimeo.

Moser, Caroline O.N. (1993). Gender Planning and Development: Theory, Practice & Training. Routledge, London.

NABARD (1990), Financing programmes for poverty alleviation—problems and issues, in: *Journal of Rural Development,* NIRD, Hyderabad, Vol. 9 (1).

Nagaraj, B.S. (1997), AP to abandon prohibition for development's sake, in: *The Indian Express,* 20 March.

Nayyar, R. (1996), New initiatives for poverty alleviation in India, in: Rao, C.H. & Linneman, H. (eds.), *Economic reforms and poverty alleviation in India,* New Delhi, Sage Publications.

Ninan, K.N. (1998), An assessment of European-aided watershed development projects in India from the perspective of poverty reduction and the poor. CDR Working Paper 98.3. Copenhagen.

NIRD (1990), *Journal of Rural Development* (theme: poverty alleviation—special issue), Hyderabad, NIRD, Vol. 9 (1), January.

Oakley, P. and Marsden, D. (1984), *Approaches to participation in rural development,* Geneva, ILO (published on behalf of the ACC Task Force on Rural Development).

ODA (1995), A Guide to Social Analysis for Projects in Developing Countries. London, HMSO.

OECD (1977), Geographical distribution of financial flows to developing countries—data on disbursements 1969 to 1975, Paris, OECD.

OECD (1978), Geographical distribution of financial flows to developing countries—data on disbursements 1971 to 1975, Paris, OECD.

OECD (1982), Geographical distribution of financial flows to developing countries—disbursements, commitments, external debt, economic indicators 1978/1981, Paris, OECD.

OECD (1986a), Geographical distribution of financial flows to developing countries—disbursements, commitments, economic indicators 1981/1984, Paris, OECD.

OECD (1987), Geographical distribution of financial flows to developing countries—disbursements, commitments, economic indicators 1982/1985, Paris, OECD.

OECD (1989), Sustainability in development programmes: A compendium of evaluation experience (Selected Issues in Aid Evaluation - 1), Paris, OECD, January.

OECD (1990), Geographical distribution of financial flows to developing countries—disbursements, commitments, economic indicators 1985/1988, Paris, OECD.

OECD (1991), Geographical distribution of financial flows to developing countries—disbursements, commitments, economic indicators 1986/1989, Paris, OECD.

OECD (1992), Geographical distribution of financial flows to developing countries—disbursements, commitments, economic indicators 1987/1990, Paris, OECD.

OECD (1993), Geographical distribution of financial flows to developing countries—disbursements, commitments, economic indicators 1988/1991, Paris, OECD.

OECD (1995), Geographical distribution of financial flows to developing countries—disbursements, commitments, country indicators 1989/1993, Paris, OECD.

OECD (1996), Shaping the 21st century: The contribution of development cooperation, Paris, OECD/DAC, May.

OECD (1999), Geographical distribution of financial flows to aid recipients—disbursements, commitments, country indicators. Paris, OECD.

Oommen, M.A. (1997), Foreign Aid and Poverty Reduction—A Critique of the Indian Perspective. Institute of Social Sciences, New Delhi.

Parikh, Kirit S., ed. 1997. *India Development Report 1997.* Oxford University press, Delhi.

Planning Commission (GoI) (1992), *Directory of schemes for voluntary agencies,* New Delhi, National Informatics Centre & Voluntary Action Coordination Cell (Planning Commission).

Planning Commission (GoI) (1993), *Report of the Expert Group on Estimation of Proportion and Number of Poor,* New Delhi, Perspective Planning Division.

Prabhu, K.S. (1996a), The impact of structural adjustment on social sector expenditure: evidence from Indian states, in: Rao, C.H. & Linneman, H. (eds.), *Economic reforms and poverty alleviation in India,* New Delhi, Sage Publications.

Prasad, A. (1992), Rural Development in India, in: UN/Interagency Committee on Integrated Rural Development for Asia and the Pacific, *Partners in Rural Poverty Alleviation - NGO cooperation,* New York, United Nations.

Putnam, R.D. & Raffaella, N. (1993), *Making Democracy Work: Civic Traditions in Modern Italy,* Princeton University Press.

Radhakrishna, G.S. & Mainak, D. (1997), Andhra and Orissa lead the way, in: Business World, March, pp. 26-28.

Rajamma, G. (1997), An Assessment of European Aided Women Training Projects in India and their Relevance to Poverty Reduction. Unpublished report.

Rao, C.H. (1996), Economic reforms, agricultural growth and rural poverty, in: *Indian Economic Journal,* April-June 1995-1996.

Rajasekhar, D. (1997), Poverty component in NGO Projects. mimeo.

Rath, N. (1985), Garibi hatao: can IRDP do it?, in: *Economic and Political Weekly,* Vol. XX, No. 6, February 9: 238-246.

Razavi, Sharashoub & Carol Miller (1995). From WID to GAD: conceptual shifts in the women and development discourse. UNRISD, Geneva.

Reddy, S. (1997), Irrigation: a comparative study of European aid for poverty reduction in India, Bangalore, mimeo.

Reddy, S. & Rajasekhar, D. (1996) Development Programmes and NGOs, BCO, Bangalore.

Shah, G. (1991), *Non-Governmental organisations in India,* Oegstgeest, NGO country study India as part of the Impact-study Co-financingprogramme, June.

Sida (1997a), Sharing Challenges: The Indo-Swedish Development Cooperation Programme. Ministry of Foreign Affairs. Stockholm.

Sida (1997b), Rajasthan. A State Study. Embassy of Sweden, Development Cooperation Section. New Delhi.

Srivastava, Ravi S. (1997), *Poverty in India: A Review of Nature, Trends and Eradication Strategies.* Report Prepared for the Research Project on: A Comparative Study of European Aid for Poverty Reduction in India. Allahabad, University of Allahabad..

Stiefel, M. and Wolfe, M. (1994), *A voice for the excluded - popular participation in development: utopia or necessity?* London, Zed Books Ltd in association with the United Nations Research Institute for Social Development.

Tendler, J. (1989), Whatever happened to poverty alleviation, in: *World Development,* July: 1033-1045.

Thin, N. (1998), *Social Development Policies, Results and Learning: Experiences from European Agencies.* Social Development Division, Department for International Development. London, DFID.

UNDP (1993), *Human Development Report 1993,* New York, Oxford University Press.

UNDP (1997a), *Human Development Report 1997.* Oxford University Press, New York.

UNDP (1997b), India: The Road to Human Development. New Delhi.

van Diesen, A. (1998), *The Quality of British Aid to India.* Christian Aid: London.

Varghese, N.V. (1997), Investment in Education and Implications for Poverty Reduction in India: A Study of Primary Education Projects Funded by the European Countries. National Institute of Educational Planning and Administration, New Delhi.

Wignaraja, P. (1991), Towards praxis and participatory development, in: P. Wignaraja, A. Hussain, H. Sethi and G. Wignaraja, *Participatory Development - learning from South Asia,* Oxford, Oxford University Press.

World Bank (1984), As the Planning Commission views the concept! - interview with CH Hanumantha Rao (member of the Planning Commission), in: *Yojana,* November: 5.

World Bank (1990), *World Development Report.* Washington D.C.

World Bank (1991), Gender and Poverty in India - A World Bank Country Study. Washington, D.C.

World Bank (1995), The World Bank and Gender in India. New Delhi.

World Bank (1995a), Strengthening the Effectiveness of Aid - lessons for donors, Washington D.C., World Bank.

World Bank (1996), *India: country economic memorandum,* Washington D.C.,

World Bank (1996), Poverty Reduction and the World Bank: Progress and Challenges in the 1990s. Washington D.C.

World Bank (1997), India. Achievements and Challenges in Reducing Poverty. Washington D.C.

World Bank (1998), *World Development Report 1997,* Washington D.C., The World Bank.

INDEX